SPEAKING
IN OUR
TONGUES

Proceedings of a Colloquium on
Medieval Dialectology and Related Disciplines

Medieval Dialectology and Related Disciplines was the theme of an international Colloquium which took place at the University of Edinburgh in April 1992. It was hosted by the Institute for Historical Dialectology, School of Scottish Studies, and held in the Institute for Advanced Studies in the Humanities.

The Colloquium's purpose was to examine the place of medieval dialectology within the wider realms of historical linguistics and medieval studies. The Colloquium brought together participants whose interests covered philology, textual studies, codicology and palaeography, onomastics, word geography, lexicography, history and ethnology. They also brought expertise in different languages: English, Scots, French, Dutch, the Celtic and Scandinavian languages and Latin. This breadth of interest is reflected throughout the present volume.

Papers were presented within the framework of four panels, each panel being followed by a lengthy discussion period which was tape-recorded. There was also a keynote address on 'Historical dialectology and literary text traditions' by Anthonij Dees. This volume contains edited versions of the thirteen papers and the discussions.

Under the heading of Panel I, Taxonomy and Typology in Medieval Dialect Studies, appear papers by Hans F. Nielsen, 'On the origin and spread of initial voiced fricatives and the phonemic split of fricatives in English and Dutch'; Pieter van Reenen, 'The study of medieval language in the Low Countries: the good, the bad and the future' and Michael Benskin, 'Descriptions of dialect and areal distributions'. Panel II, Manuscript Studies and Literary Geography, has contributions by Richard Beadle, 'Middle English texts and their transmission, 1350–1500: some geographical criteria', A.I. Doyle, 'A Palaeographer's view' and Jeremy Smith, 'A Philologist's view'. Panel III, Languages in Contact, is represented by Angus McIntosh on 'Codes and cultures', William Gillies on 'The Celtic languages: some current and some neglected questions' and Helmut Gneuss on 'Language contact in early medieval England: Latin and Old English'. Panel IV, Word Geography, contains Terry Hoad's 'Word geography: previous approaches and achievements', Robert Lewis's 'Sources and techniques for the study of Middle English word geography' and Gillian Fellows-Jensen's 'Place-names and word geography: some words of warning'.

SPEAKING IN OUR TONGUES

Proceedings of a Colloquium on
Medieval Dialectology and Related Disciplines

Edited by

MARGARET LAING
and
KEITH WILLIAMSON

D. S. BREWER

First published 1994
D. S. Brewer, Cambridge

ISBN 0 85991 403 8

D. S. Brewer is an imprint of Boydell & Brewer Ltd
PO Box 9, Woodbridge, Suffolk IP12 3DF, UK
and of Boydell & Brewer Inc.
PO Box 41026, Rochester, NY 14604, USA

British Library Cataloguing-in-Publication Data
A catalogue record for this book is available
from the British Library

Library of Congress Cataloging-in-Publication Data applied for

The paper used in this publication meets the minimum requirements
of American National Standard for Information Sciences –
Permanence of Paper for Printed Library Materials, ANSI Z39.48-1984

Printed in Great Britain by
St Edmundsbury Press Ltd, Bury St Edmunds, Suffolk

CONTENTS

LIST OF ILLUSTRATIONS

I.R   *Descriptions of Dialect and Areal Distributions*

CONTRIBUTORS

Richard Beadle, Fellow of St. John's College and University Lecturer in English, University of Cambridge

Michael Benskin, Professor of Older English Language, University of Oslo

Anthonij Dees, Emeritus Professor of Medieval French Philology, Faculty of Letters, Free University of Amsterdam

A.I. Doyle, Reader in Bibliography, University of Durham

Gillian Fellows-Jensen, Docent, Director of the Institute for Name Research, University of Copenhagen

William Gillies, Professor of Celtic, University of Edinburgh

Helmut Gneuss, Professor of English Philology, University of Munich

Terry Hoad, Fellow of St. Peter's College and University Lecturer in English, University of Oxford

Robert E. Lewis, Editor-in-Chief, Middle English Dictionary, University of Michigan

Angus McIntosh, Emeritus Professor of English Language, University of Edinburgh

Hans F. Nielsen, Docent, Institute of Language and Communication, University of Odense

Jeremy J. Smith, Senior Lecturer in English Language, University of Glasgow

Pieter Th. van Reenen, Professor of Linguistics, Faculty of Letters, Free University of Amsterdam

PARTICIPANTS

Professor A.J. Aitken, University of Edinburgh — history of Scots; lexicography

Professor Geoffrey Barrow, University of Edinburgh — Scottish history and palaeography

Dr Richard Beadle*, University of Cambridge — Middle English dialectology in relation to literary texts

Professor Michael Benskin*, University of Oslo — medieval English language; numerical taxonomy

Mr Derek Britton, University of Edinburgh — history of Modern English dialects

Professor Graham Caie†, University of Glasgow — Old and Middle English Literature

Professor Anthonij Dees*, Free University of Amsterdam — historical dialectology of French; stemmatology

Dr A.I. Doyle*, University of Durham — dating and provenance of Middle English manuscripts; palaeography

Dr Dorrit Einersen, University of Copenhagen — Middle English literature

Dr Gillian Fellows-Jensen*, University of Copenhagen — place-names in Scandinavia and the British Isles

Professor Alexander Fenton†, University of Edinburgh — ethnology

Professor William Gillies*, University of Edinburgh — historical dialectology of Gaelic

Professor Helmut Gneuss*, University of Munich — lexicography of Old English; editions of Old English texts

Mr Richard Hamer†, University of Oxford — Old and Middle English language and literature

Mr Terry Hoad*, University of Oxford — Old and Middle English language; etymology and lexicology

Mr George Jack, University of St Andrews — Middle English syntax

Ms Christian Kay, University of Glasgow —historical lexicography and semantics

Professor Gillis Kristensson, University of Stockholm — Middle English dialectology

Dr Margaret Laing, University of Edinburgh — Middle English dialectology

Professor Robert E. Lewis*, Middle English Dictionary, University of Michigan — lexicology of Middle English

Dr Kathryn Lowe, University of Glasgow — medieval cartulary copies of Old English charters

Professor Angus McIntosh*†, University of Edinburgh — Middle English dialectology

Professor Manfred Markus, University of Innsbruck — historical linguistics; Middle English literature; diachronic corpus linguistics

Dr Hans F. Nielsen*, University of Odense — early comparative Germanic language history

Professor Matti Rissanen†, University of Helsinki — historical linguistics; diachronic corpus compilation

Dr Jeremy J. Smith*, University of Glasgow — historical dialectology of English; medieval English textual studies

Professor Pieter van Reenen*, Free University of Amsterdam — historical dialectology of the Low Countries

Mr Harry Watson, Dictionary of the Older Scottish Tongue, University of Edinburgh — lexicography of Older Scots

Dr Keith Williamson, University of Edinburgh — linguistic analysis of Older Scots

* Contributor   † Chairman

ACKNOWLEDGEMENTS

The Colloquium on Medieval Dialectology and Related Disciplines, held at the University of Edinburgh, 10–12 April 1992, was hosted by the Institute for Historical Dialectology, School of Scottish Studies. We would like to thank Mr Derek Britton for his part in its organisation, our colleagues in the English Language Department, University of Glasgow for their collaboration and Professors Angus McIntosh and Alexander Fenton for their help and encouragement.

We gratefully acknowledge sponsorship and financial support of the Colloquium from the Royal Society of Edinburgh and from the British Academy. We also thank Mr Colin MacLean, formerly of Aberdeen University Press.

We are grateful for assistance from the University of Edinburgh. We wish especially to thank Professor Peter Jones and Mrs Anthea Taylor of the Institute for Advanced Studies in the Humanities, Mrs Sheila Nimmo and the staff at Pollock Halls of Residence, Mr Andrew Millar and Audio Visual Services, Mrs Simpson and the Edinburgh University Students' Association.

The Glenmorangie Distillery Coy provided much appreciated assistance towards the social programme which was further enhanced by the expertise of Pinkerton's Cooks and Caterers and by musical contributions from Dr Ian Laing and Mrs Isobel Mieras.

Margaret Laing
Keith Williamson

Institute for Historical Dialectology
School of Scottish Studies
University of Edinburgh
October 1993

Introduction

Als þai to-togedir talked sua,
þai loked þam on ferrum fra . . .
(*Cursor Mundi*, 11744–745)

1. Objectives of the Colloquium

The 'conference' figures ever greater as an event in the academic
calends. Scholars feel an ever pressing urge to be heard by, or to be
seen amongst, their peers if not the great and the good of their
particular disciplinary sect. Aacademic gatherings are proliferating, not
least within the field of English studies (literature, language and
linguistics). A feature of the conference circuit in the 1980s and 1990s
has been the increasing scale of many events. Striking examples are
the *MLA* conventions where attendance numbers over 5,000 and the
English 'fair' at Kalamazoo with some 2,000 participants. However, at
such large-scale events (or even not so large ones) it is extremely
difficult to interrelate the disparate, often narrowly focused, concerns
of individual speakers. Frequently, by far the most useful part of the
proceedings arises from informal discussion during leisure time.

The organisers of the event whose proceedings are published in the
present volume were anxious to stress to the invitees that it was *not* a
conference. The emphasis was to be very much on discussion and the
title 'Colloquium' was adopted. The overall purpose of the
Colloquium was to examine the place of medieval dialectology not
only within dialectology and historical linguistics in general but also
within the wider realm of medieval studies. More particularly, we
sought to provide a forum for a liberal exchange of views on two
major themes: (1) problems and concerns common to the
investigation of different medieval vernaculars; (2) how the study of
language variation might be more fully integrated with the divers
related disciplines which contribute to define its historical, cultural

and social context. Although papers by individual participants were to be presented, these were intended to be brief. Their purpose was to set out some ideas on a given topic on which the whole gathering might focus its attention for discussion and debate.

The Colloquium took place over two days, 11th and 12th April, 1992 in the Institute for Advanced Studies at the University of Edinburgh. We have here in Scotland (and notably at Edinburgh) strong traditions both in dialectology and lexicography, particularly in English, Scots and Gaelic. These disciplines encompass linguistic study in both its historical and geographical dimensions; but interests are not confined to the distribution and evolution of language varieties. For this reason, the participants were invited as representatives of disciplines which the organisers believe to be mutually informative within the broad field of medieval linguistic studies: philology, textual studies, codicology and palaeography, onomastics, word geography, lexicography, history, ethnology.[1] They also brought expertise in different languages: English, Scots, French, Dutch, the Celtic and Scandinavian languages and Latin.

To focus thinking further, we envisaged that the two themes stated above might be considered in terms of a set of topics:

(1) the investigation of medieval vernaculars

    (a) types of source material
    (b) methods of analysis
    (c) the relationship between diachronic and diatopic variation
    (d) translation and standardisation
    (e) dialectal patterning across political and cultural boundaries
    (f) ethnographic problems and the movement of populations
    (g) word geography
    (h) the integration of place-name (and personal-name) studies
        into dialectology as a whole;

(2) related disciplines

    (a) palaeography
    (b) codicology
    (c) stemmatology
    (d) historical linguistics

---

[1] A list of participants is given on pp. x–xi.

(e) medieval literature, including textual studies
(f) lexicography, including thesaurus work
(g) local history, especially as it relates to language and how
different languages interact within a society.

These topics were to be approached within the framework of four panels:

I   taxonomy and typology in medieval dialect studies
II   manuscript studies and literary geography
III languages in contact
IV   Middle English word geography.

There was also a 'keynote' paper by a Romance scholar, Professor Anthonij Dees of the Free University of Amsterdam. Each panel opened with the presentation of short papers (up to 15 minutes), followed by 45 minutes of discussion. That the results of the discussions might not evaporate into the ether, or only reside in variant fragments in individual memories, the presentation of the papers and the ensuing discussions were tape-recorded.[2] The present volume contains edited versions both of the papers and the transcriptions of the discussions. A résumé of the papers is given below.

The organisers hoped that the Colloquium might be a first step towards the promotion of interdisciplinary studies and collaboration between institutions and individuals across areas of common interest. Among the practical benefits of collaboration would be sharing of data, methods and results and a clearer understanding of what new projects could profitably be undertaken, with consequently stronger concerted efforts in seeking funding for them. Historical linguists and other students of medieval culture have often drawn upon the work of other disciplines. But the time may have come when this should be done more systematically and at a more formal level. Future large-scale projects would, we believe, benefit from planned inter-disciplinary collaboration.[3] The Colloquium was a modest attempt to set people thinking in these terms, with a view to setting an agenda for further meetings, correspondence and collaboration.

---

[2] This task was done by the University of Edinburgh's Audio-Visual Services.
[3] See William Gillies' paper, III.2, pp. 139–47.

2. Why an Interdisciplinary Approach is Important

At the heart of the disciplines represented at the Colloquium is language and the users of a language in its various forms, how they use it (in speech and writing) and what their perceptions of it are. As historical linguists with a special interest in how a given language shows variation across space and time and within speech communities, the organisers believe that it is essential to investigate linguistic phenomena not only as structures and systems, but also in their social and cultural context; '. . . the history of language (whatever its physiological, physical and perceptual substrates) is in essence culture history' (Lass 1980: 3).

The language varieties which we study are preserved in manuscripts which might be anything from a fragment to a large, bound, illuminated volume. The manuscripts are often the product of more than one scribe, the scribes not necessarily being coeval contributors. A manuscript may be a compilation of originally separate ones or the result of breaking up a larger single manuscript. They may contain more than one text and that text may have been written by more than one hand. Literary manuscripts in particular are commonly not original compositions in the writing or language of their author, but copies, possibly several removes from the original and reproduced by scribes whose language may be quite different in many respects from that of the author and/or previous copyists. This gives just a hint of the codicological complexities of late medieval manuscripts. To begin to understand the varieties of language one must understand something of the manuscripts, their contents, their production, their dissemination, the scribes and their practices and the social structure and culture of late medieval Europe.

A text may contain different strands of language which have to be teased out and unravelled.[4] In the compilation of *A Linguistic Atlas of Late Mediaeval English* (McIntosh et al. 1986) an understanding of the context of the manuscript sources became essential. The kind of texts most readily localised were legal and administrative documents. With these one is able to look at the non-linguistic evidence they offer for their potential provenance. This comprises personal-names (parties to a transaction, witnesses, notaries) and place-names (territorial designations of people mentioned, lands which are the subject of

---

[4] For detailed discussion of some of the problems of dealing with the language of Middle English texts see McIntosh 1973 [1989a]; Benskin and Laing 1981.

transaction, the place at which the document is made or signed or sealed). Such evidence may or may not provide a clear prima facie indication of the document's provenance. If it does, then this evidence can be weighed against the evidence of the language of the document when compared with the language of other documents of already established provenance. But identification of the people and places referred to in a document is not always straightforward. For example, there may be more than one landed family or branch of a family bearing the same name in a region, or more than one place with the same name. In such cases historical and onomastic research will be needed to resolve ambiguous references.[5]

Local documents are one class of material. The other major class of material, literary texts, pose their own problems. For example, dating of a manuscript containing a literary text may depend solely on the type of script. Here the skill and experience of the palaeographer must be called on.

Palaeographical knowledge can also identify formerly unrelated manuscripts as the product of the same scribe. Such identifications are clearly of great interest to the linguist and also the literary scholar. The 'Hengwrt' and 'Ellesmere' manuscripts of the *Canterbury Tales*[6] (along with hand B of Cambridge, Trinity College R.3.2) were identified as the work of the same scribe by palaeographical analysis (Doyle and Parkes 1978). When the languages of the manuscripts were later analysed they were found not only to be remarkably similar, so confirming the identity, but the differences of practice by the scribe in the manuscripts revealed a great deal about his linguistic behaviour in relation to his exemplars and his linguistic milieu as defined by other manuscripts (Samuels 1983 [1988]).

Just as the historical dialectologist must draw on language-external data, so detailed linguistic analysis of a text may reveal information about manuscript transmission and relationships as well as provenance, and so inform the literary scholar or the historian. The series of studies by McIntosh, Samuels, Laing and Smith (in Laing 1989a; Smith 1988), based on the methods and principles of *LALME* give ample evidence of what may be achieved. As examples one may note Margaret Laing's study of the language of Richard Misyn's translations of works by Richard Rolle in three manuscripts, which

---

[5] For a detailed discussion with examples of some of the problems presented by this class of material see *LALME*, vol. 1, Introduction to the Index of Sources.

[6] Hengwrt = National Library of Wales, Peniarth 392; Ellesmere = Huntington Library, San Marino, EL 26.C.9

reveals one of the manuscripts was the direct exemplar for the other two (Laing 1989b); Angus McIntosh's unravelling of the linguistic complexities of the Scottish *Troy Book* (McIntosh 1979 [1989a]); and M.L. Samuels and Jeremy Smith's analysis and clarification of the language of William Gower (Samuels and Smith 1981 [1988]). Independently, but with parallel results, the data furnished by the two atlases for Old French made by Anthonij Dees and his team in Amsterdam have led to important insights into medieval French texts (Dees, van Reenen and De Vries 1980; Dees, Huber and van Reenen-Stein 1987).

For the medieval dialectologist to interpret the varieties of language which are the object of study it is necessary to go beyond the purely linguistic not only to understand the diplomatic but also the broader social and cultural context. This kind of approach to language study is in contrast to that of other historical linguists where the object of study is a closed, autonomous, uniform system — the kind characterised (if not caricatured) by the notion of 'ideal speaker-listener, in a completely homogeneous speech-community' (Chomsky 1965: 3). In a recent paper on the interpretation of language change James Milroy observes:

> if we focus on linguistic change alone (excluding other aspects of language), we can indeed propose sophisticated descriptions of attested changes and go on to propose even more sophisticated theories of change. However, if we pose the more basic question why some forms and varieties are maintained while others change, we cannot avoid reference to society.
>
> (Milroy 1992: 75–76)

The autonomist view leaves out of consideration a great deal that is clearly important to an understanding of language variation and change. Language must also be described in its use as well as its apparent structure and theory needs ultimately to take account of that. However abstract the levels of analysis become, there has to be reference back to speaker–listeners and writer–readers and how they use their language. Language is a human faculty. The study of language and languages, if it has any purpose, is to contribute to the wider science of humanity and therefore it is part of a much greater epistemology. The kind of interchange between the practitioners of the different branches of inquiry represented at the Colloquium reflects in part the wider picture albeit on a small scale.

3. Panel I: Taxonomy and Typology in Medieval Dialect Studies

The intention was to open the programme with consideration of the nature of medieval dialects, and indeed to question the sense of this notion. This task was to have been undertaken by Michael Benskin. However, a bout of illness on the opening day caused his contribution to be postponed until the second day of proceedings. His paper is discussed below.

The first paper, presented by Hans Frede Nielsen, seeks to look anew at an old philological problem: the origin and spread of initial voiced fricatives and the phonemic split of fricatives in English. He compares it with the same phenomenon in the history of Dutch and demonstrates that though it occurred in two closely related varieties of West Germanic with similarly structured phonological systems it had different outcomes in the two languages. He argues that in England the greater prevalence of adopting French loanwords strengthened and confirmed the phonemicisation of voiced and voiceless fricatives, a colonisation of what in Old English was 'empty' phonological space. Middle Dutch was less influenced by borrowing from French with, moreover, quite separate development of members of its fricative set. His paper challenges the conclusions of Kurath's (1956) account of the phenomenon in English.

Pieter van Reenen critically surveys the study of Medieval Dutch and makes some trenchant comments on methodology. Van Reenen belongs to what we may call 'the Amsterdam School of historical dialectology'; he was a member of the team which produced the first of the two important atlases for Old French (Dees et al. 1980). He has been applying the same methods to Middle Dutch (van Reenen et al. 1985). The 'Amsterdam School' and the 'Edinburgh School' (McIntosh, Samuels, Benskin, et al.) — in which the organisers claim enrolment — have developed independently similar methods of tackling the 'dialectal' analysis of medieval vernaculars. There are important differences and emphases, but the two approaches are in broad agreement. We at Edinburgh endorse van Reenen's views on the selection of data, his distrust of manuals and printed texts as data-sources for theorising and the problems of channelling the results of research into mainstream teaching. However, we believe that studying orthographic variation in its own right should not be neglected. It is evident from the analysis of late Middle English that written conventions can often show geographically patterned variation, in situations where it is not possible to adduce underlying differences in the spoken language to account for the variants. The relative distributions for ‹y› and ‹þ› provide a striking example (see Benskin 1982; and *LALME*, vol. 2, maps for items 2 THESE, 7 THEY, 8 THEM, 31 THAN, 32 THOUGH, 235 THITHER).

The 'Amsterdam School' is experienced in the computer storage and analysis of texts. At Edinburgh also we are developing computer-aided methods. However, we are very dubious about the possibility of 'standardising' the encoding of texts. It does not seem to us practical. Research projects, even collaborative ventures, tend to be sui generis. The kind of coding required for the lexico-morphological analysis of texts, such as both Amsterdam and Edinburgh are engaged in, is quite different from what might be required for a palaeographical analysis (cf. Arn 1985) or a stylistic analysis (cf. e.g. Meurman-Solin 1993). The creation of, or ability to reconstitute, basic texts in ASCII format would seems to us a more realistic approach to moving data between computer systems.

4. Panel II: Manuscript Studies and Literary Geography

Richard Beadle considers the question of geographical dissemination of texts in the late 14th and the 15th centuries. He contrasts the situation resulting form the establishment of a strong, London-centred printing industry with its standardising influence on English at the end of the 15th century with the earlier regional origination and copying of texts in manuscript. Drawing on the notion of 'criterio geografico', more familiar in relation to Biblical and Classical texts, Beadle suggests that manuscripts of a text were disseminated through copies being made in neighbouring localities. In this way texts spread out in a graduated way from the place of authorial origin. The ability to determine patterns of distribution of a text depends upon a high rate of survival of manuscript copies and evidence, linguistic and non-linguistic, for localisation of the copies. (How many manuscripts does one need to show a coherent pattern of dissemination?) Beadle illustrates his argument with three texts which have survived in a number of copies and which have received considerable scholarly attention — the *Prick of Conscience, Piers Plowman* and John Mirk's *Festial*. In two appendices he proposes distributions for *Speculum Vitae* and *Speculum Christiani* which he considers as good candidates for further study.

Taking a palaeographer's view, Ian Doyle examines the educational background to manuscript production in the late Middle Ages and the teaching of writing. He stresses the need for investigation of the possibility of regional variation in scripts and of the relationship of script to spelling. Doyle also points out the limitations of graphetic profiles (cf. McIntosh 1974 [1989a]). Indeed, if the computer is to be brought to bear on the analysis and comparison of scripts in individual texts then a coding procedure (such as that produced, for example, by Arn 1985) may not be adequate. Procedures involving the scanning of manuscripts and analysis by means of graphics software may be the way forward.

Jeremy Smith considers the relationship between modern linguistic theory and traditional philology. Smith believes that there must be an awareness of 'underlying theoretical orientations'. But the reality of language — its 'buzz and hum', its mix of order and mess — must not be ignored in theorising. Theories must be able to account for the confusion and complexity as well as the simple regularities.

In the study of medieval vernaculars our data comes in the form of written texts. Smith asserts that 'every text has its own history'. The interpretation of individual texts requires an understanding of the wider context. He illustrates his point with three examples: the language of Gower and its scribal treatment by copyists; the Anglo-Scots linguistic curiosity *Lancelot of the Laik*; and the linguistic behaviour of the Rushworth Gospel scribe, Farman.

As a future prospect Smith proposes a series of regional studies, 'whereby codicological and philological interests could combine to recreate the linguistic and literary geography of the medieval period'.

5. Keynote Address

Anthonij Dees of the Free University of Amsterdam gave a 'keynote' paper. As the majority of the participants were Anglicists, we believed it would be instructive to hear from a scholar within another tradition — Romance linguistics — and one who has developed new ideas and techniques of analysis in two important areas of study. Anthonij Dees has been responsible with a team of researchers for revolutionising the understanding of linguistic variation in Old French texts, both literary and non-literary, of the late 13th and early 14th centuries. The fruits of this research are published in two linguistic atlases for Old French and a series of papers by Dees and his collaborators on dialectal distribution of forms and sound-changes. In addition, Dees has developed a novel and controversial approach to the study and construction of textual stemmata.

In his paper Dees gives a sketch of his work on these two topics. He and his colleagues in their work on dialectal variation in Older French (late 13th and early 14th century) have challenged the received view of the dissemination of Parisian French in the provinces, where, it is held, it gradually diluted and eliminated regional written forms. The dialect atlases reveal rather a picture of geographically patterned variation of written forms right across the country. Dees outlines the motives for his approach and states the principles underlying his dialectological procedures.

Turning to the reconstruction of textual stemmata, Dees advocates a quite different approach to the usual one, practised within both the Anglicist and Romance philological traditions. He is extremely sceptical of relying on comparisons of common error and contamination as a means of constructing a single genealogical tree for a manuscript tradition. Dees proposes that, in fact, more than one tree may be required to account for manuscript kinships.

6. Panel III: Languages in Contact

The study of 'languages in contact' is a particulary interesting field for medieval studies. The British Isles has always been a multi-cultural and multi-lingual area, no less so than the rest of Europe. As an antidote to monolinguistic and anglocentric perceptions of British culture and society, it should be remembered that indigenous Celtic languages still survive and that in the 20th century immigrant communities have introduced, and their descendants maintained, their languages and cultures. In the Middle Ages plurality of cultures and languages is not in doubt.

Angus McIntosh in 'Codes and Cultures' questions the practice of treating language as somehow quite separate from its speakers. 'fundamentally, what we mean by *languages in contact is users of language in contact.*'[7]

McIntosh's point may seem obvious, even trivial. It is not. The tenet of studying language as an autonomous system underpins a great deal of 20th-century linguistic theory. Yet, as stated above, it is plain

---

[7] Cf. James Milroy (1992) on the usefulness of distinguishing 'speaker' and 'system'.

from the work of sociolinguists (and indeed from commonsense observation) that changes which affect the structure of language appear to correlate with extralinguistic factors. Speakers' attitudes to their culture and society, their aspirations, their perceptions of their roles and relationships have a bearing on their use of the language or languages which they speak. And we cannot account for a great deal of observable linguistic variation unless such factors are taken into account, no less so in relation to present-day language than to those of the Middle Ages.

William Gillies reviews the past and present states of study of the Celtic languages, pointing up the complexity of relationships between speakers of these languages in the British Isles both with each other and with their Germanic neighbours. Gillies argues that it is time for a comprehensive synthesis of recent research along the lines of Kenneth Jackson's *Language and History in Early Britain* (1953). However, he regards this as most likely to be achieved by an interdisciplinary team of scholars rather than an individual. And (echoing McIntosh) they would need to be open to 'the dynamic quality of the language (or languages), as spoken by real speakers...'.

Helmut Gneuss addresses the issue of contact between Latin and Old English in early medieval England and particularly the borrowing of Latin words into Old English. Although he regards much of the pioneering work of a century ago as still 'sound and valid', new evidence has led to revision in our understanding. Gneuss considers some important seams of evidence which have been opened up or developed further for investigating loanwords and their dating: (1) archaeological evidence; (2) historical linguistics, particularly work on linguistic interference, bilingualism, semantic borrowing and loan-formations; (3) manuscript evidence, with a wider range of data now available in textual editions and corpora. Gneuss also considers early treatment of Latin loanwords in Old English and the possibility of their regional distribution.

Latin influenced all European vernaculars for which we have evidence in the Middle Ages and its relationship to and effect on them is of great interest. Nor is the influence all one way: the vernaculars must in turn have influenced the writing and also the speaking of Latin. The use of vernacular words in Latin texts is a common phenomenon (e.g. in Scottish texts) with sometimes switching between, or even mixing of, Latin and vernacular (e.g. in Irish and

German texts[8]). Comparison of such vernacular–Latin interaction would enhance our understanding both of the vernaculars and of medieval Latin.

7. Panel I Revisited: On Dialects and Dialectology

To hold a colloquium on 'medieval dialectology' presupposes that the organisers, if not the participants, are agreed that the notion of 'dialect' is valid in the interpretation of some linguistic phenomena of the Middle Ages. The notion of dialect as a determinable entity, linguistic-ally or non-linguistically, is challenged by Michael Benskin. Rightly, in our view, he takes to task scholars who conceive of dialects as discrete entitites, pre-defined according to non-linguistic criteria (e.g. an administrative county or a putative area of historical settlement) or linguistic (e.g. a philological category such as the reflexes of WGmc ǎ). Benskin argues that the distributions of linguistic forms should be determined first before worrying about classification of linguistic features in terms of non-linguistic criteria.

We have stressed the importance of considering linguistic material in the light of non-linguistic factors; that is at the heart of the Colloquium.   But the nature of the relationship has to be carefully considered. Dialectology, medieval or otherwise, deals with the facts of linguistic variation and their interpretation as linguistic data. That is where it begins. Until the linguistic facts have been determined we cannot see how they may relate to any non-linguistic phenomena. In effect, dialectology can be carried out without the notion of 'dialect'.

Benskin also argues for the application of statistical methods in the comparision of areal distributions of linguistic forms. The general ready availability of computers makes it possible to tackle such comparisions in a systematic and rigorous way rather than relying on impressionistic assessments of similarity or dissimilarity.

8. Panel IV: Word Geography

Terry Hoad offers a brief retrospective on the history of word-geographical studies in Middle English and concludes that the result to

---

[8] For the development of the vernacular alongside Latin in a class of 14th-century south-west German texts, see W. Kleiber et al. 1979: vol. 1, Introduction § 1.4.1.

date is disappointing. As a field of study it has been neglected and work so far has been rudimentary, nor have the aims of word geography been clear, he believes. Hoad cites two paradigms within which word geography has been tackled. The first, pioneered by Kaiser in his study of scribal treatment of northern vocabulary in the southerly versions of *Cursor Mundi*, might be termed 'translation tolerance'. The second is that which underpins the *Linguistic Atlas of Late Mediaeval English* — the creation of a large corpus of localised texts in which 'the occurrence of particular words can be observed'.

It may be observed that *LALME* in itself is of limited use in word-geographical studies, since it deals with a defined set of vocabulary items, albeit numbering 280. However, the texts localised in the atlas could be scanned beyond these items for new data. The early Middle English and Older Scots projects currently under way in Edinburgh will offer more scope for word-geographical study since the corpora will contain complete texts, fully tagged.

If much systematic data collection for word geography still lies ahead, Robert E. Lewis assesses what is now available and what can be done with it. There is, he asserts, enough data collected for a start to be made. In addition to the set of localised texts in *LALME*, he cites the increasing availability of machine-readable Middle English texts. There are also numerous printed editions with glossaries and concordances of texts in multiple versions. And there is the *Middle English Dictionary*. Of course, there are limitations with even these materials, as Lewis makes clear. But he exemplifies what can be done by examining the verb *tharnen* 'to lack, lose'.

The important resource of place-name evidence is discussed by Gillian Fellows-Jensen. In particular, she highlights the value of field names as sources of localisable vocabulary elements and suggests ways in which these can be exploited.

9. Editing of the Proceedings

The task of editing the proceedings of the Colloquium has been more complex than if we had confined ourselves just to publication of the papers. The papers, after all, were intended as lead-ins to the main business of the Colloquium — discussion. Those participants who gave papers had the opportunity to revise their contributions for publication and it is the revised texts that are published here. Our biggest problem was how best to treat and present the taped discussions.

The tapes of the discussion sessions were transcribed by the editors. To publish a verbatim transcript would not have made an easily readable text. The hesitations, repetitions and false starts that are part and parcel of 'real speech' had to be filtered out. Also, the text was emended where it was felt necessary to clarify arguments and points made in contributions. Our aim has been to present a text for reading which nevertheless retains a strong flavour of the spoken interchanges. Each participant was sent copies of the transcriptions and given the opportunity to comment on their contributions and to add information, including references, and to correct errors (sometimes of transcription). Some re-expression of arguments was permitted; in such cases, the essence of what was said originally has always been retained. In one or two cases contributions were re-ordered where they did not relate to the surrounding contributions, but where they were taken up later in the discussion.

Keith   Williamson
Margaret Laing

References

Arn M.-J. 1985 The systematic representation of early manuscripts in computer form: a proposal. In: Arn M.-J. and Wirtjes H. (eds.) *Historical and Editorial Studies in Medieval and Early Modern English for Johan Gerritson.* Wolters–Noordhoff: Groningen

Benskin M. 1982 The letters ⟨þ⟩ and ⟨y⟩ in later Middle English, and some related matters. *Journal of the Society of Archivists* 7: 13–30

Benskin M., Laing M. 1981 Translations and *Mischsprachen* in Middle English manuscripts. In: Benskin M. and Samuels M.L. (eds.) *So meny people longages and tonges: Philolgical Essays in Scots and Mediaeval English presented to Angus McIntosh.* Published by the editors: Edinburgh

Chomsky N. 1965 *Aspects of the Theory of Syntax.* MIT Press: Cambridge, Mass.

Dees A., with Reenen P.Th. van and De Vries J.A. 1980 *Atlas des formes et constructions des chartes françaises du 13e siècle.* Niemeyer: Tübingen

Dees A., with Dekker M., Hubber O., and Reenen-Stein K. van 1987 *Atlas des formes linguistiques des textes littéraires de l'ancien français.* Niemeyer: Tübingen

Doyle A.I. and Parkes M.B. 1978 The production of copies of the *Canterbury Tales* and *Confessio Amantis* in the early fifteenth century. In: Parkes M.B. and Watson A.G. (eds.) *Mediæval Scribes, Manuscripts and Libraries: Essays presented to N.R. Ker.* Scolar Press: London, pp. 163–210

Jackson K.H. 1953 *Language and History in Early Britain.* Edinburgh University Press: Edinburgh

Kleiber W., Kunze K., Löffler H. 1979 *Historischer Südwestdeutscher Sprachatlas*, vol. 1. Francke Verlag: Berne and Munich

Laing M. (ed.) 1989a *Middle English Dialectology: essays in some principles and problems*. Aberdeen University Press: Aberdeen

Laing M. 1989b Linguistic profiles and textual criticism: the translations by Richard Misyn of Rolle's *Incendium Amoris* and *Emendatio Vitae*. In: Laing M. 1989a, pp. 188–223

Lass R. 1980 *On Explaining Language Change*. Cambridge University Press: Cambridge

McIntosh A. 1973 [1989a] Word geography in the lexicography of mediaeval English. *Annals of the New York Academy of Sciences* 211: 55–66; repr. in Laing M. 1989a, pp. 86–97

McIntosh A. 1974 [1989a] Towards an inventory of Middle English scribes. *Neuphilologische Mitteilungen* 75: 602–24; repr. in Laing M. 1989a, pp. 46–63

McIntosh A. 1979 [1989a] Some notes on the language and textual transmission of the *Scottish Troy Book*. *Archivum Linguisticum* NS 10: 1–19; repr. in Laing M. 1989a, pp. 237–55

McIntosh A., Samuels M.L., Benskin M. with Laing M., Williamson K. 1986 *A Linguistic Atlas of Late Mediaeval English*, 4 vols. Aberdeen University Press: Aberdeen

Meurman-Solin A. 1993 *Variation and Change in Early Scottish Prose*. Academia Scientiarum Fennica: Helsinki

Milroy J. 1992 A social model for the interpretation of language change. In: Rissanen M., Ihalainen O., Nevalainen T. and Taavitsainen I. (eds.) *History of Englishes: New Methods and Interpretations in Historical Linguistics*. Mouton de Gruyter: Berlin

Reenen P.Th. van, Hogenhout-Mulder M.J., Dekker M., Huber O. 1985 Towards a data base of Middle Dutch dialects on the basis of 14th century charters. *Vrije Universiteit Working Papers in Linguistics* 18. Department of General Linguistics, Vrije Universiteit, Amsterdam

Samuels M.L. 1983 [1988] The scribe of the Hengwrt and Ellesmere Manuscript of *The Canterbury Tales*. *Studies in the Age of Chaucer* 5: 49–65; repr. in Smith J.J. 1988, pp. 38–50

Samuels M.L., Smith J.J. 1981 [1988] The language of Gower. *Neuphilologische Mitteilungen* 82: 294–304; repr. in Smith J.J. 1988, pp. 13–22

Smith J.J. (ed.) 1988 *The English of Chaucer and his Contemporaries*. Aberdeen University Press: Aberdeen

Panel I

TAXONOMY AND TYPOLOGY IN MEDIEVAL DIALECT STUDIES

I.1 On the Origin and Spread of Initial Voiced Fricatives and the Phonemic Split of Fricatives in English and Dutch[1]

Hans F. Nielsen

0. Introduction

One of the difficult problems of early Middle English dialectology is the voicing of initial fricatives. It is the aim of this paper first to survey the research history of the origin of initial voicing, taking into account similar developments on the European continent, and secondly to compare the systemic split of fricatives in Middle English to that in a closely related continental language, Middle Dutch, with a view to determining the possible cause(s) of the split (and its success) in English. Finally, the paper offers suggestions as to why initial voicing proved unable to spread into the northern and north-east Midland dialects of Middle English.

1. The Origin of Initial Voiced Fricatives

Over the last one hundred years numerous attempts have been made to account for the voicing of initial fricatives as manifested in the southern and south-western dialects of Middle English and early Dutch, cf. $f, s, þ > v, z, ð$ (Middle Kentish *vader, verste; zelve, zoþe; þe, þyef* and Old Low Franconian (Old Dutch) *vogala* (Old West Flemish), *Velthem* (Old Ghentish); Middle Dutch *zegghen, zo; daer, dief* ($d < ð$), cf. van Bree 1987: 156–60). Not surprisingly, this parallel has been

---

[1] Only section 2 of this paper as it appears in this volume was delivered at the Colloquium.

interpreted in terms of shared inheritance exhibited by two closely related languages, i.e. as a change that took place in Germanic or West Germanic (cf. Sweet 1876: 76–79, 1888: 139; and Ellis 1889: 832), and which was brought to England by the Anglo-Saxon colonisers. In his doctoral dissertation from 1917 Brøndal also attributed the parallel to a common background, although not to one for which the Germanic *Stammbaum* could be employed as an explanatory model. According to Brøndal (1917: 102–110), the voicing of fricatives in English and Dutch was the result of an increase of sonority in these two Germanic idioms that should ultimately be ascribed to Celtic substrata in England and in the Low Countries.

A scholar working in the border area between the *Stammbaum* and the more recent methods of dialect geography is W.H. Bennett, who agreed with Sweet and Ellis in dating the voicing of initial fricatives to the pre-invasion period, but who thought that the Jutes on their way from Jutland to Kent and the Saxons en route to the *Litus Saxonum* and the south-west of England had passed through the lower Rhenish area (Bennett 1969 [1955]: 351) and thereby acquired voicing of initial *f*, *s*, *þ*. Bennett thus combined spread of features through emigration of speakers with spread through contact. But it is significant that Bennett (1969 [1955]: 353–54) considers 'the Channel and the Strait of Dover ... effective barriers against the ingress of linguistic influences'. Bennett seems to be unaware of the fact that actual contact is decisive for the spread of linguistic features. The sea does not in itself prevent spread as is convincingly demonstrated by Hans Kuhn (1955: 16–44). In principle, the possibility of post-invasion cross-Channel diffusion must be accepted, and this is precisely what lies behind the hypothesis that initially voiced fricatives spread from Old Low Franconian into late Old English/early Middle English (cf. Luick 1940: §703 Anm. 8 and Markey 1976: 37–78, esp. 72). According to Samuels, the 'Kerngebiet for this voicing appears to have been Franconian' (Samuels 1971: 8), but it cannot, in his view, be settled whether its attestation in English dialects was due to pre-invasion inheritance or post-invasion contacts. As pointed out by Braune/Eggers (1987: §102a), fricatives were exposed to lenition in all West Germanic languages and in Old Danish, lenition reaching Old High German from the north. In Franconian lenition was only a step on the way to fricative voicing. Fisiak (1985) has interpreted the voicing of initial fricatives in English as the result of a unitary lenition process that may or may not be attributable to continental influence. See also Kristensson (1992).

The first scholar to suggest that the voicing of initial fricatives in English was an independent process was, to my knowledge, Otto Jespersen, who in his doctoral dissertation from 1891 argues that initial *f* (and presumably *s-* and *þ-*; cf. 1891: 176) was voiced south of the Thames when the preceding word ended in a vowel; cf. *Ancrene Riwle* (1225) spellings such as *ilke uondunges, one ureond* vs. *þeos fondunges, mot fleon* (Jespersen 1891: 173–76).[2] Jespersen is aware that the rule is not found consistently in 13th-century southern Middle English manuscripts but he assumes that the voiced sound was eventually generalized, cf. the modern south-western dialects (Jespersen 1909: 42). The traditional historical grammars have tended to see no explicitly foreign inspiration in the voicing of initial fricatives in English (cf. Wright 1905: §278, §320; 1928: §236; Brunner 1965: §192, Anm. 1; etc.), assigning the voicing process to late Old English/early Middle English — and certainly to the pre-Norman era because words of French origin were generally not affected. Jespersen's parole-based view of the origin of voiced initial fricatives has been more or less repeated by Moore et al. (1935: 15), Luick (1940: §703), Wakelin/Barry (1968: 59) and Wakelin (1972: 92). In the last-mentioned scholar's words initial voicing may first have arisen 'in the sentence in intervocalic positions'. In a later book Wakelin called the origin of voicing 'obscure' (1975: 161), and most recently (Wakelin 1982: 9) it is stated that the change arose in Old English, 'in or near the Devon area, where it is still most vigorous'. To Jespersen, Moore et al., Luick, Wakelin/Barry and Wakelin (1972) the origin of voicing should be ascribed to sentence assimilation, a type of change which is likely to have developed independently in English. Contact need not be assumed to account for such a conditioned change in the spoken chain.

2. The Phonemic Split of Fricatives in English and Dutch

As far as the systemic split of /f/, /s/ (and /þ/) into voiceless and voiced phonemes is concerned, no scholar has, to my knowledge, ever ascribed this specific process to contact between Dutch and English.

---

2 In view of Sweet's own continental Germanic derivation of the initial voiced fricatives in early English, cf. above, it is hardly surprising that he is not convinced by Jespersen's observation, even if in a letter to Jespersen he calls it 'very interesting' and 'new' (Jespersen 1891: 176 fn. 2). It is noteworthy, however, that in a subsequent work Sweet assigns the voicing to the Middle English period (1900: 262, cf. 242) and without offering any explanation as to its origin.

Traditionally, this phonemic contrast in Dutch has been associated with the introduction of loanwords in *f-* and *s-* from, e.g., French, which disrupted the complementary distribution of respectively [-f] [(-)v-] and [-s] [(-)z-], cf. *fier* 'proud', *sier* 'cheer' (< French) vs. indigenous Dutch *vier* 'four', *zier* 'whit' (van Bree 1987: 157, 160 and esp. 196; Schönfeld/van Loey 1970: §50 opm. 1, §86; Goossens 1974: 73, 75, 84).

Similarly, the split of Old English /f/ and /s/ into Middle English /f/, /v/ and /s/, /z/ has often been connected with the introduction of French loanwords which, in terms of voicing, had initial fricatives contrasting with the native ones, cf. ME *fain* (< OE *fægen*) vs. *vain* (< OF *vain*) and ME *sele* 'sele' vs. *zele* 'zeal' (< OF)[3] (Samuels 1972: 95; Lucas 1991: 52–54; cf. also Schibsbye 1972: 85; Jordan/Crook 1974: 192; and Steponavičius 1987: 171).

According to Kurath (1969 [1956]), however, voiced fricatives first became phonemicised in intervocalic position in the north-east Midlands and some northern dialects in early Middle English (by 1200). In these dialects all short vowels were lengthened in open syllables, and this led to the shortening of long consonant phonemes which up to this point had been retained in intervocalic positions: /v́ccv/ (cf. OE *bannan*) no longer contrasted with /v́cv/ but only /v́vcv/ (cf. OE *bana*, which in eME acquired the same vowel length as the reflex of OE *stānas*), and /v́ccv/ was therefore simplified to /v́cv/. Up to this time /v́ccv/ had been the only possible environment of occurrence for long consonant phonemes, but to retain their phonemic status had become pointless because vowel length had now become an unequivocal distinguishing factor, cf. /v́vc/ vs. /vc/ as in eME *bǭk* vs. *buk*. Orthographically, the systemic realignment led to the use of double consonants as markers of preceding short vowels. The shortened voiceless reflexes of /-ff-/, /-ss-/ and /-þþ-/ in the dialects in question therefore came to contrast with the intervocalic voiced allophones of /f, s, þ/. The phonemic split into /f, s, þ/ and /v, z, ð/ was eventually reinforced by the adoption of French loanwords with *v-* and *z-* in initial position[4] and the loss of final /-ə/ from ca. 1300 in the northern half of England which resulted in voiced final fricatives contrasting with voiceless ones (Kurath 1969 [1956]: 144–46).

---

[3] In the southern and south-western dialects of Middle English, French loanwords in /f-/ and /s-/ would contrast with local forms in /v-/ and /z-/.

[4] Initial /ð/ arose later in the unaccented, pronominal words *the, thou, thy, that*, etc. in accordance with the principles of 'Jespersen's Law' (cf. Jespersen 1909: 199–208 and Schibsbye 1972: 84–85).

In the south Midland and southern dialects long consonants survived for a bit longer. Here only /e, o, a/ were lengthened in open syllables but not /i/ and /u/ which in the sequences /icə, ucə/ continued to contrast with /iccə, uccə/. It is generally believed that in the south long phonemic consonants disappeared only ca. 1400 with the loss of final /-ə/ (cf. /v́ccə/ > /v́c/) in combination with analogical pressures. In London, it might be added, north Midland forms co-occurred with the dominant south Midland type (Kurath 1969 [1956]: 147–49).

If once again we return to Dutch, let us examine to what extent Kurath's view of the phonemic split of fricatives in Middle English can be applied to the Dutch material. The West Germanic geminated consonants are likely to have become independent phonemes only in Old Dutch when the reflex of the West Germanic conditioning factor (-*j*-) disappeared (van Bree 1987: 155; Schönfeld/van Loey 1970: 59; and Goossens 1974: 94–95). In medial position Middle Dutch at first retains regular geminated spellings (van Bree 1987: 155), but later Middle Dutch spellings suggest that double consonants had come to designate preceding short vowels — and single consonants, preceding long ones (Schönfeld/van Loey 1970: 106); cf. *heffen* vs. *geven* and *vlassen* vs. *glazen*. It would seem that in Middle Dutch vowel lengthening in open syllables (cf. Goossens 1974: 41–42) was followed by shortening of long consonant phonemes[5] just as in Middle English. Medial long consonants may have lost their phonemic status in the same way as suggested by Kurath for the north Midland and northern dialects of English: vowel quantity became the dominant distinguishing factor, and voiceless shortened fricatives thereby came to contrast with medial voiced ones. However, the overall picture in Dutch differs a good deal from what we find in English.

It is true that the adoption of French loanwords paved the way for the implementation of the phonemic split into /f/ and /v/ and into /s/ and /z/ in initial position, but the opposition between voiceless and voiced fricatives did not become nearly as well integrated into the Dutch phonemic system as it did in English. Whereas in the latter language the loss of final /-ə/ put voiced fricatives in final position, in Dutch the unaccented vowel was retained for somewhat longer, and when it was eventually exposed to apocope in Modern Dutch, the fricative became voiceless in final position, cf. MDu *ic scrive* 'I write',

---

5   Or, alternatively, that MDu vowel lengthening and shortening of geminated consonants were interdependent changes, cf. Goossens 1974: 74.

neve 'nephew' vs. ModDu *ik schrijf, neef.* And whereas in English the phonemic opposition between voiceless and voiced fricatives was reinforced by the inclusion of /ʃ/ ≠ /ʒ/ (cf. Fisiak 1985: 13–14; Lucas 1991: 56–57), there was not even a split in Dutch of /þ/ into /þ/ and /ð/; cf. the opposition developing in Middle English. On the contrary, the reflex of ODu /þ/ had merged with /d/ both initially and medially in Middle Dutch (*drie* 'three', *oude* 'old'), and in final position it had become /t/ (MDu *doot* 'death' vs. *dodes* 'death's'). The geminated consonant /-þþ-/ changed to /-s(s)-/, cf. MDu *smisse* 'smithy' (van Bree 1987: 157; Schönfeld/van Loey 1970: 57–58). It might also be mentioned that *z*-spellings to denote the reflex of ODu /s/ initially are rare in Middle Dutch and only emerge in considerable number in Modern Dutch; cf. Franck (1910: 74). According to Goossens (1974: 84, 75), the opposition /s/ ≠ /z/ did not come into existence until the Modern Dutch period and most probably subsequent to the split between /f/ and /v/. It is interesting that in present-day Dutch there is a tendency, apparently spreading from Amsterdam (van Bree 1987: 203), among some speakers to give up the opposition between voiceless and voiced fricatives, the voiceless pronunciation being prevalent. If we are to believe Schönfeld/van Loey (1970: 56) this coalescence is by no means disastrous, for the functional yield of the phonemic distinction in question is relatively low in Dutch.

We may sum up by saying that voicing processes were at work in both the Low Countries and the south of England, *f, s, þ* becoming voiced initially in both Old Dutch (van Bree 1987: 156–60) and late Old English/early Middle English. In my view, the significance of this voicing or lenition process should not be overrated, for it involves only an extension of the phonological space occupied by the three phonemes /f, s, þ/. But why did the phonemic patterns emerging from the split into voiceless and voiced fricatives come out so differently in English and Dutch? The potentiality for a split was present in both languages (Moulton 1972: 152; van Bree 1987: 201) in that other obstruents, namely the stop consonants, exhibited the opposition voice ≠ voiceless. And the input was in both cases not all that different: /f, s, þ/ were present in both languages and lengthening of short vowels in open syllables as well as shortening of long medial fricative consonants to voiceless medial fricatives took place in both Dutch and English. This would seem to suggest that Kurath is not right in his (otherwise fascinating) structural exposition of the emergence of voiced fricatives in English contrasting with voiceless ones. Rather, it would imply that the massive influx of French loanwords into Middle English, a borrowing process quantitatively far from being paralleled by Middle Dutch, played a much greater role than anticipated by Kurath. Thus the phonemic opposition between voiceless and voiced fricatives[6] could simply have been imported along with the numerous loans.[7]

3. The Spread of Initial Voiced Fricatives and the Danelaw

Let us finally discuss the hypothesis recently advanced by Poussa concerning the voicing of initial fricatives that 'what checked the northward expansion of the lenition innovation was most probably its encounter with a belt of Scandinavian-influenced (creolised) dialects' (1985: 238); cf. also Lucas 1991: 57–58. Poussa takes inspiration for her theory in Kristensson's tentative isophones (based on Lay Subsidy Rolls) for the spread of initial *v*- and *z*- in the West Midlands (see Fisiak 1985: 10–12 and Map 4) which lie further north than hitherto assumed and which, significantly, seem 'to correspond so clearly with the western end of the Danelaw boundary in the OE period' (Poussa 1985: 238). Poussa envisages a scenario where in the Danelaw, on the verge of language death, bilingual Danish speakers would 'relexify their language to English, while retaining their own phonological system'. Here (and elsewhere) Poussa appears not to distinguish between the lenition process itself and the phonemic split of fricatives into voiceless and voiced entities. But by saying that initial /ð/ arose in *the, that, this* 'in later OE', Poussa (1985: 240) makes not only what amounts to a phonemic statement (borrowed from Brunner 1960: 376 and ultimately from Sievers, cf. Brunner 1965: §200 Anm. 1), but also one that deviates sharply from the prevalent view (cf., for example, Fisiak 1985: 13–14; Jespersen 1909: §6.53; and above n. 4 and 6). What is the explanation of this? The obvious answer is that Poussa *needs* a voiced initial fricative phoneme in order to show that it becomes devoiced in the *Orrmulum*, the 'best evidence for the phonology of an

---

6 As Lucas (1991: 54–55) points out, there could have been no (direct) French influence in the split of /þ/ into /þ/ and /ð/. Lucas connects the split especially with the initial voicing to /ð/ in weakly stressed words ('Jespersen's Law', see above n. 4), cf. *thy* vs. *thigh*, and the loss of final /ə/ which put /ð/ in final position in, e.g., *bathe* (vs. *bath*).

7 Cf. , e.g., *vine* 'vine', *fine* 'end'. And not infrequently borrowings would have become homonymous with native words, had it not been for their voicing contrast, cf. French loan words like *vain* 'vain' and *zele* 'zeal' (vs. *fain* < OE *fægen* and *sele* 'seal').

early ME Danelaw dialect'; cf. such spellings as *þe~te, þatt~tatt, þis~tis* (Poussa 1985: 240–41). As she points out herself, the 'other fricatives are invariably spelled with *f, s* and *sh* ...' If, as most scholars believe today, devoicing did not take place, this would only mean that the Danes and their descendants held on to a pronunciation pattern identical with that inherited from Old English, namely one that exhibited initial voiceless fricatives.

It is interesting that Kristensson's ME Lay Subsidy Rolls survey, when eventually published in 1987, showed that in Staffordshire, there were occurrences of initial *v-* and *z-* north of Watling Street (1987: 201–208 and 247 (Map 14). Kristensson even suggests that the *v-, z-* area in the West Midlands may have extended somewhat further north than attested by his survey (1986: 7). A systematic analysis of the place-name material in the county volumes of the *English Place-Name Society* by Michael Weber pushes the northern boundary of the voicing area further north also towards the east. In his presentation of Weber's survey, Voitl (1988: 568 and 585 (Map 1)) includes all of Essex and all of Hertfordshire in the voicing area and suggests that the northern boundary may have to be redrawn still further north[8] if, e.g., Weber had been able to include the material for Suffolk, for which no *EPNS* volume was available.

To me it would seem that in the north-east Midland and northern dialects initial *f-* and *s-*, apart from being voiceless retentions of OE (and Scandinavian) fricatives, were prevented from taking part in the voicing (lenition) process spreading north once the phonemic split into voiceless and voiced fricatives had gone into operation in the dialects in question. And although I believe that the split is likely to have been triggered by French lexical influence (cf. above), I think that /f/, /v/ and /s/, /z/ became independent phonemes earlier in the North and (North-)East than in the area where lenition prevailed. It is a fact (a) that short vowels were lengthened earlier and more consistently in the north-east Midland and northern dialects (see, e.g., Jordan/Crook 1974: §§ 25–26); (b) that geminated consonants lost their phonemic value earlier in these dialects;[9] and (c) that final /-ə/ was

---

[8] Kristensson's Lay Subsidy Roll material for the East Midland counties (not yet published) shows that *f-* in fact became *v-* in the southern parts of Suffolk and Cambridgeshire as well as in northern Hertfordshire and all of Essex. Kristensson links this to the rare occurrences (or virtual absence) of Scandinavian settlement names near the south-eastern limit of the Danelaw, cf. Hugh Smith's famous map. See Kristensson (1992).

[9] The loss of long consonants should probably be seen in close connexion with the lengthening of short vowels in open syllables and the subsequent systemic realignment,

first dropped towards the North and much later in the southern and south-western dialects.[10] There is considerable irony in the assumption that the retention of the old (voiceless) pronunciation of initial fricatives is (at least in part) associated with a phonemic split which has itself been accelerated by the rate of linguistic innovation in the dialects concerned.

4. Conclusion

It is interesting, but perhaps not surprising, that the history of linguistic science is so well reflected in the explanations offered by scholars of the origin of early initial fricative voicing: *Stammbaum* inheritance, substratum influence and contact of dialects or languages are all there along with explanations in terms of independent development or conditioned change and subsequent generalisation and spread. However, there is no evidence which forces us to assume either independent parallel change or continental influence on English (cf. Fisiak 1985: 5), but it should be noted that initial voicing had no immediate bearing on the early southern Middle English or on the early Dutch fricative system: it simply took advantage of the phonological space available.

As for the systemic split into voiceless and voiced fricatives in Middle English and Middle Dutch, we have seen that there is remarkable similarity between the processes leading up to the split in the two languages: lengthening of short vowels in open syllables, shortening of long intervocalic consonant (fricative) phonemes and loss of final unaccented /-ə/. However, we do not agree with Kurath that it was the loss of the long intervocalic fricatives that triggered the phonemic split in the northern and north-east Midland dialects of England and the (later) loss of final /-ə/ which was responsible for the

---

cf. Kurath above. It is noteworthy that consonant lengthening may have been very close to losing its phonemic value in Northumbria as early as in the 10th century, cf. the following unetymological spellings in the gloss of the *Lindisfarne Gospels*: ðidder, cymmende, spreccende, frumma, nomma, etc. (S.M. Kuhn 1970: 49).

[10] According to Jordan/Crook (1974: §141) /-ə/ disappeared in the North from the 13th century, and at first formerly medial intervocalic fricatives came out with -*f*, cf. Northern *luf* 'love', *abof* 'above', *gif* 'give', etc. (1974: §217, §209), which suggests that phonemicisation might not yet have taken place. Forms in -*v* (cf. the ModE spellings) only cropped up later in the Middle English period. See also above, §2. It might be added that Minkova (1982: 42–52) regards open syllable lengthening and the loss of /-ə/ as simultaneous and interdependent processes.

split in the South and the South-West. To Kurath the introduction of French loanwords into English with /f-, s-/ ≠ /v-, z-/ only established the phonemic opposition in initial position. Comparison with Dutch suggests that the French lexical impact on English played a decisive role for the fricative split in this language. In Dutch, contrasting fricatives did not become nearly as well integrated in the phonemic system, and it would appear that the outspoken differences of degree of French influence on the two languages could explain the diverging fates of the fricative splits. After all, only England was invaded and ruled by the Norman French.

Finally, doubt is raised as to whether the Danelaw boundary was of any real significance for checking the northward spread of initial voiced fricatives as claimed by Poussa (1985). There are indications that in some cases voicing crossed Watling Street and, further east, even penetrated into Essex and beyond. To me it is very tempting to connect the failure of initial voiced fricatives to spread into the northern and north-east Midland dialects of Middle English with the phonemic split of fricatives which must have taken place earlier in these dialects than further south and south-west. The speed of change was generally higher here and the way had been paved, as it were, for the fricative split although itself sparked off by French influence. The phonological space necessary for the further northward expansion of the initial voicing process was no longer available. Whether the later retreat of initial voicing had anything to do with the advance of the fricative split is unknown, but sociolinguistic factors may well have played a role as suggested by Voitl (1988). London with its great influx of northern and north Midland speakers and prestigious initial voiceless fricatives eventually came to exercise considerable linguistic influence, and in the Midlands /f-, s-, þ-, ʃ-/ spread to neighbouring dialects, the voiceless fricative pronunciation being identical with that of London (Voitl 1988: 575–80).

References

Bennett W.H. 1969 [1955] The Southern English development of Germanic initial [f s þ]. In: Lass R. (ed.), *Approaches to English Historical Linguistics*. Holt, Rinehart & Winston: New York, pp. 349–54; first publ. *Language* 31: 367–71

Braune W./Eggers H. 1987 *Althochdeutsche Grammatik*, 14th edn. Niemeyer: Tübingen

Bree C. van 1987 *Historische Grammatica van het Nederlands*. Foris: Dordrecht

Brøndal V. 1917 *Substrater og Laan i Romansk og Germansk*. G.E.C. Gad: Copenhagen

Brunner K. 1960 *Die englische Sprache*, vol. I, 2nd edn. Niemeyer: Tübingen

Brunner K. 1965 *Altenglische Grammatik*, 3rd edn. Niemeyer: Tübingen

Ellis A.J. 1889 *On Early English Pronunciation*, vol. V. Philological Society: London

Fisiak J. 1985 The voicing of initial fricatives in Middle English. *Studia Anglica Posnaniensia* 17: 3–16

Franck J. 1910 *Mittelniederländische Grammatik*, 2nd edn. Tauchnitz: Leipzig

Goossens J. 1974 *Historische Phonologie des Niederländischen*. Niemeyer: Tübingen

Jespersen O. 1891 *Studier over engelske kasus*. Klein: Copenhagen

Jespersen O. 1909 *A Modern English Grammar on Historical Principles*, vol. I. Allen & Unwin: London; Munksgaard: Copenhagen

Jordan R./ Crook E.J. 1974 *Handbook of Middle English Grammar: Phonology*. Mouton: The Hague

Kristensson G. 1986 On voicing of initial fricatives in Middle English. *Studia Anglica Posnaniensia* 19: 3–10

Kristensson G. 1987 *A Survey of Middle English Dialects 1290–1350: the West Midland Counties*. Lund University Press: Lund

Kristensson G. [forthcoming 1992] Voicing of initial fricatives revisited. In: *In Memoriam John Dodgson*

Kuhn H. 1955 Zur Gliederung der germanischen Sprachen. *Zeitschrift für deutsches Altertum und deutsche Literatur* 86: 1–47

Kuhn S.M. 1970 On the consonantal phonemes of Old English. In: Rosier J.L. (ed.) *Philological Essays. Studies in Old and Middle English Language and Literature in Honour of H.D. Meritt*. Mouton: The Hague, pp. 16–49

Kurath H. 1969 [1956] The loss of long consonants and the rise of voiced fricatives in Middle English. In: Lass R. (ed.) *Approaches to English Historical Linguistics*. Holt, Rinehart & Winston: New York, pp. 142–53; first publ. *Language* 32: 435–45

Lucas P.J. 1991 Some aspects of the historical development of English consonant phonemes. *Transactions of the Philological Society* 89(1): 37–64

Luick K. 1940 *Historische Grammatik der englischen Sprache*, I.2. Tauchnitz: Leipzig

Markey T.L. 1976 *Germanic Dialect Grouping and the Position of Ingvæonic*. Inst. für Sprachwiss. d. Univ.: Innsbruck

Minkova D. 1982 The environment for open syllable lengthening in Middle English. *Folia Linguistica Historica* 3(1): 29–58

Moore S., Meech S.B., Whitehall H. 1935 *Middle English Dialect Characteristics and Dialect Boundaries*. University of Michigan Publications. Language and Literature 13: Ann Arbor

Moulton W.G. 1972. The Proto-Germanic non-syllabics (consonants). In: Coetsem F.v., Kufner H.L. (eds.) *Toward a Grammar of Proto-Germanic*. Niemeyer: Tübingen, pp. 141–73

Poussa P. 1985. A note on the voicing of initial fricatives in Middle English. In: Eaton R. et al. (eds.) *Papers from the 4th International Conference on English Historical Linguistics*. Benjamins: Amsterdam, pp. 235–52

Samuels M.L 1971 Kent and the Low Countries: some linguistic evidence. In: Aitken A.J., McIntosh A., Pálsson H. (eds.) *Edinburgh Studies in English and Scots*. Longman: London, pp. 3–19

Samuels M.L. 1972 *Linguistic Evolution*. Cambridge University Press: Cambridge

Schibsbye K. 1972. *Origin and Development of the English Language*, I. Nordisk Sprog- og Kulturforlag: Copenhagen

Schönfeld's Historische Grammatica van het Nederlands 1970. 8e druk verzorgd door A. van Loey. Thieme: Zutphen

Steponavičius A. 1987 *English Historical Phonology*. 'Vysšaja škola': Moscow

Sweet H. 1888 [1876] *A History of English Sounds*. Clarendon Press: Oxford; 1st edn. 1876

Sweet H. 1900 *A New English Grammar*, I. Clarendon Press: Oxford

Voitl H. 1988 The history of voicing of initial fricatives in Southern England: a case of conflict between regional and social dialect. In: Fisiak J. (ed.) *Historical Dialectology: Regional and Social*. Mouton: Berlin, pp. 565–600

Wakelin M.F. 1972 *English Dialects*. The Athlone Press: London

Wakelin M.F. 1975 *Language and History in Cornwall*. Leicester University Press: Leicester

Wakelin M.F. 1982 Evidence for spoken regional English in the 16th century. *Revista Canaria de Estudios Ingleses* 5: 1–25

Wakelin M.F./Barry M.V. 1968 The voicing of initial fricative consonants in present-day dialectal English. *Leeds Studies in English. New Series* 2: 47–63

Wright J. 1905 *The English Dialect Grammar*. Frowde: Oxford

Wright J., Wright E.M. 1928 *An Elementary Middle English Grammar*, 2nd edn. Oxford University Press: Oxford

I.2 The Study of Medieval Language in the Low Countries: the Good, the Bad and the Future

P. Th. van Reenen

I am invited to this Colloquium as a specialist in historical dialectology of the Low Countries. I certainly feel flattered, since there are many extremely competent colleagues in the field. I am also a specialist in computer linguistics, dealing especially with the treatment of corpora: large quantities of language data. In this latter quality I will present a brief diagnosis of the field of Middle Dutch, followed by a sketch of two future scenarios plus an illustration of what is possible, with a view to a long-term strategy. Since the realisation of this aim is quite ambitious in 10 to 15 minutes, I will simply skip all subtleties and refrain from more than incidental illustration. What is at stake in my opinion — and this is my starting point — is a redefinition of how research in the field should be carried out, a field that is in need of resurrection. Essentially I will make three main points.

- positive developments in the field;
- factors preventing progress;
- the future.

1. Positive Developments in the Field

Perhaps more than any other medieval language, the oldest documents (charters and literary texts) of Middle Dutch are accessible for research to a very large extent. Many have been published, and many are stored on computer. And many are both. The charters on computer are tagged morphologically or are in the process of being tagged. Essentially two corpora of charters are available:

- About 2,000 charters of the 13th century. These charters have been published in Gysseling (1977). The corpus comprises essentially all 13th-century charters in Middle Dutch which still exist. They are all morphologically coded on computer at the Instituut voor Nederlandse Lexicologie (INL). The great majority were written in Flanders, mainly Brugge, at some distance followed by Gand. In the Northern Netherlands only Dordrecht is reliably and sufficiently documented with 59 charters. There are also many charters from the Count of Holland which may often represent the language of The Hague, but this is not certain since the Count did not necessarily recruit his scribes from this area. On the basis of this corpus already two dialect atlases have been published, see Berteloot (1984b) and Mooyaart (1992), and a number of smaller studies, see for instance Goossens (1979) and Berteloot (1984a).

- About 2,500 charters of the 14th century. This corpus covers the whole Dutch speaking area, including Overijssel, Drente and Groningen. For the greater part the corpus has not been published yet. It is available on computer at the Free University, Amsterdam and is in the process of being morphologically tagged. Essentially the same system is being used as with respect to the 13th-century charters of the Corpus Gysseling (see above), the coding system for both projects being developed in collaboration with the INL. My colleague Maaike Mulder and I started to collect the 14th-century data more than 10 years ago. Map 1 gives some idea of how the charters are distributed over the Dutch speaking area. Some studies based upon this corpus are van Reenen and Wattel (1992), van Reenen and Wijnands (1993), van Reenen and Mulder (1993).

There is also a Middle Dutch corpus of early literary texts, published in Gysseling (1980–87), and available on computer at the INL. These texts have not yet been placed systematically, the date and place of production often being not known in detail. Since March 1993 a project for the localisation of such texts is being carried out at the Free University (NWO ST 300–172–019). This project is inspired by the methods developed for Old French (see Dees et al. 1987) and Middle English (see Benskin 1988). It will serve not only to localise literary (and historical) texts but also to test the localisation of the charters of the Count of Holland: is the language of these charters closer to the

Map 1.

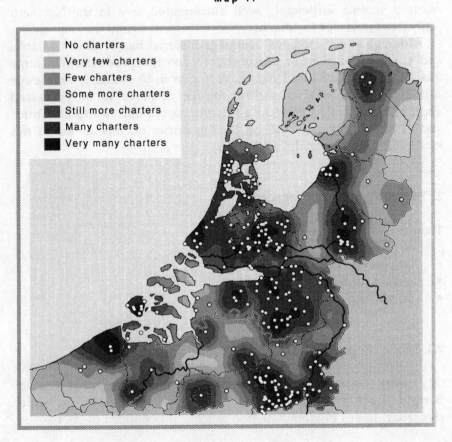

Frequency distribution of 14·th century charters per

locality/region.

language of The Hague village than to any other locality, i.e. are they from The Hague or from other localities? Since these charters are dated it may be possible to add a reliable series of charters to those already accepted as such and, as far as the 13th century is concerned, to create a second sufficiently well documented area in the Northern Netherlands besides Dordrecht.

Although much medieval language material has become available, and the most important preconditions for the production of large quantities of systematised data have begun to be fulfilled, even more 14th-century material is waiting in the archives to be processed appropriately, with a view to a reliable description of Middle Dutch and its many dialects. And for later centuries documentation of this kind is almost completely lacking yet.

2. Factors Preventing Progress

The main factors preventing progress are

- lack of respect for data;
- respect for the wrong data;
- problems of data processing.

2.1 *Lack of Respect for Data*

'My theory is not confirmed by the data. Let us look for other data' (cf. Bertold Brecht). The approach is typical for studies in which theoretical issues predominate (too much). It is implicit of course.

2.2 *Respect for the Wrong Data*

I distinguish three cases: written language instead of spoken language; present-day opinions instead of medieval realities; manuals instead of manuscripts.

2.2.1 *Written Language instead of Spoken Language*

The focus is on the spelling and writing, not on the speech. The implicit reasoning is: since we have no spoken language left, we should not examine speech, but letters, spelling, text. We should examine questions like the influence of the writing system developed in one city on the writing system developed in the other, instead of an analysis of the influence of the speech of one city on the speech of another. In this approach the problem of dialectal transition zones has been reduced to a spelling problem instead of a sound problem.

2.2.2 *Present-day Opinions instead of Medieval Realities*

Present-day opinions are projected in the past without any guarantee that these opinions represent genuine medieval realities. Two of the best known notions, especially in the French tradition, but also elsewhere, are 'koine' and 'scripta'. Thanks to Dees (1985) these pseudo-notions are not taken seriously any longer.

Recently I have come across another, in my opinion rather mythic, notion in connexion with medieval charters: that of 'city hall language', instead of the, in my opinion, much more realistic notion of 'city language' (see Niebaum 1991).

Quite common and seductive is our wishful thinking that we know better than our predecessors. Once a colleague warned me against Erasmus. What he said was approximately: 'Admittedly, Erasmus was a great humanist, but he did not understand language and linguistics as well as we do. Consequently, we had better not trust [as we did in van Reenen and Wijnands 1993] the description Erasmus provides of the pronunciation of *uy* in his time'.

A last example illustrates, I think, the very common, usually implicit, opinion that language is homogeneous. The medieval pronunciation of [s] and [z] before a vowel is a good example. Franck (1910: 74) observed that *s* preceding a vowel in Middle Dutch is pronounced as [z], although it was spelled both *z* and *s*. For instance *z* and *s* in *sal, zal* 'shall, will' are both pronounced [z]. Apparently, in Franck's view scribes could not spell very well: 'Diese Schreibung . . . wird selten konsequent, sondern in willkürlichem Wechsel mit *s* angewandt'. As a neogrammarian, Franck did not take into account the possibility that the pronunciation might have been both [s] and [z], i.e heterogeneous, instead of homogeneous, as it still is today (see van Reenen and Wattel 1992).

2.2.3 *Manuals instead of Manuscripts*

In many publications in the field, linguists and philologists follow implicitly the guideline 'Trust the manuals not the manuscripts!', a complete reversal of values. Three points illustrate this attitude.

- Handbooks repeat each other. The pronunciation of *s* and *z* preceding a vowel is again a good example. Without any exception, all the later manuals have the same opinion as Franck (see above). There is one difference, however. They are more polite than Franck. Franck's blunt but perfectly logical conclusion (following from his wrong premise) about the lack of professional qualities of medieval scribes is not repeated.

- Historical linguists with an interest in data rely blindly on handbooks. For many of them these manuals, so easy to consult, have replaced the medieval reality of the manuscripts, usually not easily accessible in any systematic way. These linguists are not aware of the fact that handbooks reflect the older languages in a seriously biased way. In their view the handbooks function as the norm, a status these studies do not deserve (and sometimes do not claim to have). As a consequence, many a linguistic statement, even language universals, have been proposed which are only to be found in these manuals, but cannot be traced in medieval texts.

- Text editors tend to adapt editions of medieval texts to the handbooks. Many an edition of a medieval text does not distinguish between the part of the modern scholar and the part of the medieval manuscript. Especially the so-called abbreviations the scribes have used are often supplemented by the modern scholar without notice. The reader of such editions risks being informed about linguistic aspects which were never present in the medieval manuscript, but which via the intervention of the scholar come directly from the manuals. Proper names especially tend to be assigned systematic aspects they never had in medieval texts, a pure artefact of the manuals.

2.3 *Problems of Data Processing*

I have observed already that existing knowledge often is not reliable. This is due to a large extent to the problem of data processing: the classification of medieval manuscripts and the systematisation of the speech in the manuscripts. I will mention three specific points:

- the lack of knowledge of how to process the relevant data;
- the impossibility of processing data appropriately;
- the impossibility of applying present-day research methods.

For more about these problems the reader is referred to van Reenen (1985), van Reenen and Schøsler (1990).

2.3.1 *Lack of Knowledge of How to Process the Relevant Data*

There is often little or no serious reflection on the reliability of the documents to be used. This lack of reflection on data contrasts sharply with the ingenious proposals to be found in the field of theoretical linguistics. However, since theories are to be (dis)confirmed by data, the outcome of the verification procedure is usually far from satisfactory, if any verification is possible at all.

It is often not felt that the language of original, local charters is more reliable than the language of literary texts, which are usually undated copies and hard to localise. It is sometimes not even felt that the language of both types of texts is more reliable than subjective present-day opinion.

In a study of the verb *zullen* 'shall, will', De Vriendt-de Man (1952: 22–23) observes that texts reproducing the *Theater of the Rhetoricians* are hardly or not useful for linguistic research, since 'it may sometimes be very difficult to indicate the area of origin and to distinguish northern and southern publications'. As a consequence, 'reliable and dated pieces of the *Theater of the Rhetoricians* are rare'.[1] We cannot but agree with this observation. However, the same scepticism is found with respect to charters: 'The language of the official documents . . . teems with traditional formulas and archaic turns, often slavishly

---

[1] Translations by PvR.

copied from an older, similar piece'. For instance, the form *zelen* in a document dated 19 May 1589, Brussels, is, allegedly, slavishly transcribed from an earlier redaction dated 1446. However, how does the author know that *zelen* was acceptable in 1446, but is not any longer 143 years later? The author does not make clear at all why the scribe in 1589 should have used, in an official document, a speech form which was not longer current any more. A case of completely unjustified apriorism!

The author, however, lacks methodological knowledge to the extent that the arguments mentioned are not even taken seriously. Since the study is to be based upon, in the author's view, unreliable sources of information, one wonders why the author has undertaken it at all. It would have been good logic to abandon the study completely, as the author does indeed with respect to the pronunciation of the first consonant of the verb *zullen*, i.e. *s* or *z* preceding a vowel, possibly in the wake of Franck (1910); see above.

2.3.2 *The Impossibility of Processing Data Appropriately*

Present-day linguistic knowledge of the past is to a large extent based upon data which, instead of being representative of the old language, are both incorrect and incomplete. The reason why this is so is not always lack of knowledge of how to process data. Since medieval manuscripts — consisting of text written for other purposes than linguistic analysis — do not provide linguistic information in any systematic way, the process of systematising the speech forms they contain could not be carried out on a sufficiently large scale in the pre-computer age. But already Fallot (1839) had the right view of how to proceed.

Studies of the verb *zullen* may illustrate the point for Middle Dutch. Van Loey (1952, 1966) and especially van den Berg and Vermeulen (1973) use a correct research strategy. But even in these studies we do not find a more or less complete picture of what the medieval sources have to offer. And several observations turn out to be hardly representative or even to be incorrect.

When these studies were written, computer science could not yet provide its powerful search and select capacities on large quantities of data, in order to enable the linguist to detect the patterns in the speech forms, and to check their ideas and intuitions about the distributions of these forms.

As a result, much of what could have been observed on the distribution of *zal* versus *zel*, *zullen* versus *zellen*, *zolen* versus *zoelen* or *zelen*, forms with *-ll-* (mainly *zullen*, *zellen*) versus forms with *-l-* (mainly *zoelen*, *zolen*, *zelen*), is either lacking or incorrect.

2.3.3 *The Impossibility of Applying Present-day Research Methods*

Linguistics started as a science of the older phases of languages, and methods and habits in philology were developed in this early period. Later, interest shifted towards research on present-day language. New methods of research were developed in view of this. Thanks to Labov (see for instance Labov 1972), methods and data processing have been quite succesful in sociolinguistics, and still are, see for instance Gregersen and Pedersen (1991). These results are highly inspiring, also for those working on older language stages.

The research on present-day language may help us to understand problems of the past indeed. But beware! Present-day strategies of research are not always relevant for research of the language of the past. There are considerable differences in the production of the systematised data. The processes for data-collecting for languages of the past are often completely different from those for data-collecting for present-day speech. Another difference concerns the fact that research on present-day speech is usually in apparent time, whereas research on older speech can be carried out in real time. A notion such as standard language usually goes no further back in history than the beginnings of industrialization. And where appropriate statistics are available for present-day speech research, they are not always with respect to languages of the past. (See van Reenen and Wattel 1992.)

3. The Future

I have three points to make:

- without renewal the future will be ugly; but
- when auxiliary sciences are used appropriately the future will be bright;
- an illustration: the modal verb marking future tense, *zullen*.

3.1 *The Future May Be Ugly*

With few exceptions, the teaching of Middle Dutch in the Low Countries is restricted to medieval literature. If medieval language is on the programme at all there is often no connexion with empirical research. This has been so for quite a number of years. Even if we want to change this deplorable state of affairs there may be hardly any competent teachers available. The field is dying, not for lack of potential research areas, but for lack of the renewal which makes re-animation possible.

Many linguists have the wrong mentality. Large scale empirical research is outside their scope. They have no idea of, or experience in, systematising large quantities of data. They sometimes say they are proud not to know how to do mathematics very well: it is a figure of speech to pretend so when starting a discussion on numbers and figures. But nobody would ever dream of starting a discussion by observing that he is not able to spell.

Of course, it is only a figure of speech, and more than once I have observed that it is used by colleagues who show great insight into what the figures are about. However, when other colleagues warn us, and especially the youngsters among us, that we should not believe that the computer can take over thinking, we are listening to those colleagues who usually have not even the slightest idea of what they are talking about. The best they can do for the field is immediately retire, or at least keep silent.

3.2 *The Future May Be Bright*

In the first half of the 19th century, Louis Fallot (1839) defined a programme of research which could not be carried out for practical reasons. Today the programme can be carried out. Computer science and statistics have brought about this change. How do you organise research on languages of the past when you cannot use your intuition? Train students

- in methods of data selection;
- how to handle large quantities of data and to be familiar with notions of probability;
- how to systematise, to refine and to represent data.

Students must not only have knowledge of Middle Dutch. They should know how to handle the computer, how to produce a corpus; how to enrich a corpus; how to ask questions of a corpus; and how to process the answers.

Teachers should create standardisation procedures for that. Initiatives such as the Text Encoding Initiative should be welcomed, supported and completed. In the Low Countries a special foundation, the STDH, is actively favouring this aspect of research.[2]

Language is created in the present. It is conserved as past. Both aspects are objects of research with their own research methodology. The study of the two aspects complement each other. By combining them, we come as close as possible to understanding language and its variations.

3.3 *An Illustration: the Modal Verb marking Future Tense,* zullen

What computer science can be used for is demonstrated in Maps 2 through 7.[3] Map 2 concerns the two vowel qualities of the singular forms, *zal* versus *zel*, '(I or he) will, shall'. Maps 3 through 6 concern plural forms or the form of the infinitive of the verb *zullen*. All the forms may also begin with s. Maps 2 and 3 show that the area of *zellen* does not cover completely that of *zel*. Maps 4 and 5 show that *zoelen* and especially *zolen* are found in the East, and show the distribution of the stressed vowels of the auxiliary verb *zullen* in the 14th century. Finally, Maps 6 and 7 show that forms with -*ll*-, i.e. forms with a preceding short vowel, are taking over from the forms with -*l*-, i.e. forms with a preceding long vowel, especially in the North and in Noord-Brabant. Other maps and tables are to be found in van Reenen and Mulder (1993) for the vowels in the verb, and in van Reenen and Wattel (1992) for the first consonant: [s] or [z]. The maps provide an accurate picture of what have been the forms of the old language, as far as they are found in the charters.

---

[2] See the reference to the Policy Document, STDH 1992.

[3] The maps were produced by my colleague Evert Wattel.

Map 2.

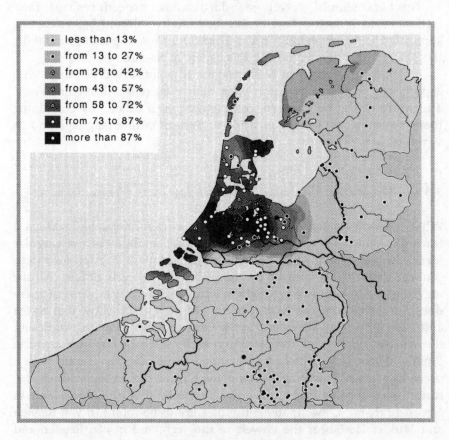

Zel (dark) versus **zal** (light) during the 14th-century.

Map 3.

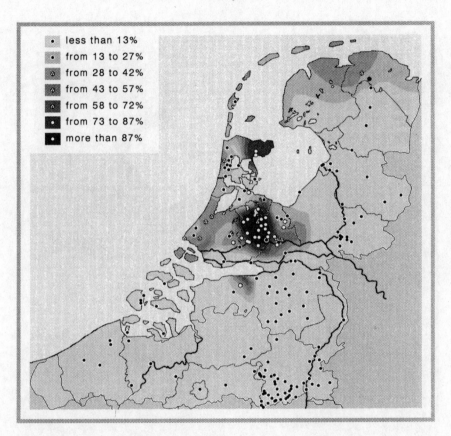

Legend:
- less than 13%
- from 13 to 27%
- from 28 to 42%
- from 43 to 57%
- from 58 to 72%
- from 73 to 87%
- more than 87%

Zellen (dark) versus the other plural/infinitive forms during the

14th-century.

Map 4.

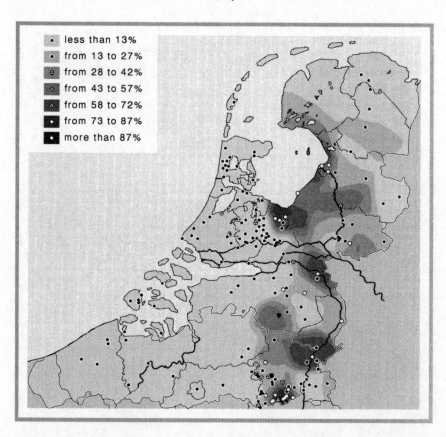

Zoelen (dark) versus the other plural/infinitive forms during the 14th-century.

Map 5.

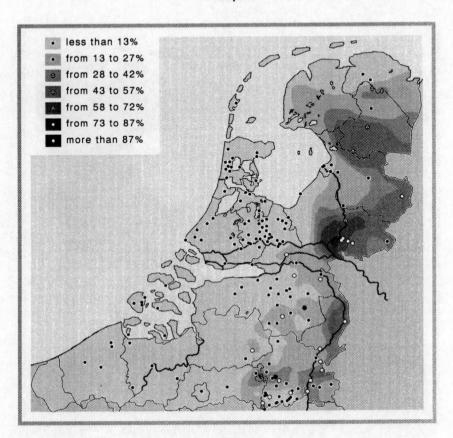

Zolen (dark) versus the other plural/infinitive forms during the

14th-century.

Map 6.

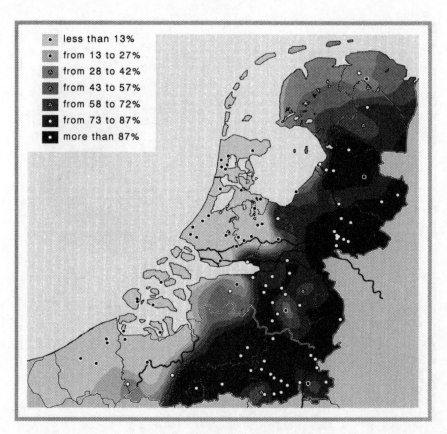

less than 13%
from 13 to 27%
from 28 to 42%
from 43 to 57%
from 58 to 72%
from 73 to 87%
more than 87%

Forms with **-l-** (dark, mainly **zelen, zolen zoelen**) versus forms with **-ll-** (light, mainly **zullen, zellen**) during the period 1301-1370

Map 7.

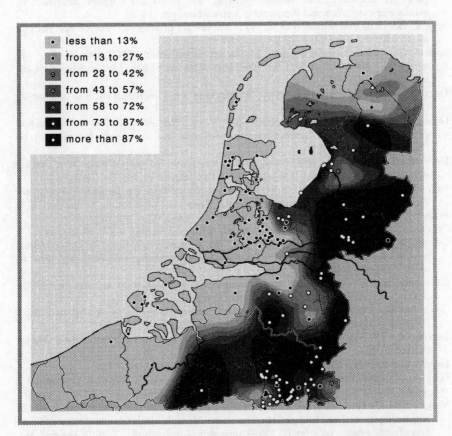

Forms with **-l-** (dark, mainly **zelen, zolen zoelen**) versus forms

with **-ll-** (light, mainly **zullen, zellen**) during the period 1371-1400

References

Benskin M. 1988 The numerical classification of languages, and dialect maps for the past. In: Reenen P. van, Reenen-Stein K. van *Spatial and temporal distributions, manuscript constellations*. Benjamins: Amsterdam, pp. 13–38

Berg B. van den, Vermeulen A.G.M. 1973 'Zullen' als proefgeval. *De Nieuwe Taalgids* **66**: 445–52

Berteloot A. 1984a Overwegingen bij de 'Lieden/luden'–kaart. *TNTL* **100**: 29–45

Berteloot A. 1984b *Bijdrage tot een klankatlas van het 13de-eeuwse Middelnederlands*. KANTL: Gent

Dees A. 1985 Dialectes et scriptae à l'époque de l'ancien français. *Revue de Linguistique Romane* **49**: 87–117

Dees A., Dekker M., Huber O., Reenen-Stein K. van 1987 *Atlas des formes linguistiques des textes littéraires de l'ancien français*. Beihefte zur Zeitschrift für romanische Philologie 212: Tübingen

De Vriendt-de Man M.J. 1958 *Bijdrage tot de kennis van het gebruik en de flexie van het werkwoord ZULLEN in de 16de eeuw*. KVAT&L, Reeks VI, Nr. 81: Gent

Fallot G. 1839 *Recherches sur les formes grammaticales de la langue française et de ses dialectes au 13e siècle*. Imprimerie royale: Paris

Franck J. 1910 *Mittelniederlaendische Grammatik*. Tauchnitz: Leipzig

Goossens J. 1979 De ambtelijke teksten van het corpus-Gysseling. *TNTL* **95**: 216–61

Gregersen F., Pedersen I.P. (eds.) 1991 *The Copenhagen Study in Urban Sociolinguistics, Parts 1 & 2*. Institut for dansk Dialektforsknings publikationer, serie A, nr 30. Reitzel: Copenhagen

Gysseling M. 1977 *Corpus van Middelnederlandse teksten (tot en met het jaar 1300), Reeks I: Ambtelijke bescheiden*. Nijhoff: The Hague

Gysseling M. 1980–88 *Corpus van Middelnederlandse teksten (tot en met het jaar 1300), Reeks II: Literaire handschriften*. Nijhoff: The Hague

Labov W. 1972 *Sociolinguistc Patterns*. University of Pennsylvania Press: Philadelphia

Loey A. van 1952 Een en ander over Mnl. *Sullen*. *VMA*: 919–22

Loey A. van 1966 *Middelnederlandse Spraakkunst, I Vormleer, 5*. Wolters: Groningen

Mooyaart M.A 1992 *Atlas van Vroegmiddelnederlandse Taalvarianten*. LEd: Utrecht

Niebaum H. 1991 Review of: Leuvensteijn J.A. van 1988 (ed.) *Uitgangspunten en toepassingen. Taalkundige studies over Middelnederlands en zestiende- en zeventiende-eeuw Nederlands*. Vu-Uitgeverij: Amsterdam. *Taal & Tongval*, pp. 222–26

Reenen P. van 1985 La linguistique des langues anciennes et la systématisation de ses données. In: *Actes du IVe Colloque International sur le Moyen Français 1982*. Rodopi: Amsterdam, pp. 433–70

Reenen P. van, Schøsler L. 1990 Le problème de la prolifération des explications. *Travaux de Linguistique et de Philologie* **28**: 221–38

Reenen P. van, Wattel E. 1992 *De uitspraak van /s/ en /z/ voor klinker in het Nederlands: zes eeuwen variatie*. In: *De binnenbouw van het Nederlands Festschrift Paardekooper*

Reenen P. van, Wijnands A. 1993 Early diphthongizations of palatalized West Germanic [uː], The spelling *uy* in Middle Dutch. In: Aertsen H., Jeffers G. *Proceedings of the 9th International Conference on Historical Linguistics*. Benjamins: Amsterdam, pp. 389–415

Reenen P. van, Mulder M. 1993 *Een gegevensbank van 14de-eeuwse Middelnederlandse dialecten op computer.* Lexikos

STDH 1992 *Stichting Tekstcorpora en Databestanden in de Humaniora* (Association for Text corpora and Databases in the Humanities, Policy Document). Vakgroep Computer & Letteren RUU: Utrecht

Panel I TAXONOMY AND TYPOLOGY IN MEDIEVAL DIALECT STUDIES

Discussion

chaired by *Matti Rissanen*

Gillis Kristensson: I listened with great interest to Hans Frede Nielsen's theories[1] and I think there are two problems. First, the phonemisation of the old [f s] sounds and the comparisons with Dutch. I think there are similarities and that they could very well be due to direct influence from Dutch. But they show a quality immanent in all West Germanic languages: namely the tendency for voicing of fricatives. This is in contradistinction to the North Germanic languages, where voicing did not exist, at least not in initial position. It could occur in the medial position. That is one problem; but rising out of that there is the other very interesting problem, namely the phonetic question: why was [f s θ] voiced, probably in late Old English, in what part of England did it take place and why did it recede?

There are lots of different theories. There are those who think that it was taken over by the immigrants to southern England, and those who even speak about Celtic influence. I think this second aspect is quite as interesting as the one you took up. Your theory is mainly concerned with a phonological point of view: the question of whether we are dealing with phonemes or allophones. But when the connective process took place — certainly in late Old English — we are dealing with allophones. It was not until much later, however, that we can talk about phonemes — in late Middle English or perhaps earlier. I have devoted a lot of time lately to Kurath's[2] article. And I

---

[1] Note that only section 2 of Hans Frede Nielsen's paper as printed in this volume was delivered for discussion at the Colloquium.

[2] H. Kurath 1969 [1956] The loss of long consonants and the rise of voiced fricatives in Middle English. In: R. Lass (ed.) *Approaches to English Historical Linguistics.* Holt, Rinehart & Winston: New York, pp. 142–53; first publ. *Language* 32: 435–45.

think in a way his argument is extremely good and interesting, but it is based on very fragile evidence, namely the theory of the lengthening of short *i* and short *u*. Actually we know very little about that and unfortunately I think there is little possibility for us ever to get exact knowledge about it.

The question is, if there was ever a lengthening of short *i* and short *u* where did it take place? Was it limited to northern England, as Luick has taught us? Or perhaps it took place in other parts, but there are no traces of it in the spelling. It might be that short *i* became lengthened and the old spelling was kept so that is why we shan't ever get to know about it. I entirely agree with your opinion that the Kurath article, however valuable, is not quite correct, and probably indeed it is because of French influence that we have phonemes here much earlier than we could have through lengthening.

Hans Frede Nielsen: You are quite right; my paper only dealt with the phonemic aspect. It didn't deal as such with initial voicing of fricatives, although I see it all in context and that is how I began by looking at it. If we discuss first the voicing of initial fricatives it is, from the viewpoint of the history of linguistics, a very interesting topic to follow. You can follow in handbooks and articles the way that the signs developed and you find people advocating *Stammbaum* explanations, that voicing was brought over to England by settlers. This would be speech analysis. You have people working within a dialect-geography framework who suggest that it spread either across the Channel or started in England and spread from there.

You also touched on the substratum theory, that it was due to Celtic influence — Celtic sonority — underlying voiced-initial fricatives both on the Continent and in England. Lately, most scholars have stuck to the notion of independent developments — that is, initial voicing might have developed independently on the Continent and in England. And I think that this kind of explanation has something to be said for it. If you look at it structurally you could argue that it was likely to happen since there was a voicing distinction in stop consonants that might eventually also become a voicing distinction in fricatives.

Also, I don't know whether you noticed this, but I used the notion of phonological space, although this is not a notion normally used in connexion with consonants. It is not really so strange that voicing took place: a word could not be misconstrued because the initial fricative was voiced — it didn't really matter; this was something that might happen, something that might not happen. The interesting thing is really, what stops the spread of voicing in England? And did phonemicisation, perhaps, have something to do with the stopping of the voicing process? I know that Professor Kristensson is in favour of Danelaw influence being decisive for the sort of borderline between initial voiced fricatives and initial voiced or voiceless fricatives. This is also a view that has been put forward recently by Poussa.[3] What struck me about some of your material from the West Midlands published in your Lay Subsidy Roll book[4] is that actually you have voicing on the other side of Watling Street; that Watling Street is not a sharp line of division between voicing and non-voicing.

Kristensson: Actually, I now have a map of the voicing process in the south-east of England and it is remarkable that we find voicing exactly in that very area where the Vikings did *not* settle. But in the area where we know there was heavy Scandinavian settlement there is no single incidence of voicing. There was one clash, namely in Essex. Essex is within the Danelaw, but I have examined it and it appears that there was only slight Scandinavian settlement in Essex. Ekwall even says that it seems to have been just a military settlement of that area. But apart from that there is a very high degree of coincidence between the Scandinavian settlement area, where there is no voicing, and the remainder of England with clear incidence of voicing.

Nielsen: You said that voicing took place in parts of the Danelaw where there are no Danish place-names. But where there are Danish place-names, can these be taken as evidence that Danish was actually spoken there? The second point is that lenition actually took place in Old Danish also.

Kristensson: Not in initial position.

Nielsen: No, not initial position except possibly in demonstrative pronouns where instead of [θuː] you say [du] and in the definite article [de], [det] instead of [θɛt]. This is a kind of lenition.

---

3 P. Poussa 1985 A note on the voicing of initial fricatives in Middle English. In: R. Eaton et al. (eds.) *Papers from the 4th International Conference on English Historical Linguistics*. Benjamins: Amsterdam, pp. 235–52.
4 G. Kristensson 1987 *A Survey of Middle English Dialects 1290–1350: the West Midland Counties*. University Press: Lund.

Pieter van Reenen: I would like to comment a little bit on this notion of the clash between West Germanic and North Germanic. In Dutch you have oppositions like [pɪt] and [bɪt] which are quite clear, although there is no aspiration as in English [pʰɪt]. But in my speech I have oppositions like [zeːvən] and [seːvəntəx] — and I pronounce them like that. But that is just in my part of the country, i.e. The Hague. In Amsterdam, many people say either [seːvən] and [seːvəntəx], and other people, or even the same people sometimes, [zeːvən] and [zeːvəntəx]. Now these people don't have two phonemes — maybe they have [s], maybe they have [z]: they don't know and we don't know. But it's one phoneme — it's just variation of style. That's like North Germanic and my speech is more West Germanic in your classification. Even if for me the opposition between [z] and [s] is existent, I am much more tolerant about changing them around than in the case with [p] and [b] — it's a completely different notion of phonemisation. I have the impression that something like that is going on with your problem.

Margaret Laing: If you had lived in the 13th century you would probably have been accused of being one of those scribes who couldn't spell at all.

I wonder if I might raise a different point and ask you something about the 13th-century charter material in the Low Countries. You mentioned that it had been called 'city hall' language. We also have a similar label in the description of English — 'chancery standard'. I wonder whether this shows the same kind of problem, where there is an acceptance of a description of a language which may well not hold when you come to look at the individual manuscripts and the individual scribes working in administrative institutions. Do you have anything to say about this in relation to the Low Country charters?

van Reenen: Well, just a very short observation. The label 'city hall' was applied to the language of Groningen. Maaike Mulder and I were the first to examine this language. There was no reason at all to say something like that; it just comes from the implicit notions of the scholar — a German tradition actually — who termed it this.

Kathryn Lowe: I would like to take you up further on your preference for the term 'language of the city'. What exact form are your charters in? Are they single-sheet charters, contemporary with the apparent date of the text in every case?

van Reenen: They are original texts — some official — for instance, mentioning a date and implicitly or explicitly where they were written.

Lowe: And they are contemporary with the apparent date of the text?

van Reenen: I see your point. They are not copies.

Lowe: I am still worried about assuming that therefore they indicate the language of the city, because from my observations with Anglo-Saxon charters, if they are in any sense formulaic — if they tend to follow various patterns — then this might lead to conservatism, to traditional spellings which don't really reflect spoken language. Is this your observation?[5]

van Reenen: I don't know whether it is conservatism or not. But I don't want to have an opinion a priori. For instance, to come back to my [s] ~ [z] problem, I see in the same charter the same scribe writing once ‹ses›, a little bit further ‹zes›. It looks like you can change it without any reason, but then when you analyse many texts you see that there is a rule, and that, especially in one syllable words, the preference is for ‹s› and in the two or three syllable words the preference is for ‹z›. It is very significant statistically speaking. So it seems probable that because longer words have shorter syllables and less stress ‹z› comes in more easily. That makes sense in the Dutch context.

Angus McIntosh: I just wonder in view of this last very interesting observation whether it links to something that has often puzzled us in relation to Middle English, and has to do with the familiar but odd fact that we spell the word 'fox' with an ‹f› and 'vixen' with a ‹v›. 'vixen' is a disyllable and 'fox' is a monosyllable, and that might be called the 'van Reenen Law'.

van Reenen: I've never found this rule in modern dialects.

McIntosh: What we do in English is to examine whether there is any correlation of a similar sort, but not necessarily of an identical kind. It

---

5 See the end of this section for additional remarks on the linguistic conservatism of copied documents.

has often puzzled me as to why in written Middle English there should be a marked difference, scribally speaking, between the incidence of graphs indicating voiced and voiceless forms. ‹f›, as the traditional spelling, remains the favourite whichever the pronunciation. I think this needs a good deal more examination from what you have said about possible rules for the choice. I still remain puzzled why 'foxes' are ‹foxes› and 'vixens' are ‹vixens›.

Rissanen: This shows again how useful interlanguage comparisons may be in giving insights into these problems.

Derek Britton: There's one point I would like to make, Hans, which is not a criticism of your paper, but of Kurath's. I happen to think it is a very bad paper, flawed theoretically as well as in some factual things. The major flaw was first pointed out by James Sledd[6] in 1958 — that is this whole idea of the rise of voiced fricatives. Because after open-syllable lengthening you got [v] following intervocalically after a long vowel and you got geminate voiceless [ff] following the short vowel. As Sledd said, is this not a complementary distribution? So that could not possibly have had anything to do with the phonemic split between [f v], [s z], and so on.

There are other problems with the Kurath article which don't necessarily pertain to the fricatives but to the loss of gemination, which I won't go into. But it's an interesting point that in the southern area of Middle English where you got voiced initial fricatives, arguably you could have had minimal pairs there through borrowing of French vocabulary items with initial ‹f› rather than the ‹v›s in other areas of the labial contrast. But in the South you have this tendency for French words with initial [f] to be anglicised to fit the phonotactic rules of English by becoming voiced. So you get [varmər] ultimately out of [farmər]. But this did not happen in all items. Whereas, seemingly outside the South, French loanwords with initial ‹v› never appear to have been devoiced to fit in with the pattern word-initially.

Christian Kay: I was interested in Piet van Reenen's comment on the [p b] opposition being stronger than the [s z] one. And I think this is also true in Modern English, and possibly particularly in Scots where I can hear myself being inconsistent with this rule. It may have

---

6 J. Sledd 1958 Some questions of English phonology. *Language* 34: 252–58.

something to do with the fact that there are not many words with initial [z] in English and phonemes are more important in the initial position for clarification of meaning.

van Reenen: Is it only [s z] or also [f v]? Is that all there is? Or maybe also [tʃ dʒ]? Certain things like that?

Kay: Yes, I think [s z] particularly is unstable in many accents of Modern English.

Keith Williamson: To take up Christian's point there. Thinking about my own kind of speech, if you take the word 'wives', [wəifs] is quite a common form for the plural, where you don't have voicing. And it may be a stylistic thing that the Scots form is devoiced. In more formal speech one would tend towards the voiced variant — [waˑɪvz]. There is a slight difference in the vowel as well, in length and quality.

Britton: The levelling to [f] in the plural is a morphological simplification though, isn't it?

Williamson: Yes, but there is a stylistic factor in its use.

Britton: Right.

Manfred Markus: On the question of plosives versus fricatives, I think there is a universal principle, in line with Vennemann's[7] hierarchy of consonantal strength. According to this, plosives are just 'stronger' consonants than fricatives and therefore tend to be more distinguished, more marked, for instance, as to the distinction of voiced and voiceless sounds, whereas in the middle of the consonantal scale, on the level of the fricatives, many languages, I would assume, don't make this distinction; or, if the distinction is there, it is often levelled. Anyway, the lower you go on the scale the less you find the distinction. As to the nasals, for example, there were voiceless nasals in Middle English, which were later done away with. In sum, plosives are the most differentiated sounds, generally speaking.

---

7 T. Vennemann 1986 *Neuere Entwicklung in der Phonologie*. Mouton de Gruyter: Berlin, pp. 34–38; T. Vennemann 1972 On the theory of syllabic phonology. *Linguistische Berichte* **18**: 1–18.

van Reenen: I will agree, but only so far. Don't try to apply to French what I told you about Dutch. It will be completely out — they will not understand you. I'm trying to think of languages in which [p] and [b] *are* just switching around without any problem and I think there are some. Maybe there is something in this phenomenon — the law of consonantal strength, but it's not everything. There is more than that.

Helmut Gneuss: Concerning taxonomy, could I ask a question in connexion with the voicing of fricatives which may be of a more general interest? It is a problem Dr Nielsen can solve perhaps. In MS Cotton Tiberius A.iii, written in the middle of the 11th century, you find a continuous interlinear Old English gloss to the Latin *Regularis Concordia* and the Benedictine Rule, which are texts that deal with the liturgy and so very often have the Latin word *versus* 'verse'. The funny thing is that in the glosses you find a number of cases of what used to be called sound substitution, the spelling ‹fers›, since we assume that in Old English there was no voiced initial labial fricative. But there are also a number of cases in the Old English interlinear gloss where the first letter is a ‹u› which of course is identical with the ‹v›.[8] Now the question here is, would one assume that there was a scribe who was aware of the phonemic distinction in Latin and wanted to transfer this into Old English? Or was it a scribe who perhaps just introduced here a certain feature of his own dialect? I should add that this manuscript was copied at Christ Church, Canterbury. I wonder which of the two possibilities is the more probable one?

Nielsen: Normally you would expect sound substitution up to the stage where phonemic split hadn't taken place and you can see this in Old English generally — sound substitution in which you choose the phoneme which comes closest to denote the foreign sound. On the other hand, it is a difficult case here (I mean bringing Canterbury into it). I think Dr Kristensson mentioned that initial voicing took place in late Old English. It would have been taking place early enough to have been implemented in this area. But, according to what we know generally about Old English, we would not expect it to have been expressed in writing. So I recognise there is a problem but I am afraid that I can't take it any further.

---

8 'See now L. Kornexl (ed.) 1993 *Die* Regularis Concordia *und ihre altenglische Interlinearversion* (Munich), where the evidence is conveniently accessible and has been discussed in notes to lines 306 and 1293. The spelling <vers> is even more frequent in Byrhtferth's *Handboc*.' — H. Gneuss.

Gneuss: The problem is it only occurs in the word for 'verse'. I mean this is a lengthy interlinear gloss of two texts; I think 30,000 words. It only occurs in this loanword.

Ian Doyle: Is this repeatedly or as a single instance?

Gneuss: It is repeatedly.

Doyle: It's a bit like the question of the 'city hall' language, and this is a case where it may be indeterminate or indeterminable whether this problem is linguistic or palaeographical. But the interlinear glossator may be simply following the forms of his Latin text rather than expressing a phonological or other phenomenon. And we may never be able to resolve some of these problems where the palaeographical conventions cross or coincide with possible linguistic ones.

Kristensson: As far as I know the classic example of voicing occurs in a charter from Southern England and it concerns the numeral 'five' [fiːf] which was written ‹uif›. That is considered to be the first example of the voicing. I think in the examples that you give here — from Canterbury — that a few are instances of voicing, because a scribe would try to get a symbol or a letter to indicate what he heard. He wouldn't like to have an ‹f› here because it was a bit unlike his ordinary ‹f›. So he put a ‹u› for it — that, I think, is what is happening.

Rissanen: An important point in Pieter's talk was this question of spoken versus written language and it's perhaps related to Professor Gneuss's comments. Now I know that the Middle English *Atlas*[9] has a very different principle about this, and I think we all feel that it is a very sound principle indeed. But are we completely helpless concerning the spoken language of the past and to what extent should we be concerned about it? I wonder if you have any comments on that point? It seems to me that you felt that we should make a more concerted effort to recover the spoken language on the basis of writings. But what are the possibilities for that?

---

[9] A. McIntosh, M.L. Samuels and M. Benskin 1986 *A Linguistic Atlas of Late Mediaeval English*, 4 vols. Aberdeen University Press: Aberdeen.

Jeremy Smith: There are possibilities in the sense that there is a mapping relationship between the two modes. There is obviously some sort of connexion between them. The difficulty is slippage. There is always a moment when the written language may be retained or held back in some way, or even the spoken language in certain situations. The fact that there is a mapping is shown by those Runic inscriptions in which new runes appear, like the Anglo–Frisian ones. Or the reproduction of the *i*-umlaut *y* is another good example, when there has obviously been an attempt to react to a sound change. So obviously there is a kind of relationship: we always have to start off by assessing the nature of that spelling and its context and what it is actually doing there. That is the difficult thing. That's the philology and that's of course going to be a problem. But I don't think it means the position is hopeless.

Anthonij Dees: The problem is the reconstruction of spoken language in the Middle Ages and I have some experience of this. I have published some articles recently on the reconstruction of Old French. Our strategy is to have global confidence in spellings but there is a statistical check by rank probabilities in texts of known original provenance. I think these two together constitute a kind of strategy. There was one question that was raised — is there conservatism? My first observations were that there is a very strict correlation until well on in the 14th century between what you can suppose to be the spoken form and the written form.

A.J. Aitken: There are a lot of examples in Middle Scots of spellings which are very much more archaic than we must presume the speech forms to have been. One example is the north-eastern dialect. Clearly a lot of the features of spoken north-eastern Scots are developed by the 16th century. But you get glimpses of these only in very occasional spellings. Mostly the scribes are writing 'city hall' language. They are writing, in other words, a sort of standard Middle Scots and not revealing — this is in Aberdeenshire — the local pronunciation, except occasionally when, for example, they slip up and write ‹f› when they ought to be writing ‹quh›, as in the words like 'whaur', 'where', and so on.[10]

---

[10] For examples, see A.J. Aitken 1971 Variation and Variety in written Middle Scots. In: A.J. Aitken, A. McIntosh and H. Pálsson (eds.) *Edinburgh Studies in English and Scots*. Longman: London, pp. 194–95.

The other thing that you get frequently in Middle Scots is what I call reduced forms. There are lots of words in Modern Scots which have reductions of Older Scots forms, for instance, by vocalisation of a final *l*. The word for 'call' in Modern Scots is [kɔː]. Now, that pronunciation existed in Older Scots as well. But you don't get much sign of it — mostly the spelling is ‹call›. You get two signs of it: first, occasional spellings again — starting in the 15th century — and secondly, in the rhymes of certain poems, the poems that are in a specially colloquial, near-spoken form.[11] So this slippage is quite clearly evidenced there.

van Reenen: Two comments. First on your last observation about the vocalisation of *l*. You hear probably that I vocalise it as well; but you would note it as [l]. I discovered that there is just one small passage about this vocalisation in Mees and Collins's book[12] on the sounds of English and Dutch. I checked out the article. We took the western part of the country and in north Holland/south Holland 50 per cent of the people vocalise their *l* in final position following a vowel. It seems to happen in Received English as well. But nobody ever observed it and everybody is noting [l]. So on that point there is a risk and you are right.

I've also got a comment on the first thing you said about the 'city hall' language. What are the arguments on the basis of which you have decided it is 'city hall' language? That's what I am really interested in, how you show that it is 'city hall' language? What is your proof?

Aitken: Well, simply from scribes in the north-east of Scotland who we must presume to have been using spoken forms like modern north-eastern Scots forms, which are quite distinct from general written Scots. One example is the change of the [ʍ] sound to [f]. Now this is very widespread in modern north-east Scots. There are occasional spellings in Middle Scots from which we presume that this pronunciation had been reached. But the fact is that these examples are very few. Therefore, one assumes that the scribe was following the standard form for spellings and didn't reveal his pronunciation.

---

11 For further comment and examples, see ibid. pp. 196–97.
12 B. Collins and I. Mees 1984 *The Sounds of English and Dutch*, 2nd rev. edn. Brill: Leiden.

van Reenen: There is one thing which I hardly mentioned in my talk. There is the problem of homogeneous and heterogeneous. In your reasoning do you take into account that the incidence of heterogeneity in language has been underestimated? That is why I tried to save the reputation of the scribes.

Harry Watson: I would just like to substantiate Jack Aitken's point about the ‹f› spelling being a kind of slippage from the ‹quh› spelling, by quoting the famous, or infamous, example from Aberdeen Burgh Court of 1539, where two women are in court accused of flyting, or mutual exchange of insults. One of them has accused the other one of having a friar as a lover, which was rather a monstrous insult, and she has said to the other woman 'I sell leid the to the place for the freir swevit the'[13] and 'where' is spelled ‹for›. But then the scribe continues in the same breath, as it were, 'And quhar thou tynt the pendace of thi belt'[14] and 'where' is spelled ‹quhar›. Clearly he is transcribing what he hears being said in court. This is somebody's actual speech. For a moment his guard slips and he writes the ‹f›. Then he corrects himself. So even in the North-east where the pronunciation was so distinctive we have a scribe trying to adhere to this written standard and only allowing us to see in brief glimpses how people are actually speaking.

Kristensson: I would like to return to the question of dialect boundaries and isophones and isoglosses. I think it is possible to establish such boundaries, such isophones. For example, we can examine the appearance of Old English long *a* in words where it could not have been subject to shortening. If we map all the forms and if we find one area where the vowel is always spelled ‹a› and a different area where the vowel is always spelled ‹o›, we must assume that that difference has a background in a difference of pronunciation. It doesn't matter exactly how, but there must be a difference because generally a scribe didn't use different symbols for one and the same phoneme. When they are different, he tried to have different letters and symbols. So we can assume that in one area there was an [a]-like pronunciation and in the other area, where they spelled the letter ‹o›, there was an [o]-like pronunciation.

---

[13] Trans: 'I shall lead you where the friar had sex with you.'
[14] Trans: 'And where you lost the ornament off your belt.'

So we make the map. But before we draw this isophone, and above all before we make a boundary between dialects, we must examine the area itself — its geography. I examined the ‹a›/‹o› distinction in the county of Lincolnshire and I found a boundary — actually a very sharp boundary — running along the River Witham. I studied the medieval topography of that area and it was quite clear that there were very big marshes on either side of the river — such big and deep marshes that it was impossible for people to communicate across that area. I would say that there we have a very sharp dialect boundary. There are other cases where the geographical situation is different, where we have to reckon with a big boundary area — a transition area — and then the core dialect. So we must very much take into consideration the geography. I think we could establish dialect boundaries. After all, in modern dialects — in Sweden for instance — it is possible to make distinctions between them, and I think we should be able to do so for the Middle Ages.

Nielsen: I noticed in your publications on the Lay Subsidy Rolls that you draw isoglosses along the utmost boundary for the occurrence of the feature. To take the example here of fricatives, if there are voiceless and voiced fricatives, you would draw the isophone or the isogloss as far north as possible, supposing that the *fs* had become *v* in that area.

Alexander Fenton: The scribes who were lousy spellers probably had a certain amount of training and education. I've been working lately on manuscript diaries and trying to publish a complete text because I think there's a lot of material there that could be used for linguistic purposes. In particular two farm-labourers' diaries, from one rather remote part of Scotland, have been very rewarding because of the extreme variations in spelling that have been produced by the writers of these two diaries. I don't think that they're necessarily random variations — they do seem to reflect the local dialect, as I know it . So I think that if you can find writers who have a little education, but not too much, you may be able to get quite a good approach to the spoken language.

Rissanen: This brings us to the question of material and data. Would you like to comment briefly on this, Pieter?

van Reenen: I think the period I was talking about *is* the period in which writers have little education, in your terminology. That is, the idea of standardisation, at least in Dutch and also in French, comes rather late in the medieval period, or even after medieval times. But it applies exactly to 18th-century reports I have seen which were made by people constructing buildings and explaining what they want to do; they know their letters but they don't know anything about standardisation. Even during that period what we have is just pure dialect, I think. Within the medieval period it's true of everybody — nobody is interested in standardisation — it's not an idea anyone had.

Gillian Fellows-Jensen: I was interested in the last comment in Piet van Reenen's paper, the appeal for standardisation in the computerisation of linguistic material. Isn't it rather late to come with this appeal? And isn't it rather difficult? I speak as one who came to computerisation at a late stage of life, when I have been very dependent on my university for what hardware and software it would put at my disposition and what advice it would give me. Even within a fairly limited field like place-name research, it is very difficult to find two universities using the same system. Have you any good advice?

van Reenen: Not in one minute. But the kind of problem is quite familiar. I do not put anything forward other than just to talk about this kind of problem. And I refer to the Association for Text Corpora and Databases in the Humanities. The Association has been founded in the Netherlands in order to encourage standardisation of procedures.[15]

Rissanen: I think that for all of us who are involved in computerised corpora this is a very urgent appeal indeed.

It's time for a very brief summing up. We discussed at great length and in great depth the voicing of fricatives and all the implications of that in the questions of change and implementation of change. We also discussed clashes, not only of dialects but also of languages and with reference to major distinctions between the Germanic languages, the North Germanic ones and the West Germanic, in particular. That was perhaps the core part of our discussion.

---

[15] At this moment the address of the Association is:
Vakgroep Computer en Letteren RUU, Achter de Dom 22–24, 3512 JP Utrecht, The Netherlands. Tel. +31.30.536417 or +31.30.536426.

Then fairly shortly we talked about the problem of spoken language. I for one have all my life been frustrated about this situation — that we all know that language essentially is spoken language. Language develops, changes and lives in speech mostly. On the other hand, we only have the written version of it to base our studies on. It was quite interesting that all the comments on the relations between written and spoken language referred to phonology — to spellings and pronunciations — which is the most difficult part of it. We are on a bit less uncertain ground if we talk in terms of syntax or lexis or even morphology. I have sometimes suggested a comparison to this question of reconstructing spoken expression on the basis of writings. It is like the work of an astronomer who tries to define invisible stars on the basis of the effect of the irregularities they cause on the movements of the visible stars. I don't think we should lose faith and hope.

The final aspect in our discussion concerned Pieter's points about corpora. For most of us a computer corpus is nothing but a highly sophisticated pack of index cards, but in 15 minutes now we can get information that would take months to collect in any other ways. And that may put us in a completely new and more hopeful situation to find something about those invisible stars — that is the spoken varieties of the language of the past, and also the questions of dialects or the typology of the bundles of features. But what this needs is a lot of work, a lot of standardisation in a certain sense of the word, and indeed a lot of co-operation among not only those of us who are working with corpora but also with others. This discussion has shown that the problems of typology and taxonomy can be better solved if we have meetings of this kind where not only the scholars of one language, be it English, be it any other, but scholars representing the study of various languages meet.

* * * * * *

Kathryn Lowe adds this comment to the discussion on pp. 54–55:

The problem facing those working on the proposed *Linguistic Atlas of Early Medieval English* as regards 'anchor-texts' cannot be overestimated (see M. Benskin 1977 Local archives and Middle English dialects. *Journal of the Society of Archivists* **5**: 500–14 (501–2); A. McIntosh, M.L. Samuels, M. Benskin 1986 *Linguistic Atlas of Late Mediaeval English*, Aberdeen University Press: Aberdeen, 1, §2.3.3). In contrast to the later period, texts which can be confidently associated with a particular place are few in number and are in the main Middle English cartulary copies of charters dating within the Anglo-Saxon period. Recent study has shown that all scribes copying this type of material are constrained to a greater or lesser degree by the linguistic form of their exemplar (see K. Lowe 1993 'As Fre as Thowt?': some medieval copies and translations of Old English wills. *English Manuscript Studies 1100–1700* **4**: 1–23). The linguistic conservatism that these scribes display will inevitably affect the value of their work for Middle English dialect studies.

Margaret Laing replies:

This somewhat negative view of the early Middle English documentary sources is perhaps premature (see M. Laing 1993 *Catalogue of Sources for a Linguistic Atlas of Early Medieval English.* D.S. Brewer: Cambridge). Copied documentary texts must certainly be treated with caution but much more work needs to be done on the language in them before their collective witness need be jettisoned. Recent work by Peter Kitson on Old English dialects suggests that there is a great deal more regionally conditioned linguistic variation in the texts and boundary clauses of Old English charters than has been previously assumed (see P. Kitson 1990 Old English nouns of more than one gender. *English Studies* **71**: 185–221; id. 1990[92] Old English dialects and the stages of transmission to Middle English. *Folia Linguistica Historica* **11**: 27–87; id. 1993 Geographical variation in Old English prepositions and the location of Ælfric's and other literary dialects. *English Studies* **74**: 1–50).

At least some early Middle English copies of Old English documents may be expected to reflect this variation, whether or not a copyist attempts to update the language of his exemplar. Such copies may contain language that is mixed both chronologically and regionally but comparison with earlier and later texts of known origins can help to differentiate these linguistic strata. Moreover, 'anchor texts' need not always be documents. Literary manuscripts can sometimes be associated confidently with particular religious houses and, subject to the usual cautions, the language of the texts in them may be taken to represent the language of that area (see M. Laing 1991 Anchor texts and literary manuscripts in early Middle English in F. Riddy (ed.) *Regionalism in Late Medieval Manuscripts and Texts.* D.S. Brewer: Cambridge, pp. 27–52 (44)).

Panel II

MANUSCRIPT STUDIES AND LITERARY GEOGRAPHY

Part II

MANUSCRIPT STUDIES AND LITERARY GEOGRAPHY

II.1 Middle English Texts and their Transmission, 1350 – 1500: some Geographical Criteria

Richard Beadle

The gradual abandonment of many regional varieties of written English, and the simultaneous adoption of a range of forms to which the term 'standard' is now often applied, had been taking place over several decades prior to the establishment of the earliest printing presses in England. The scribal practice of translating, or partially translating a text from one regionally delimited spelling system into another still continued, but the likelihood that regional forms could be replaced in some proportion by items from a standard repertoire naturally increased as time went by. During the third quarter of the 15th century, new commercial imperatives provided a marked linguistic constraint upon the early printers. It was plainly in the financial interest of Caxton and his followers to print certain texts, which had hitherto been composed and circulated with one provincial linguistic complexion or another, in the form most likely to be acceptable to the widest possible reading and book-buying public. For example, the largely standardised and dialectally colourless language in which Caxton, in 1482, presented his edition of John Trevisa's translation of Higden's *Polychronicon* (1387), stands in marked contrast to the south-west and south Midland complexion of most of the extant manuscripts (Mossé 1952: 285–89; Waldron 1991) Even a major text such as Malory's *Morte Darthur*, evidently composed in a more dilute form of a north midland dialect only a matter of a decade or so before Caxton printed it, was afforded much the same treatment (McIntosh 1968; Smith 1986).

Early English printed texts that strongly preserve the dialectal characteristics of their original author or a prior manuscript copy are very rare. The unique 1485 issue of *The Revelation of St Nicholas to a*

Monk of Evesham [sc. 'Eynsham'] (*STC*^{2} no. 20917) is exceptional in retaining the north-west Worcestershire dialect of its exemplar (Samuels 1981 [1988]: 43). It was one of a number of rather haphazard products of the short-lived London printing business occupied by William de Machlinia, a Belgian, who on this sort of evidence would appear not to have registered the linguistic factors that other printers of the time were taking into account. Manuscript copies made from early printed texts are also of some interest in this connexion, since scribes occasionally took steps to translate what was printed in a more or less standard form of the language back into a regional form more suitable for local use. Cambridge, St John's College MS G.19, for example, contains a copy of Mirk's *Festial* and the *Quattuor Sermones* taken by a Scottish scribe, sometime before 1513, from the Rouen issue of 1499, one of a number of descendants of Caxton's *editio princeps* of 1483 (*STC*^{2} nos. 17957–66). Despite their linguistic interest, examples of this kind are exceptional. The establishment of the earliest printing businesses in London made it inevitable that publication proper and the widespread dissemination of texts would, from the late 1470s onwards, be mainly a metropolitan affair, and it was natural that provincial printers, wherever they might set up, should follow the central example rather than revert to any dialectal orthographic habits that might have survived locally.

A century earlier, the picture was very different. At the turn of the 14th century the various written forms of the language in use in London had no particular prestige in relation to, and indeed no influence upon, those of other parts of the country, whilst the book-trade in the capital had hardly begun to exploit the commercial potential offered by the sudden widespread growth of English vernacular writing and reading. At this time, the 'publication' of literary compositions in English proceeded less from what are sometimes called 'centres' of book production, than from the sometimes almost arbitrary locations where authors happened to live — rural or urban, conventual or secular, provincial or metropolitan, as the case might be. Subsequent routes of textual transmission varied according to a range of factors, including the nature of the composition itself and its intended audience in which, for example, the interest of a particular religious order or a network of personal patronage played a significant part. But any marked removal of a text from the immediate neighbourhood in which it was first composed would be very likely to entail translation into the written form of English most familiar to readers at its intended destination. Such long-distance removals undoubtedly took place, but a commoner mode of transmission is likely to have been the repeated copying of a work in the area in which it was first composed, with more gradual lateral dissemination through immediately adjacent neighbourhoods whose written language was less significantly different from that of the original. I shall consider some reasonably large-scale examples of these alternative modes of transmission across space in a moment.

Every new reader of Middle English soon acquires a sense of the intensely regional character of literature written in the period ensuing upon the Norman Conquest and down to the middle of the 15th century, enshrined for many of us in the map prefacing Kenneth Sisam's *Fourteenth Century Verse and Prose*, first published in 1921, and still in print. Eventually, it ought to be possible to produce a much more detailed and refined account of this 'literary geography' of later medieval England, and the data recently assembled in the *Linguistic Atlas of Late Mediaeval English* will undoubtedly have a significant part to play in the process. Until then we must be content with a rather impressionistic account of how it developed, and our explanations of how and why a particular pattern of regional literary activity arose, flourished, and declined will remain decidedly cloudy. A few basic pieces of the jigsaw are already in place. The west and south-west Midlands provide a starting point in the early to mid 13th century, with the *Ancrene Wisse*, the *Katherine* group, Laȝamon's *Brut*, and, slightly later, the texts in MS Bodleian Digby 86 and the *South English Legendary*. It would appear that at this time the apparatus for disseminating writings in English was better developed in the Herefordshire–Worcestershire–Gloucestershire area than elsewhere. By contrast, many singly surviving earlier Middle English texts, from the late 12th-century *Ormulum* (south Lincolnshire) to the mid 14th-century *Aȝenbite of Inwit* (Canterbury, Kent), stand out like erratics in the broader landscape of Latin and Anglo-Norman transmissional activity, and it is probably no coincidence that these two particular examples should have come down to us as autographs, textual curiosities with no known and indeed no likely progeny.

From about 1300, however, the emphasis shifts towards the North, perhaps mainly to Yorkshire, for the composition of a number of basic instructional or devotional texts, the numerous later copies of which account for a significant proportion of the surviving corpus of Middle English manuscripts: the *Prick of Conscience*, *Speculum Vitae*, the *Cursor Mundi*, and the large body of writings, some associated rightly and some wrongly with the name of Richard Rolle, are the principal representatives. The impulse to compose, and, by the standards of the time, effectively to mass-produce some of these texts, undoubtedly came originally from institutionalised religion. The Fourth Lateran Council of 1215, and more locally the Lambeth Constitutions of 1281 instituted a systematic campaign to instruct the laity, in the vernacular, as to the requirements of the faith (Pantin 1955; Boyle 1985). Many copies of texts in this class continued to be intensively produced in the North over the subsequent century and a half, but it is noticeable that the earliest printers did not on the whole make any effort to issue editions of such writings, popular though they must have been.

Somewhat later in the 14th century, and not so far in the North, it is possible to point to the development of a more sophisticated variety of devotional writing, best represented by the works of Walter Hilton and the author of the *Cloud of Unknowing*, whose origin and early dissemination the present evidence associates with the north-eastern and east Midland counties of Nottinghamshire, Lincolnshire, Huntingdonshire and Cambridgeshire. From the 1380s onwards, however, the much greater bulk of writing generated by the Wycliffite movement starts to yield a mass of manuscripts from across the central Midland counties — Oxfordshire, Warwickshire, Northamptonshire, Leicestershire, Bedfordshire — often produced to a standard of codicological, textual and linguistic consistency that suggests a high degree of local organisation in the business of transmission (Hudson 1989). The orthodox counterpoise to the Lollard Bible, Nicholas Love's *Mirror of the Blessed Life of Jesus Christ*, though perhaps composed by a Midlander resident in Yorkshire, belongs in some respects with the Hilton–*Cloud* group. It seems to have been to some extent systematically disseminated from metropolitan sources, and doubtless received much impetus for its wide circulation in the Midlands and the eastern counties from the official licence granted by Archbishop Arundel in 1410.

It is nevertheless surprising that, down to the end of the 14th century, the greater London area looks strikingly under-represented as a source of the production of vernacular manuscripts, judging by the surviving examples. In 1963, M.L. Samuels drew attention to a group of eight mid 14th-century manuscripts whose language ('Type II') may be associated with London and its environs, but their contents are for the most part an adventitious assortment, and suggest nothing remotely resembling the widespread and systematic promotions of vernacular writing that had manifested themselves successively in the west Midlands and the North by this time (Samuels 1963 [1989], 1983

[1988]). Large-scale production of vernacular literary manuscripts in circumstances that can be described in some ways as 'commercial' is not evidenced in London until around the turn of the 14th century. Its inception was undoubtedly connected with the growth in the posthumous literary reputations of Geoffrey Chaucer and John Gower (Doyle and Parkes 1978 [1991]), and it was given further impetus by the sudden simultaneous availability of major, provincially composed texts for which there was a growing demand, notably *Piers Plowman*, John Trevisa's massive translations of Higden's *Polychronicon* and the *De Proprietatibus Rerum* of Bartholomaeus Anglicus, and Love's *Mirror*. In the first decades of the new century, London's new pre-eminence was nourished by the voluminous writings of authors with strong court connexions, principally Thomas Hoccleve and John Lydgate, and, with the appearance there of a standard form of the language, it was natural that the capital should become a national centre of the vernacular manuscript book trade (Christianson 1989).

On the other hand, the 15th century was also the time of burgeoning general literacy, especially amongst the laity, and the re-duplication of vernacular texts in a variety of semi-professional and informal circumstances became widespread in London and the provinces alike (Bühler 1960: 22–4; Parkes 1973 [1991]). In such circumstances, certain regional literary movements and patterns of transmissional activity retained a notable degree of strength and independence. Evidence for the continuity of interest in alliterative compositions across north-western and northern areas of England, with strong Scottish connexions, is fragmentary but clearly identifiable (Turville-Petre 1977: 122–25). East Anglia developed a thriving literary culture of its own, much of it surviving in the form of a large body of manuscripts which preserve the distinctive spelling systems of the area until well into the period of 'standardisation' and the coming of the printed book (Beadle 1991).

This sketch of the development of the literary geography of England from the 13th to the 15th century leaves very ample scope for refinement and elaboration. It also returns us pointedly to the rather infrequently articulated issue adumbrated above, of precisely how English texts were transmitted across space in circumstances where the written language of different localities and communities tended to differ increasingly, and to differ in what often appear to be random ways, the further apart they stood. Since the publication of *LALME* and studies ancillary to it, much more is coming to light about the scribal practices involved in the translation of Middle English texts from one dialect to another — what the orthographic form of a given text looked like when it left one place, and what it was turned into when it arrived in, or was recast for use in, another (Benskin and Laing 1981). But we still know remarkably little about the comings and goings of the manuscripts themselves across space; that is, the physical objects as distinct from the written substances that they contain.

The silence of the historical record on this point is in no way surprising since the scribes of vernacular manuscripts, or those who organised their activities, had little or no reason to leave any trace of where or how they had obtained their exemplars. In some contexts, practices resembling or derived from the traditional operations of monastic scriptoria, or from the newer *pecia* system of the university environment, were evidently present. But it is equally certain that for a good majority of the texts that have come down to us, a vast invisible network of loans, borrowings, exchanges, sales, purchases and other less formal arrangements underpinned the spatial dissemination of Middle English compositions from around 1350 onwards. In terms of their specific relationships to one another, the manuscripts themselves only seldom yield any help in tracing this network, since the existence of an exemplar, together with a copy which is demonstrably its direct and immediate descendant, is a very rarely noticed phenomenon in this period.

Examples of copies that have survived alongside their immediate ancestors are for various reasons better attested, and have been more extensively addressed, in textual and palaeographical studies of Classical and earlier Latin writings (Reynolds and Wilson 1991: 320; Ker 1960: 12–14; Ker 1972 [1985]; Ker 1979 [1985]). In their study of the 60 or so surviving complete copies and fragments of the *Canterbury Tales*, Manly and Rickert record only one instance of a pair of manuscripts where such a relationship may be thought to exist, and further instances are not easy to trace (Manly and Rickert 1940 i: 185). Such a dearth of extant Middle English manuscripts with their immediate exemplars surviving alongside them is one of a number of comparable signs that point towards a difficult question which will prove to be of relevance to many different levels of enquiry in this field, especially those of taxonomic or statistical intent. It may be crudely framed as follows: what proportion of the total number of Middle English manuscripts once extant is represented by the surviving corpus?

II

Some idea of the kind of refinement that has been wrought in our perception of the literary and linguistic geography of later medieval England by the publication of *LALME* can be gained by considering the case of *Piers Plowman*. This long and difficult work in alliterative verse comes down to us in what are probably three versions (A, B and C), thought to be the result of successive revisions by the author, and found in 50 more or less complete copies and three fragments. Almost nothing is known of the author from external evidence (Kane 1965), but literary–historical tradition, allusions in the poem, and information derived from the dialects of the manuscripts combine to associate the text with two quite different localities, namely the area of the Malvern Hills in Worcestershire, and London. It was evidently for these reasons that Sisam, when he came to represent *Piers Plowman* on the map prefacing his student's reader, drew a large sausage-shaped area, with Worcestershire at one end and London at the other, to designate the poem's likely area of circulation and influence.

Since Sisam's time, M.L. Samuels has given detailed attention to the dialects of the manuscripts (1985 [1988]; 1988). The great majority of them are not composites of more than one of the versions of the poem, and of these, 34 present a written language whose orthography can be localised and plotted on a map (Map 1 — after Samuels 1988: 207).

The manuscripts shown represent a proportion only, and perhaps a small proportion, of the total number of *Piers Plowman* manuscripts that existed in the later 14th and 15th centuries. But we have no reason to think that they survived on anything other than a random basis, and thus the pattern of their spatial distribution becomes a matter of some interest. With a text that exists in more than one version, one of the relevant considerations is the 'geographical criterion' sometimes invoked in relation to the transmission of Biblical and Classical texts, and Professor Samuels himself alludes to one form of it with respect to the manuscripts of A-version: 'they demonstrate a situation that is found elsewhere, in which the oldest manuscripts of a work (or their descendants) are found on the periphery of a culture' (Samuels 1988: 206).

The basic assumption implied in Pasquali's well-known discussion of the 'criterio geografico' in his *Storia della tradizione e critica del testo* (1952: 156–83), is that where the previous or sometimes the present spatial locations of manuscripts can, by one means or another,

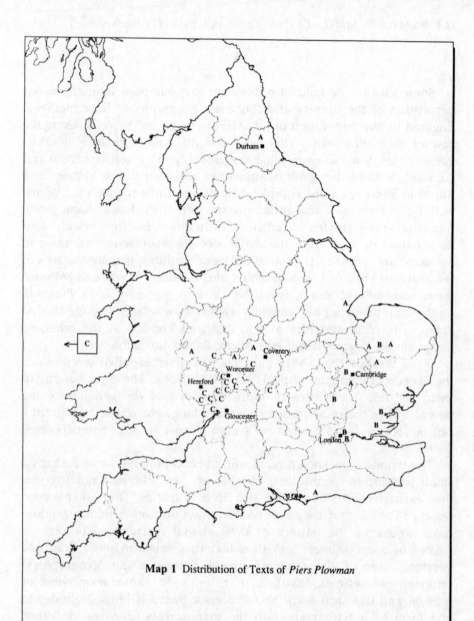

Map 1 Distribution of Texts of *Piers Plowman*

be established, such information may have consequences for the history of the texts that they contain. An important part of his discussion is concerned with the relationship between the nature and quality of texts preserved in manuscripts located in peripheral regions, as opposed to those connected with some significant geographical or cultural centre, and he demonstrates how manuscripts found in places remote from such centres can exhibit valuable readings and early versions of texts. Conversely, these remoter witnesses tend not to have been affected by such later developments of the text as may have emanated from the centre after their spatial removal took place. The issue of what constitutes a significant geographical or cultural centre in Middle English textual studies is obviously rather different from Pasquali's concern with the transmission of Classical texts in much broader Western European and Near-Eastern contexts. Nevertheless, there is no reason why some of the basic principles underlying the geographical criterion should not be tested, elaborated or refined in this field where our knowledge of the spatial distributions of texts has been so massively enhanced by the publication of *LALME* and related work.

The question of what constitutes a 'centre' where the study of the transmission of *Piers Plowman* is concerned takes an interesting form if we return to the distributions shown on Map 1. By 'centre' we may mean the place or places where Langland's successive working copies or autographs of the B and C versions lay at the point where their respective disseminations began. Of this we know nothing, though London or the Malvern area are in principle both candidates, in either case, for reasons mentioned briefly above. On the other hand, if by 'centre' we mean the locality where most of the surviving manuscripts were copied, then the centre for the B-version is evidently London and the adjacent counties immediately to the north: Hertfordshire, Essex, Cambridgeshire and west Norfolk; and for the C-version, the west Midland counties in the neighbourhood of the Malvern Hills: predominantly Worcestershire, Herefordshire, Gloucestershire and Oxfordshire. Either way, the evidence of the map points to a surprisingly discrete circulation of the B and C-versions of *Piers Plowman*, from 'centres' in the east and west respectively, and tends to support the suggestion that neither of these later versions circulated in such a way as to supplant the A-text that had already reached outlying counties.

A further point deserving remark concerns the transmission of the B and C versions of *Piers Plowman* on a specifically local level. On

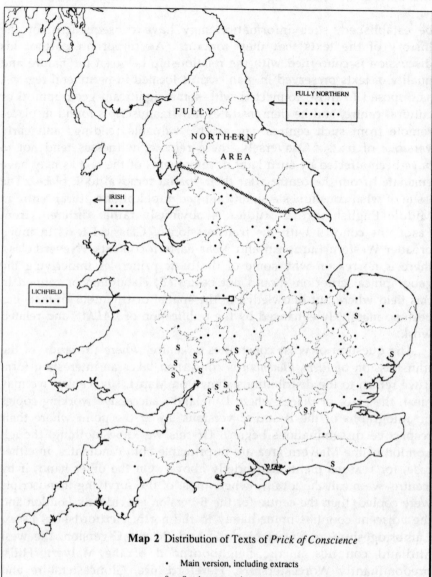

Map 2 Distribution of Texts of *Prick of Conscience*

· Main version, including extracts

s Southern recension

FULLY NORTHERN
· · · · · · · · ·
· · · · · · · ·

IRISH
· · ·

LICHFIELD
· · · · ·

FULLY

NORTHERN

AREA

this evidence, it looks as if exemplars moved out from the centre in some sort of graduated way, through counties adjacent to one another, rather than by leaps and 'bounds across wider areas of space. Recent mappings of other texts surviving in multiple copies suggest that this is likely to have been a standard mode (though it was doubtless not the only one) in which Middle English writings made their way from their place of origin to other locations.

Map 2 is a schematic representation of the scribal distribution of the very numerous manuscripts of the *Prick of Conscience*, based on that published in 1982 by Robert E. Lewis and Angus McIntosh. The *Prick* was by far the most widely circulated poem of the time, surviving in around 115 complete manuscripts or fragments. It is a fairly long (9,000+ lines) and entirely didactic composition of limited literary aspirations, as compared for example with *Piers Plowman*, and nothing whatsoever is known of its authorship. Nevertheless, early ownership marks in the manuscripts and other contemporary evidence suggest that the *Prick*'s 'audience' probably had much in common with that of Langland's more ambitious work, and consisted of people such as lower-ranking secular clergy, as well as those in orders, together with the kind of pious laymen and women who were rapidly acquiring literacy in the half-century or so after the time of its composition, probably towards the middle of the 14th century. Like any text of the time, it must sometimes have been read privately, but, in common with other didactic compositions such as the *Cursor Mundi*, *Speculum Vitae*, or the *Northern Passion*, designed as pious alternatives to the literature of secular narrative entertainment, the *Prick* must often have been read aloud. A good many of the surviving manuscripts were, as Lewis and McIntosh remark, probably made by 'local scribes . . . for edificatory use in their own district' (Lewis and McIntosh 1982: 17).

The numerous locations shown on Map 2 provide what appears to be a gratifyingly full indication of where these districts are likely to have have lain, and, as the *Descriptive Guide* shows, there is sometimes a useful correlation between the location of the scribal dialect and other contemporary evidence of provenance. There has long been general agreement, on linguistic grounds, that the *Prick* is very likely to have been composed in the north of England, probably in Yorkshire, and perhaps within the area where the 'fully northern' manuscripts (whose more precise distribution remains to be worked out) are shown on the map. The 'centre' from which it emanated must have lain in that region, and the distribution gradually thins as it moves southwards, though by no means evenly. East Anglia, an area with which a conspicuously large number of surviving Middle English manuscripts can be associated on dialectal and other grounds (Beadle 1991), shows a particular concentration, and the perhaps adventitious survival of a variant version in a group comprising five manuscripts associated with Lichfield (Dareau and McIntosh 1971) lends strength to a comparable but less dense concentration in the north-west Midland counties. It is noticeable that the southward progress, as it were, of the main version of the *Prick* in these western counties is interrupted in Shropshire and north Worcestershire. It seems that in Herefordshire, Monmouthshire, south Worcestershire and Gloucestershire, the abridged and fairly thoroughly revised version known as the Southern Recension was preferred, and that the 'centre' for this regional revision by someone other than the original author must have lain somewhere in this area.

The identification of the Lichfield group, together with the more recent recognition of an interpolated version represented by four manuscripts lying in a band stretching as it were from north-west Worcestershire through south Gloucestershire to the Somerset/east Devon border (McIntosh 1976 [1989]), indicate that the *Prick* was liable to local revision and re-dissemination on a much smaller scale than the Southern Recension. In this respect, its distribution has a miniature resemblance to the variation of the geographical criterion sometimes brought into discussions of the text of the New Testament, where the regional affiliations of the manuscripts are taken into account when considering the relative merits of the Western, Caesarean, and Alexandrian witnesses (Metzger 1968: 213–17).

The scribal distribution of the surviving manuscripts of the *Prick of Conscience*, then, reinforces the impression that a text of this type is likely to have progressed outwards (or in this case, predominantly southwards) in a gradual way from its 'centre', giving rise at the same time to both major and minor variant versions. But though the distribution gives some impression of fulness, it also prompts a return to our earlier question as to how many pieces of the jig-saw puzzle are missing? Angus McIntosh has pursued by statistical means the number of missing manuscripts that might be required to explain the range of variant readings amongst the four surviving manuscripts in the Worcester–Gloucestershire–Devonshire band, and suggests that the proportion of survivals to losses may be, roughly, upwards of 1 : 20 (McIntosh 1976 [1989]: 129).

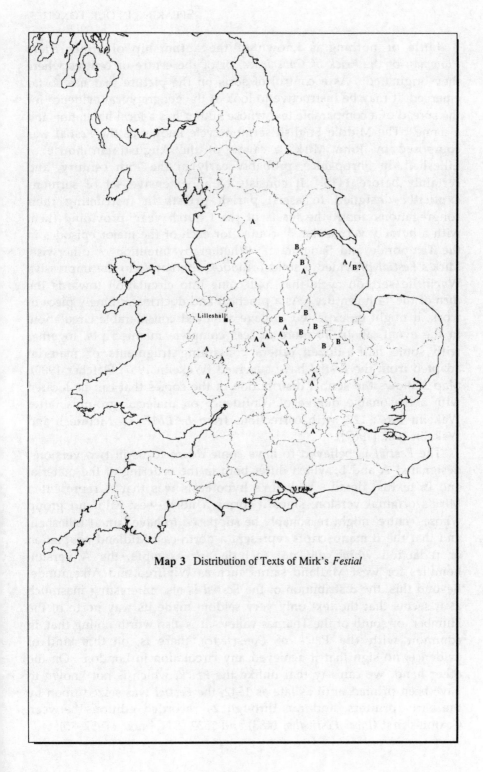

Map 3 Distribution of Texts of Mirk's *Festial*

Little or nothing is known of the authorship of either *Piers Plowman* or the *Prick of Conscience*, or of the centre or centres where they originated. As a control of sorts on the picture that has so far emerged, it may be instructive to look at the geographical evidence for the spread of a comparable text whose author has a local habitation and a name. The Middle English sermon cycle known as the *Festial* was composed by John Mirk, a canon of the Augustinian house of Lilleshall, in Shropshire, probably early in the 15th century, and certainly before 1415. It consists of an extensive set of sermons explicitly designed to assist parish priests in instructing their congregations about the feasts of the Church year, providing them with a homely vernacular discourse for each of the major episodes in the Temporale and Sanctorale. Whether by intention or otherwise, Mirk's *Festial* provided a solid orthodox alternative to the impressive Wycliffite sermon cycle that had come into circulation towards the turn of the 14th century. As a practical and doctrinally timely piece of work, it might be expected to have achieved considerable circulation. In the event, about 30 more or less complete manuscripts, together with some half-a-dozen others containing fragments or material adapted from the *Festial* have survived (Wakelin 1967; Fletcher 1980). Map 3 shows the scribal distribution of the copies that can be located with a reasonable degree of confidence on dialectal grounds (after Wakelin 1967: 127, with corrections from *LALME*; cf. McIntosh and Wakelin 1982 [1989]).

The *Festial* is believed to have come down to us in two versions, designated A and B, which differ both in the ordering of the material and in textual detail. Wakelin's hypothesis was that A represented Mirk's original version, since it forms a north-west Midland group whose 'centre' might reasonably be supposed to have lain at Lilleshall, and that the B manuscripts represent a north-east Midland adaptation or redaction which did not include, for example, the A version homilies for west Midland saints such as Winifred and Alkemunde. Beyond this, the distribution of the *Festial* is also interesting inasmuch as it seems that the text only very seldom made its way north of the Humber, or south of the Thames valley. It is also worth noting that, in common with the *Prick of Conscience*, there is, on this kind of evidence, no sign that it achieved any circulation in London. On the other hand, we can say that unlike the *Prick*, which is not known to have been printed until as late as 1542, the *Festial* was seized upon by the early printers, and ran through 24 recorded editions between Caxton's first (*Liber Festivalis*, 1483) and 1532 (*STC*[2] nos. 17957–75).

III

The relationships between the geographical and textual affinities of the great majority of writings in Middle English remain to be elucidated. The irresolvable issue of how many manuscripts have been lost for each one that survives, and our almost non-existent specific understanding of how exemplars of vernacular writings were obtained and circulated, are amongst the major factors militating against any firm guarantee that the establishment of the geographical propinquity of two extant manuscripts will have consequences for our knowledge of their textual relationship. Nevertheless, the point is always worth pursuing, since there is an inherent likelihood in the idea that a significant proportion of our surviving manuscripts must have been copied from exemplars that lay in neighbouring places. The foregoing discussion of some published scribal distributions for specific Middle English works suggests, even if in occluded or varied form, the operation of geographical criteria resembling those that have been longer and more widely recognised in the study of Classical and Biblical texts. Further studies of this kind may most appropriately be directed, in the first instance, towards Middle English texts that survive in a sufficiently large number of copies whose distribution by scribal dialect has proved to be determinable. Appendices A and B offer a schematic approach to two possible examples, the *Speculum Vitae,* and *Speculum Christiani.*

Appendix A: *Speculum Vitae*

The *Speculum Vitae* (Raymo 1986: 2261–62, 2479–80) is an unpublished Middle English didactic verse composition of around 16,000 lines, probably written in the north of England during the third quarter of the 14th century. The identity of the author is unknown, but he states that the text is intended to be read aloud to instruct the illiterate who know neither Latin nor French. It survives in 38 complete copies and two fragments, the following of which are assigned to county locations (and in some cases with greater exactitude) in *LALME*, on the basis of their scribal dialects.

P	Aberystwyth, National Library of Wales, Peniarth 395.D (Staffordshire).
Mc	Cambridge, Fitzwilliam Museum, McLean 130 (Lincolnshire).
Cs	Cambridge, Gonville and Caius College 160 (Yorkshire WR).
Tr^1	Cambridge, Trinity College R.3.13 (Yorkshire WR).
Tr^2	Cambridge, Trinity College R.3.23 (Ely).
C^6	Cambridge, University Library Additional 2823 (Northern area).
C^7	Cambridge, University Library Additional 6686 (Lincolnshire).
C^1	Cambridge, University Library Ff.iv.9 (Leicestershire).
C^2	Cambridge, University Library Gg.i.7 (Yorkshire NR).
C^3	Cambridge, University Library Gg.i.14 (Yorkshire NR).
C^4	Cambridge, University Library Ii.i.36 (Ely).
C^5	Cambridge, University Library Ll.i.8 (Norfolk).
D^1	Dublin, Trinity College 76 (Derbyshire).
D^2	Dublin, Trinity College 155 (Derbyshire).
D^3	Dublin, Trinity College 423 (Cambridgeshire).
Hu	Glasgow, University Library, Hunterian 89 (Lincolnshire).
L	Liverpool, University Library F.4.9 (Yorkshire WR).
Ad^1	London, British Library Additional 8151 (Leicestershire).
Ad^2	London, British Library Additional 22558 (Northern area).
Ad^3	London, British Library Additional 33995 (NW Yorkshire).
H^1	London, British Library Harley 435 (Ely).
H^2	London, British Library Harley 2260 (Lincolnshire).
R	London, British Library Royal 17C.viii (Northern area).
Sl	London, British Library Sloane 1785 (Leicestershire).
St	London, British Library Stowe 951 (Yorkshire WR).
W	Nottingham, University Library Middleton Mi LM.9 (Leicestershire).
B^2	Oxford, Bodleian Bodley 446 (Lincolnshire).
V	Oxford, Bodleian Eng. poet. a.1, Vernon (Worcestershire).
B^6	Oxford, Bodleian Eng. poet. d.5 (Northern area).
G	Oxford, Bodleian Greaves 43 (Yorkshire WR).
Ha	Oxford, Bodleian Hatton 18 (Suffolk).
B^5	Oxford, Bodleian Hatton 19 (Worcestershire).
B^7	Oxford, Bodleian Lyell 28 (Northern area).
R^2	Oxford, Bodleian Rawlinson C.890 (Nottinghamshire).
A	Princeton University Library, Mr Robert Taylor (NW Yorkshire).
X^1	Tokyo, Professor T. Takamiya 15 (Yorkshire WR).

Map 4 shows the sigla for these manuscripts placed simply within the boundary of their assigned counties, rather than at any particular point therein, except for several belonging to places or areas as yet undefined to the north of the Humber. A distribution similar to but more limited than the *Prick of Conscience* is disclosed, with a centre which is likely to have been in Yorkshire. The textual relationships of these and other manuscripts of the *Speculum Vitae* have yet to be investigated.

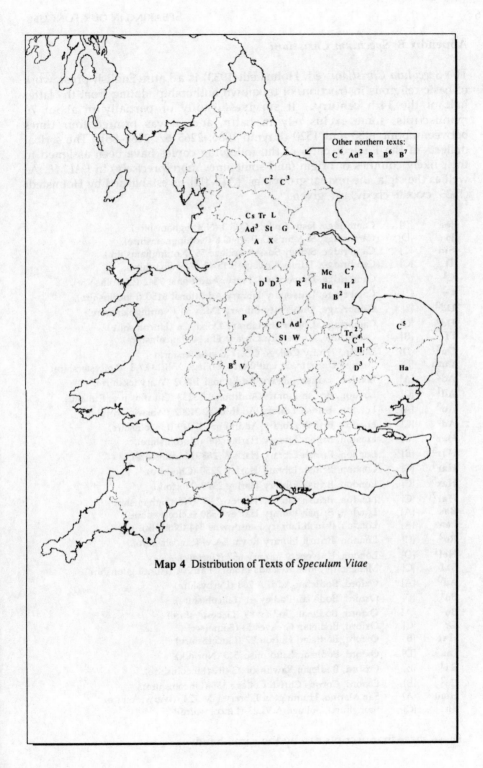

Other northern texts:
C⁶ Ad² R B⁶ B⁷

C² C³

Cs Tr L
Ad³ St G
A X

Mc C⁷
D¹ D² R² Hu H²
B²

P C¹ Ad¹ C⁵
Sl W Tr²
C⁴
H¹

B⁵ V D³ Ha

Map 4 Distribution of Texts of *Speculum Vitae*

Appendix B: *Speculum Christiani*

The *Speculum Christiani* (ed. Holmstedt 1933) is a Latin–English prose work of basic religious instruction, of unknown authorship, dating from the latter half of the 14th century. It survives wholly or partially in about 70 manuscripts, some exclusively in Latin, and it was printed four times between about 1480 and 1520 (Raymo 1986: 2265–67, 2484–85). The scribal dialects of the English parts of the following copies have been assigned to their likely counties of origin (and sometimes more precisely) in *LALME*. As well as the sigla, the textual groupings, [A] – [D], as established by Holmstedt (1933: cxxxiii–clxxiv) are given.

Jes	[B]	Cambridge, Jesus College Q.G.3 (Nottinghamshire).
Jo	[D]	Cambridge, St John's College G.8 (Nottinghamshire).
Sid	[C]	Cambridge, Sidney Sussex College 55 (Nottinghamshire).
Tr	[C]	Cambridge, Trinity College B.15.42 (Warwickshire).
C^1	[?]	Cambridge, University Library, Additional 3042 (Lincolnshire).
C^2	[?]	Cambridge, University Library Additional 6150 (Lincolnshire).
Dd^2	[?]	Cambridge, University Library Dd.iv.51 (Nottinghamshire).
Dd^1	[C]	Cambridge, University Library Dd.xiv.26 (Lincolnshire).
Ff	[B]	Cambridge, University Library Ff.i.14 (Lincolnshire).
Du^2	[D]	Dublin, Trinity College C.5.17 (Leicestershire).
Cuth	[D]	Ushaw, Durham, St Cuthbert's College XVIII.D.7.8 (Leicestershire).
Ad^2	[A]	London, British Library Additional 10052 (Warwickshire).*
Ad^1	[C]	London, British Library Additional 15237 (Lincolnshire/Rutland).
Ad^3	[A]	London, British Library Additional 21202 (Warwickshire).*
Ad^5	[C]	London, British Library Additional 37049 (Lincolnshire).
Har^1	[B]	London, British Library Harley 206 (Lincolnshire).
Har^3	[B]	London, British Library Harley 1288 (Lincolnshire).
Har^4	[C]	London, British Library Harley 2250 (Cheshire).
Har^5	[C]	London, British Library Harley 2379 (Norfolk).
Har^7	[C]	London, British Library Harley 2388 (Nottinghamshire).
Bas	[A]	London, British Library Harley 6580 (Leicestershire).
Lan	[A]	London, British Library Lansdowne 344 (Norfolk).
Ro^2	[C]	London, British Library Royal 5A.vi (Lincolnshire).
Hel^1	[D]	London, University Library 657 (Norfolk).
Sal	[C]	Manchester, John Rylands Library Lat. 201 (Huntingdonshire).
Ad^0	[A]	Oxford, Bodleian Add. A.268 (Derbyshire).
Bo^1	[C]	Oxford, Bodleian Bodley 61 (Lincolnshire).
Bo^2	[A]	Oxford, Bodleian Bodley 89 (Leicestershire).
Gr	[C]	Oxford, Bodleian Greaves 54 (Somerset).
Hat	[B]	Oxford, Bodleian Hatton 97 (Lincolnshire).
Lau^2	[D]	Oxford, Bodleian Laud misc. 513 (Norfolk).
Ra^1	[B]	Oxford, Bodleian Rawlinson C.401 (Lincolnshire).
Co^2	[B]	Oxford, Corpus Christi College 155 (Lincolnshire).
Hunt	[A]	San Marino, Huntington Library HM 124 (Warwickshire).*
Sh	[C]	Stonyhurst College A.VI.23 (Lincolnshire).

* These three manuscripts are by the same hand.

Map 5 *Speculum Christiani* : Manuscripts

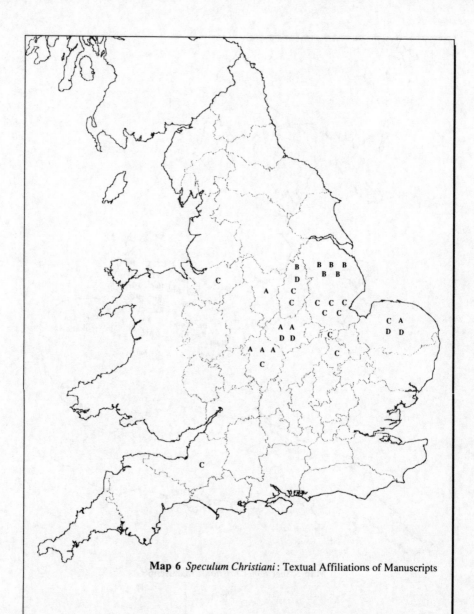

Map 6 *Speculum Christiani*: Textual Affiliations of Manuscripts

Two schematic representations of the distribution of the *Speculum Christiani* are given in maps 5 and 6. The first gives the sigla of the manuscripts within their assigned counties, but without reference to specific points within those areas. The second shows most of the same manuscripts in terms of one of the four textual groupings indicated by Holmstedt. Judging by map 5, and considerations advanced earlier in this paper, the centre of origin for the text would appear to have lain in the Lincolnshire–Nottinghamshire area. (Compare Laing 1978 i: 253–61, upon which many of the NE Midland localisations in *LALME* are based, for more precise placings and further discussion.) Its failure to be represented north of the Humber is striking, the more so given the view of Dr Vincent Gillespie (quoted in Raymo 1986: 2266), whose study of the cultural milieu and sources led him to the conclusion that the *Speculum* might have been the work of someone such as a Carthusian of Mount Grace, or a secular canon of York Minster. Map 6 provides a useful illustration of the relevance of aspects of the geographical criteria discussed above, especially in respect of groups B and C. Holmstedt represents group D, as compared with the other groups, as relatively inchoate, but emphasises the textual affinity of **Du**[2] with **Cuth**, and **Hel**[1] with **Lau**[2]. The locations of these pairs in Leicestershire and Norfolk respectively is a useful corroboration of his work.

Abbreviated titles

LALME McIntosh A., Samuels M.L., Benskin M. 1986 *A Linguistic Atlas of Late Mediaeval English*, 4 vols. Aberdeen University Press: Aberdeen

STC[2] Pollard A.W., Redgrave G.R. [1926] 1976–91 *A Short-Title Catalogue of Books Printed in England, Scotland, & Ireland . . . 1475–1640.* 2nd edn. revised and enlarged, ed. Jackson W.A. et al., 3 vols. Bibliographical Society: London

References

Beadle R. 1991 Prolegomena to a literary geography of later medieval Norfolk. In: Riddy F. 1991, pp. 89–108

Benskin M., Laing M. 1981 Translations and *Mischsprachen* in Middle English manuscripts. In: Benskin M., Samuels M.L. 1981, pp. 55–106

Benskin M., Samuels M.L. (eds.) 1981 *So meny people longages and tonges: Philological Essays in Scots and Mediaeval English presented to Angus McIntosh.* Published by the editors: Edinburgh

Boyle L.E. 1985 The Fourth Lateran Council and manuals of popular theology. In: Heffernan T. J. (ed.) *The Popular Literature of Medieval England*. University of Tennessee Press: Knoxville, pp. 30–43

Bühler C.F. 1960 *The Fifteenth-Century Book*. University of Pennsylvania Press: Philadelphia

Christianson C.P. 1989 Evidence for the study of London's late medieval manuscript-book trade. In: Griffiths J., Pearsall D. 1989, pp. 87–108

Dareau M.G., McIntosh A. 1971 A dialect word in some West Midland manuscripts of the *Prick of Conscience*. In: Aitken A.J. et al. (eds.) *Edinburgh Studies in English and Scots*. Longmans: London, pp. 20–26

Doyle A.I., Parkes M.B. 1978 [1991] The production of copies of the *Canterbury Tales* and *Confessio Amantis* in the early fifteenth century. In: Parkes M.B., Watson A.G. 1978, pp. 163–210; repr. in Parkes M.B. 1991, pp. 201–48

Fletcher A.J. 1980 Unnoticed sermons from John Mirk's *Festial*. *Speculum* 55: 514–22

Griffiths J., Pearsall D. (eds.) 1989 *Book Production and Publishing in Britain 1375–1475*. Cambridge University Press: Cambridge

Holmstedt G. (ed.) 1933 *Speculum Christiani* EETS OS 182

Hudson A. 1989 Lollard book production. In: Griffiths J., Pearsall D. 1989, pp. 125–42

Kane G. 1965 *Piers Plowman: The Evidence for Authorship*. Athlone: London

Ker N.R. 1960 *English Manuscripts in the Century after the Norman Conquest*. Oxford University Press: Oxford

Ker N.R. 1972 [1985] Eton College MS 44 and its exemplar. In: Gumbert J.P. et al. (eds.) *Varia Codicologica. Essays presented to G.I. Lieftinck*. Litterae Textuales, vol. 1. Van Gendt: Amsterdam, pp. 48–60; repr. in Watson A.G. 1985, pp. 87–99

Ker N.R. 1979 [1985] Copying an exemplar: two manuscripts of Jerome on Habbakuk. In: Cockshaw P. et al. (eds.) *Miscellanea Codicologica F. Masai Dicata*. Les Publications de *Scriptorium* 8. Story-Scientia: Ghent, pp. 203–10; repr. in Watson A.G. 1985, pp. 75–86

Laing M. 1978 Studies in the dialect material of mediaeval Lincolnshire. Ph.D. dissertation, University of Edinburgh. Unpublished

Laing M. (ed.) 1989 *Middle English Dialectology: Essays on some principles and problems*. Aberdeen University Press: Aberdeen

Lewis R.E., McIntosh A. 1982 *A Descriptive Guide to the Manuscripts of the* Prick of Conscience. Medium Ævum Monographs NS 12: Oxford

McIntosh A. 1968 Review of W. Matthews, *The Ill-framed Knight*. *Medium Ævum* 37: 346–48

McIntosh A. 1976 [1989] Two unnoticed interpolations in four manuscripts of the *Prick of Conscience*. *Neuphilologische Mitteilungen* 77: 63–78; repr. in Laing M. 1989, pp. 123–35

McIntosh A., Wakelin M. 1982 [1989] John Mirk's *Festial* and Bodleian MS Hatton 96. *Neuphilologische Mitteilungen* 83: 443–50; repr. in Laing M. 1989, pp. 170–78

Manly J.M., Rickert E. 1940 *The Text of the Canterbury Tales*, 8 vols. University of Chicago Press: Chicago

Metzger B.M. 1968 *The Text of the New Testament*, 2nd edn. Clarendon Press: Oxford

Mossé F. 1952 *A Handbook of Middle English*. The John Hopkins Press: Baltimore

Pantin W.A. 1955 *The English Church in the Fourteenth Century*. Cambridge University Press: Cambridge

Parkes M.B. 1973 [1991] The literacy of the laity. In Daiches D., Thorlby A.K. (eds.) *Literature and Western Civilization: The Medieval World*. Aldus: London, pp. 555–76; repr. in Parkes M.B. 1991, pp. 275–97

Parkes M.B. 1991 *Scribes, Scripts and Readers: Studies in the Communication, Presentation and Dissemination of Medieval Texts.* Hambledon: London and Rio Grande

Parkes M.B., Watson A.G. (eds.) 1978 *Medieval Scribes, Manuscripts & Libraries: Essays presented to N. R. Ker.* Scolar Press: London

Pasquali G. 1952 *Storia della Tradizione e Critica del Testo,* 2nd edn. Felice Le Monnier: Florence

Raymo R.R. 1986 Works of religious and philosophical instruction. In: Hartung A.E. (ed.) *A Manual of the Writings in Middle English 1050–1500,* vol. 7. Archon: Hamden, pp. 2255–378, 2467–582

Reynolds L.D., Wilson N.G. 1991 *Scribes and Scholars: A Guide to the Transmission of Greek and Latin Literature,* 3rd edn. Clarendon Press: Oxford

Riddy, F. (ed.) 1991 *Regionalism in Late Medieval Manuscripts and Texts.* D.S. Brewer: Cambridge

Samuels M.L. 1963 [1989] Some applications of Middle English dialectology. *English Studies* **44**: 81–94; repr. in Laing M. 1989, pp. 64–80

Samuels M.L. 1981 [1988] Spelling and dialect in the late and post-Middle English periods. In: Benskin M., Samuels M.L. 1981, pp. 43–54; repr. in Smith J.J. 1988, pp. 86–95

Samuels M.L. 1983 [1988] Chaucer's spelling. In: Gray D., Stanley E.G. (eds.) *Middle English Studies presented to Norman Davis.* Clarendon Press: Oxford, pp. 17–37; repr. in Smith J.J. 1988, pp. 23–37

Samuels M.L. 1985 [1988] Langland's dialect. *Medium Ævum* **54**: 232–47; repr. in Smith J.J. 1988, pp. 70–85

Samuels M.L. 1988 [Langland's] Dialect and Grammar. In: Alford J.A. (ed.) *A Companion to* Piers Plowman. University of California Press: Berkeley, pp. 201–21

Sisam K. 1921 *Fourteenth Century Verse and Prose.* Clarendon Press: Oxford

Smith J.J. 1986 Some spellings in Caxton's Malory. *Poetica* **24**: 58–63

Smith J.J. (ed.) 1988 *The English of Chaucer and his Contemporaries.* Aberdeen University Press: Aberdeen

Turville-Petre T. 1977 *The Alliterative Revival.* D.S. Brewer: Cambridge

Wakelin M.F. 1967 The manuscripts of John Mirk's *Festial. Leeds Studies in English* NS **1**: 93–118.

Waldron R.A. 1991 Dialect aspects of the manuscripts of Trevisa's translation of the *Polychronicon.* In: Riddy F. 1991, pp. 67–87

Watson A.G. (ed.) 1985 *N.R. Ker, Books, Collectors and Libraries: Studies in the Medieval Heritage.* Hambledon: London and Ronceverte

II.2   A Palaeographer's View

A.I. Doyle

I am speaking as one of those people who have followed the gestation of the *Linguistic Atlas of Late Mediaeval English* from its earlier stages and have been excited and helped in my own studies of Middle English manuscripts by some of its findings, which are not set out fully in the *Atlas* itself but have been explored in accompanying correspondence and published articles. From one of my viewpoints, that is palaeography, there has been a very notable advance. First, in the identification of the work of individual scribes in more than one codex, either from an ensemble of spelling, confirmed by characteristics of the handwriting, or from the writing corroborated by the spelling; and, secondly, in the associations found for these and still more manuscripts, through the geographical analysis of habits of spelling, with particular places or areas of England (whether or not corroborated by independent evidence), at specific dates or within approximate periods indicated by contents and by codicology (e.g. script, watermarks, decoration, ownership). The quantity and quality of regional book production substantiated by the *Atlas* is impressive.

For the palaeographer any new connexion of one manuscript with another, and of one or more with a place or area may be a lead to seeing similarities in script or other features, both inside and beyond the limits of one language, and a clue to the intellectual and social circumstances. In England of the 13th to 15th centuries, where palaeographical attention has hitherto been concentrated chiefly on Latin manuscripts, very few distinct types of writing or single features have yet been connected uniquely or firmly with particular centres, let alone areas. This is because the limited amount of palaeographical study there has been in these centuries in England focused either on monasteries like St Albans, from which survive a fair number of manuscripts expressly made for it, or on the broad chronological

developments in script, undifferentiated geographically, and
dominated by metropolitan milieux. I think it should be a reproach to
the many archivists involved with medieval English manuscripts that
they have done nothing to work out the occurrence of changes in
details and types of script in different parts of the country at different
dates.

In an article published in 1974 Angus McIntosh proposed and
exemplified, in parallel to the *linguistic* profiles of individual scribes
he and his colleagues were compiling, a systematic collection of
graphetic profiles (which of course need not be limited to texts in
English), towards a comprehensive taxonomy of at least the cursive
scripts. This has not yet been taken up by English palaeographers, as he
hoped, though it could now be facilitated by computer, as the
evolution of 12th-century papal chancery script is being handled at
Marburg.

One might expect the shared ranges of spelling preferences,
alternatives and tolerances of scribes from the same localities would be
paralleled in shared types or ranges of writing usage but, as long as we
lack an extensive body of systematic graphetic profiles covering the
whole or much of England, it is not easy to determine even single
practices, let alone repertoires, peculiar to one locality. You may think
that some or all of those hands argued from their peculiarities of
spelling and writing to be those of single individuals in more than one
manuscript may instead be those of more than one person of identical
training; but although one must allow that possibility, one's
judgement is affected by the fact that more often than not the next
nearest congeners in spelling do *not* reveal very close likeness in
details or type of writing. Graphetic profiles cannot well record more
than a selection of forms and variants of letters and abbreviations,
within the broad morphology of the main classes of later medieval
majuscule and minuscule script, subject also to the grades of actual
performance. There is a nomenclature for some different *styles* of
littera textualis in the 13th and 14th centuries, but within them and
within the class of *cursiva anglicana* there are distinct types, even
before the influence of continental cursives multiplied the latter from
about 1375 onwards, while within the new secretary style there are
recognisably different types, apart from innumerable amalgams, for
most of which we want some way of description, besides profiles of
their constituent graphs. This is a problem towards which the fresh or
more convincing geographical distribution of manuscripts which has
been effected by the *Atlas* (and work for it) could help, in conjunction

with facsimiles, if it associated certain styles or types of script with one place or area rather than another. But so far my impression is that most styles and types are of long-established or quite rapid *national* dissemination (in which however some chronology may be traceable) and of professional, not local, determination.

Significantly there *is* one broad regional identity: from the beginning of the 15th century the types of Scottish script do become quite distinct from the English ones, and their characteristics show it must be because of increased educational and cultural links with France, the Low Countries and the Rhineland, not just independent development.

One of the questions that the work towards the *Atlas*, and its findings, provoke is how people learned to read, spell and write in the vernacular, for which there is a paucity of direct evidence. There are grounds for thinking that rather more people could read than write, and it may be surmised that at least by the early 15th century more could read English than French or Latin. Presumably the teacher of *reading* alone (whether father, mother, nanny, nun or clerk), having inculcated the shapes and names of the graphs, no doubt first in textura (for which the criss-cross row ABCs at the beginning of some devotional primers were provided), and then in cursive, and variant forms and combinations in each, went on with already-known and fresh words, saying more or less, in the Middle English situation, 'that's how so-and-so is spelled hereabouts, or else like this', but would have to add at some stage, or leave it to the pupil to discover, 'other people, in this direction or that, more or less far away, whose writing you may meet, spell it differently, thus or thus'. What the teacher of *writing* must have added, or the pupil must have picked up, to produce the effects we find, is 'these are the shapes you must imitate, with such and such variations and combinations, some of which we only use in English, and though we spell some sounds, syllables and words in these ways hereabouts, elsewhere they differ; if you have to write to strangers or for them you may have to compromise or imitate their spellings, though if you are copying a text of theirs for us, you can convert it to ours in whole or part'. That readers and scribes did have a range of tolerance of variation in spelling, and that the scribes were prepared to modify it when they moved, or for different patrons, or from different exemplars, is one of the phenomena which has been strongly demonstrated by the *Atlas* team's work, and there are certainly parallels in the modification of graphic habits in response to new and local fashions, especially metropolitan ones, from the last decade or two of the 14th century onwards.

Most of the evidence we have of the teaching of reading and *composition* in *Latin*, after the Old English period and before the middle of the 14th century, is for the direct method or via French, only afterwards increasingly with the aid of English. In private tuition, petty and grammar schools the teaching of actual *writing* must practically have accompanied it, although there is a remarkable lack of evidence in England, except from pen-trials, mostly Latin, in some manuscripts. There is not a great deal of variation in spelling of even medieval Latin, in comparison with the vernaculars, but the common texts and treatises of grammar masters discuss alternatives and prescribe forms, with reasons, so teachers and pupils must have been well aware of the problems. The *models* of script and spelling must have been in the teachers' books and performance, and from what we know of the training of grammar masters, particularly at Oxford, it is not surprising that the *styles* so conveyed and practised locally were national and conservative in character, so that it is somewhat surprising that local spelling for so long, until the middle of the 15th century or later in many places, held out against standardisation. That it must have been for long positively taught, not just tolerated, seems to me to be shown by the largest palaeographical phenomenon substantiated by the survey of the *Atlas*, previously suspected by some of us (McIntosh 1974 [1989]: 608–609 [49]), but more fully explored and mapped by Michael Benskin (Benskin 1982), the geographical predominance of the use of the letter-form ‹y› in the north-eastern half of England and in Scotland, against the runic ‹þ› in the south-western half of England, as equivalents for ‹th› (voiced and unvoiced). Although he may be right in thinking the ‹y›-usage originated from a graphic confusion in 14th-century *littera textualis*, and despite its not infrequently causing further confusions of several sorts, tabulated by Professor Benskin, it seems to me that it can only have been so widely spread and so long maintained (for up to two centuries in the Middle Ages, and later) by being prescriptively taught in its strongholds, despite the disadvantage of ambiguities avoided by the use of ‹þ› or ‹th›, which must have been obvious to readers across the isographs. But graphic conventions are often resistant to convenience.

Mapping of distinct graphs, peculiar forms and fusions of them, and of abbreviations (which the *Atlas* team has done for some things like ‹þ› with superscripts), in relation to its localisations of manuscripts, and the findings of separate research on Latin, French and Celtic ones, are the obvious avenues of approach to further advance in this field.

References

Benskin M. 1982 The letters ⟨þ⟩ and ⟨y⟩ in later Middle English, and some related matters. *Journal of the Society of Archivists* 7: 13–30

McIntosh A. 1974 [1989] Towards an inventory of Middle English scribes. *Neuphilologische Mitteilungen* 75: 602–24; repr. in Laing M. (ed.) 1989 *Middle English Dialectology: Essays on some principles and problems*. Aberdeen University Press: Aberdeen, pp. 46–63

McIntosh A., Samuels M.L., Benskin M. 1986 *A Linguistic Atlas of Late Mediaeval English*, 4 vols. Aberdeen University Press: Aberdeen

Simpson G.G. 1973 *Scottish Handwriting 1150–1650*. Bratton Publishing Ltd: Edinburgh; repr. with corrections 1986 Aberdeen University Press: Aberdeen

II.3   A Philologist's View

Jeremy J. Smith

1. Philology and Linguistics

One of the many virtues of the *Linguistic Atlas of Late Mediaeval English* (henceforth *LALME*) has been the way in which it has combined up-to-date linguistic theory with the traditional philological concerns of textual transmission and context. So that my cards are on the table, I should state right away that I am not one of those who willingly separates the study of language from the literary–historical contexts in which it is recorded: and that is why this discussion is called 'a philologist's view'. But I think we all have to recognise — 'we' being philologists like myself — that 'old-fashioned' philology of the kind so often condemned as atomistic and untouched by theoretical concerns cannot be defended very easily from the charge of triviality. As Michael Halliday put it some time ago, '...the human sciences have to assume at least an equal responsibility in establishing the foundations of knowledge...' (Halliday 1987: 152); in such a world we philologists have a duty to be aware of underlying theoretical orientations. And to quote Harré, 'the explicit identification of the structure and components of one's conceptual system releases one from bondage to it' (1972: 17, cited in Lass 1976: 220).

However, I think many rather old-fashioned philologists like myself have felt that there is sometimes a tendency in the discipline of historical linguistics to allow theory (or sometimes simply notation) to overwhelm the data — for the empirical study, which (in our view) the subject should be, to be smothered in a rationalist bind. Being in the middle of the real (rather than the abstractly reconstructed) evidence for the history of our language, 'we philologists' are daily reminded of 'the buzz and hum in which mankind has been evolving' (Halliday 1987: 135), of the messiness and complexity of real language.

Obviously, what is needed is a rapprochement between these two approaches to the history of language. Of course, I am by no means the first or the most eminent to seek such a rapprochement between philology and linguistics, and many leading scholars who have attempted and achieved such a synthesis are present at this Colloquium. Since it is invidious to make personal references to people present, however, I should like to mention briefly someone who did achieve such a synthesis (but whose health prevents him from being with us): Michael Samuels. His *Linguistic Evolution* (Samuels 1972) remains the benchmark text, I believe, for students of the history of English. Although I am entirely responsible for what follows, insights derived from Professor Samuels' work appear throughout this paper.

The approach adopted here is unambitious, in the sense that it makes no earth-shattering claims of theoretical insight; it takes, as its title suggests, a philological approach. However, despite this restriction, an attempt has been made to take broader 'linguistic' views into account. Lytton Strachey in *Eminent Victorians*, anticipating Karl Popper, wrote that

> the wise historian of a complex epoch will row over that great ocean of material, and lower down into it, here and there, a little bucket, which will bring up to the light of day some characteristic specimen, from those far depths, to be examined with a careful curiosity.
>
> (Strachey 1918:1)

I hope that at least some of the 'buckets' presented here may have the effect of 'searchlights' (see further Diller 1990).

2. Every Text has its own History

The three examples chosen here may be taken to illustrate a rephrasing of Gilliéron's classic dictum, 'every word has its own history': in this case, the philological approach as defined above requires every text to have its own history.

The first example derives from some research undertaken for my doctoral thesis in the mid-1980s, and it connects in interest with some of the points made by Dr Doyle in his paper to this Colloquium (II.2; see Smith 1985: 144–45). Oxford, Bodleian Library Arch. Selden B.11 is a mid-15th-century manuscript of John Gower's *Confessio Amantis* in its unrevised first version; that is, it contains the references to King

Richard II which the poet judiciously chose to expunge at a later date, but was unable to prevent from being widely transmitted by copyists during the reign of Richard's usurping successors. Macaulay, the great editor of Gower's works, was much puzzled by this text.

> The text is a poor one with a good many corruptions, from the first line of the Prologue ... onwards, many of them absurd ... some arising from confusion between þ, ȝ and y. Thus the scribe (who usually has th for þ and y for ȝ) is capable of writing 'aþen' for 'aȝein', 'yerof' for 'þerof', 'yeff' for 'þef', 'biþete' for 'biȝete' ... Some northern forms [appear], as 'gude' iii.1073, 'Qwhat' iii.2439.
>
> (Macaulay 1900: cl)

Since Macaulay's time, new research, notably by Michael Benskin (1982), has allowed us to interpret the copyist's behaviour in this case. The scribe writes the letters ‹þ› and ‹y› differently: thus far, we know that he does not come from one of those areas, mainly northern ones, where, in the Middle English period, these letters came to be written identically. But ‹athen› 'again', ‹yeff› 'thief' need to be accounted for. The most plausible explanation for these forms is that the Selden scribe is copying from a manuscript where ‹þ› and ‹y› are written identically, as ‹y›, and, while copying mechanically, he interprets the distribution wrongly, giving ‹y› for ‹þ›, ‹þ› for ‹y› and — by extrapolation — ‹th› for ‹y›. That this exemplar was northerly is confirmed by the presence in the Selden MS of relicts such as ‹gude›, ‹qwhat›.

This example, which as Professor Benskin points out is paralleled elsewhere in the Middle English corpus, may seem interesting but trivial: a minor example of the confusions that scribal 'translation' can bring about. But there are some wider implications. First of all, there are implications for those like Dr Beadle who are interested in literary geography: here is a text, like the *Cursor Mundi* or the *Prick of Conscience* or the *Speculum Vitae*, which experiences a wide and complex process of geographical spread in its transmission, demonstrated by the language of one MS. Then there are some interesting implications for our understanding of contemporary practices of reading and of translation. But the main inference to be drawn from this example in the context of this paper is a very obvious one: texts can arise in very individual ways, but can be accounted for only within a larger framework.

A much more intriguing example is an Older Scots one, chosen here in honour of the generous way in which Edinburgh's School of

Scottish Studies is supporting the work of the Institute for Historical Dialectology. It is the well-known text of *Lancelot of the Laik*, which survives in a large, late 15th-century composite manuscript in Cambridge University Library, Kk.I.5. (A convenient edition of the poem is Gray 1912; see also Skeat 1865. Other poems in the MS copied by the same hand appear in Lumby 1870.) More work remains to be done on this interesting MS, and I hope to pursue this in the not too distant future (see on this the seminal article by Aitken 1971 and references there cited).

Gray (1912: xx) says of the poem, perhaps a little harshly, that 'although it possesses little literary value, [it] has a considerable share of linguistic interest'. She goes on to say:

> It shows an attempt on the part of the Middle Scots writer to adopt English, and the attempt is as superficial and as little convincing in the domain of the written language as that of some of his latter-day fellow-countrymen in the domain of the spoken tongue, and might well be compared with it. Yet it may be noticed that it apparently deceived the owner of the MS., for in the list of contents ... , whereas the 'Lancelot' is described as 'an English poem', one of the other Scottish pieces is distinguished as 'Dicta Salomonis in Scotch'
>
> (Gray 1912: xx–xxi).

That this mixture is due to the author rather than the copyist is shown, on the one hand, by rhyming and metrical practices and, on the other, by the fact that the scribe, when copying other poems in the MS, does not produce a similar *Mischsprache*.

Two examples might be taken to illustrate the behaviour adopted: the use of ‹-ith› in verbs, and forms like ‹boith› 'both', ‹quhois› 'whose'. The writer freely uses ‹-ith›, which he regards as a markedly southern English form, not only as an ending for the 3rd present singular — which is 'correct' in southern English terms — but also, 'hyper-correcting', in the 1st and 2nd persons singular. Thus *the brycht and fresch illumynare / Uprisith ...* (lines 3–4) is 'correct'; but 'incorrect' are *Yhow callith* [cf. southern English ‹clepest›] *the birdis be morow fro thar bouris* (line 91), and *in the feild I walkith* [cf. southern English ‹walke›] *to and froo*. Spellings such as ‹quhois, boith› are similarly 'incorrect' in comparison with Middle Scots ‹quhais, baith›, Southern English ‹whose›, ‹both›; they are obvious blend-forms, combining Scots ‹quh-›, ‹-i-› with Southern English ‹o› for Old English *ā*.

Forms such as ‹quhois› have been commented on before, notably by Agutter (1989), who has found a number of such forms in the poetry of the makars. She suggests that Dunbar's use of the form in *The Thrissil and the Rois*, 'a poem to celebrate the marriage of the reluctant James

IV to Margaret Tudor', was 'an anti-English joke' (1989: 10). If *Lancelot of the Laik* is a joke, then it is a rather heavy-handed 3,480-line one; a peculiar if not unparalleled text, and possibly rather special, it nevertheless raises interesting questions about the relationship between English and Scots at a crucial time in the development, divergence and standardisation of these two closely connected languages.

My final example also deals with 'hypercorrection', but at a much earlier date. MS Oxford, Bodleian Library, Auct. D.2.19 (3946), an 8th/9th-century copy of the Gospels in Latin, is known as the Rushworth Gospels after an early owner. In the 10th century it was given an interlinear gloss by two scribes whose names are recorded in colophons: Farman and Owun. The colophon records that Farman wrote 'æt harawuda', usually identified with Harewood near Leeds in Yorkshire.

Farman's language long puzzled scholars, because it seemed to be a strange blend of Mercian, West Saxon and 'unhistorical' forms. That this blend was the scribe's 'own' language was shown by Menner in 1934, who compared Farman's gloss to the Gospel of Mark with that of his exemplar, the Old Northumbrian *Lindisfarne Gospels Gloss*; Farman's gloss to Matthew is independently derived. One of these curious features was Farman's use of ‹æ› for the isolative development of both WGmc *a* and WGmc *e*. For the reflexes of WGmc *a*, Farman usually followed West Saxon practice, thus: ‹dæg› 'day', ‹fæder› 'father', ‹æfter› 'after', etc., with occasional ‹e›, e.g. ‹hweþre› 'whether'. But he also used ‹æ› for that very stable sound, West Germanic *e*, in words like ‹þægn›, ‹wær›, ‹þæc›; cf. 'normal' OE ‹þegn› 'thane', ‹wer› (archaic) 'man' ‹þec› 'thee'.

This peculiar practice was accounted for by Kuhn (1945). He suggested that Farman came from an area where the sound-change known as 'second fronting' was usual; this change is found most consistently in the language of the *Vespasian Psalter Gloss*, with alternations such as ‹deg ~ dæges› 'day, days' for West Saxon ‹dæg ~ dagas›. However, as Kuhn put it,

> Farman was trying to imitate the language of his temporal and ecclesiastical superiors. As a consequence of this imitation, he introduced numerous Saxonisms into his glosses, among them *æ* instead of *e* for [WGmc] *a*. He ... carried the imitation too far, and wrote *æ* frequently for [WGmc] *e*.
>
> (Kuhn 1945: 641–42)

Farman's 'hypercorrection' in the written mode — since the work of Angus McIntosh (e.g. 1956 [1989]), we need not, like Campbell (1959: 111, n. 1) confuse his written behaviour with his speech — has many implications, but one might be pursued here. In recent work by James and Lesley Milroy (Milroy and Milroy 1985; see also Milroy 1992), the innovations which may produce linguistic change are to be found amongst those members of the speech community who are 'weakly tied', in a social sense, to their 'target' culture. Farman was not a West Saxon, but aspired to West Saxonism. This makes him a 'weakly-tied' innovator.

3. Some Ways Forward

What general conclusions can be drawn from the three examples discussed above? These may be summed up as follows: on the one hand, the interpretation of individual texts requires an understanding of their wider context, while, on the other, to understand the wider context a good deal of analysis of individual texts is needed.

This conclusion is hardly the most earth-shattering statement ever made — nor am I by any means the first to make it (see, e.g., Rissanen 1990). But it does have some implications for the ways in which the disciplines of philology and historical linguistics should be pursued, as exemplified by the creation of *LALME*. In the theoretical approaches, I should like to see a movement away from some of the rather autistic, rule-based conceptions of language which, or so it sometimes seems to me, are not able to take account of what Michael Halliday (1987: *passim*) has called 'the dynamic open system' which is language. And, in practice, I should like to see a lot more emphasis, following the lead of *LALME*, on the detailed analysis of texts in context. A fruitful development of this Colloquium, I believe, would be the emergence of a whole series of interdisciplinary projects which focus on texts. Leaving aside the atlases of early Middle English and Older Scots which are currently being constructed in succession to *LALME*, one obvious — and necessarily collaborative — venture would be a series of regional studies, whereby codicological and philological interests could combine to recreate the linguistic and literary geography of the medieval period. This is only one suggestion for future research (see Smith forthcoming for a broader programmatic account). Suffice it to say that new developments in the theory and practice of historical dialectology have produced many opportunities for exciting and non-trivial research; especially for younger scholars, these opportunities are very considerable indeed.

References

Agutter A. 1989 Standardisation and restandardisation in Middle Scots. In: Law V., et al. (eds.) *Proceedings of the Fifth International Conference on English Historical Linguistics 1987*. Benjamins: Amsterdam, pp. 1–11

Aitken A.J. 1971 Variation and variety in written Middle Scots. In: Aitken A.J., McIntosh A., Pálsson H. (eds.) *Edinburgh Studies in English and Scots*. Longmans: London, pp. 177–209

Benskin M. 1982 The letters ‹þ› and ‹y› in later Middle English, and some related matters. *Journal of the Society of Archivists* 7: 13–30

Campbell A. 1959 *Old English Grammar*. Clarendon Press: Oxford

Diller H.-J. 1990 Linguistic searchlights and philological buckets. In: Fisiak J. 1990, pp. 143–64

Fisiak J. (ed.) 1990 *Historical Linguistics and Philology*. Mouton de Gruyter: Berlin

Gray M.M. (ed.) 1912 *Lancelot of the Laik*. Scottish Text Society 2nd series. Edinburgh

Halliday M.A.K. 1987 Language and the order of nature. In: Fabb N. et al. (eds.) *The Linguistics of Writing*. Manchester University Press: Manchester, pp. 135–54

Harré R. 1972 *The Philosophies of Science: an Introductory Survey*. Oxford University Press: London

Kuhn S.M. 1945 *e* and *æ* in Farman's Mercian Glosses. *Publications of the Modern Language Association of America* 60: 631–69

Lass R. 1976 *English Phonology and Phonological Theory*. Cambridge University Press: Cambridge

Lumby J.R. (ed.) 1870 *Bernardus de Cura Rei Famuliaris, with some early Scottish Prophecies &c*. EETS OS 42. London

Macaulay G.C. (ed.) 1900 *The English Works of John Gower*. EETS ES 81, 82. London

McIntosh A. 1956 The analysis of written Middle English. *Transactions of the Philological Society*: 26–55; repr. in Laing M. (ed.) 1989 *Middle English Dialectology: Essays on some principles and problems*. Aberdeen University Press: Aberdeen, pp. 1–21

McIntosh A., Samuels M.L., Benskin M. 1986 *A Linguistic Atlas of Late Mediaeval English*. Aberdeen University Press: Aberdeen

Menner R. 1934 Farman Vindicatus. *Anglia* 58: 1–27

Milroy J., Milroy L. 1985 Linguistic change, social network and speaker innovation. *Journal of Linguistics* 21: 339–84

Milroy, J. 1992 *Linguistic Variation and Change*. Blackwell: Oxford.

Rissanen M. 1990 On the happy reunion of English philology and historical linguistics. In: Fisiak J. 1990, pp. 353–69

Samuels M.L. 1972 *Linguistic Evolution*. Cambridge University Press: Cambridge

Skeat W.W. (ed.) 1865 *Lancelot of the Laik*. EETS OS 6. London

Smith J.J. 1985 Studies in the language of some manuscripts of Gower's *Confessio Amantis*. PhD dissertation, University of Glasgow. Unpublished

Smith J.J. forthcoming *An Ecology of English*

Strachey L. 1918 *Eminent Victorians*. Chatto & Windus: London

Panel II   MANUSCRIPT STUDIES AND
LITERARY GEOGRAPHY

Discussion

chaired by *Graham Caie*

Angus McIntosh: Can I ask Professor Dees, or anyone else, about something that has long puzzled me and that is the question that Richard Beadle raised about the probable percentage of survival of medieval manuscripts.

A.J. Aitken: It's a striking fact that the survival rate in England is very much higher than in Scotland and this presumably has some sociological implication.

McIntosh: I have discussed this issue at some length, particularly with my friend Dr Peter Buneman of the Wharton School of Mathematics in Philadelphia. His view of material on which he and I worked together, the *Prick of Conscience* and one or two other texts, was that it was very unlikely that more than one manuscript in twenty of a given stemma will have survived in that period, at least in the case of literary manuscripts. If that is the case, we need some sophisticated mathematical analysis and opinions about how far we can generalise on the basis of, for instance, the Mirk maps. It seems to me that where things pattern, as the Mirk and the *Speculum Christiani* maps clearly do,[1] then that in itself might tell us something about the total number of manuscripts of the *Speculum* or of Mirk, because if the proportion was very small one wouldn't expect so striking a pattern.

Anthonij Dees: I have one comment (I can't answer your question). It is extremely difficult to find an intermediary manuscript as I understand it — an intermediary manuscript in the sense of direct

---

[1] See maps 3, 5 and 6, pp. 81, 87–88.

predecessor of one of the known manuscripts. This is extremely rare; I
hardly have found any.

Richard Beadle: As far as Middle English is concerned, it is relatively
rare to find the exemplar from which a given manuscript has been
copied. We know of a small handful of instances. Another point to
connect with what Ian Doyle was saying, is that we don't even know
the total number of manuscripts containing the English literary texts. I
suppose it must be upwards of 5,000, perhaps 6,000 or 7,000. But the
number of those manuscripts in which the work of a scribe is
recognisable in more than one is again not particularly high. A list is
being compiled[2] and I think about 100 individuals are recognisable in
more than one manuscript. At the moment as palaeographical and
linguistic protocols become more refined more individuals may be
identified.

Ian Doyle: There is a corroborative figure for a large printed book of
1493 where we know 600 copies were printed in English and only 20
copies survive. So there you've got figures for a religious text. But
every text has its history because the factors — historical, religious and
so on — which determine the survival of any particular one and the
date of its origin will vary tremendously. The case of the book of 1493
is not out of line with the sort of figures you're pointing to.

Helmut Gneuss: I should like to ask Dr Beadle about the patterns of
distribution on some of the maps. Some of these patterns are very
clearly delimited. Could at least a few of those texts be related to, say,
certain groups of religious houses or religious orders?

Beadle: There is one map [not presented here] which is for the text of
Walter Hilton's, *Scale of Perfection*. This is a mystical text, which is
considerably more sophisticated intellectually than things like the
Prick of Conscience and the other manuals of pastoral theology, the
Speculum Vitae and the *Speculum Christiani*. And there the
distribution is really rather different. There is a cluster in the
immediate centre of dissemination round one of the places where the
author is known to have lived, Thurgarton in Nottinghamshire. But
there are other patches. There is one up in the North-west —
Cumberland, North Lancashire — another right down in the south

---

[2] This was begun by Angus McIntosh, Ian Doyle and Michael Samuels.

coast in Dorset, another in East Anglia, and it is a kind of text where conventual ownership marks are occasionally found.[3] And I think in this case you have a text about which the answer to your question is probably 'yes'. I think the pattern of distribution is probably related to dissemination, to some extent, by religious orders. The manuals of popular theology and the homiletic poems, one imagines, would be more likely to be in the hands of parish priests and the dissemination would be from one parish to the next. If you could imagine one priest borrowing an exemplar from his neighbour down the road, and copying it, then it would lead to more even distribution for this kind of text in contrast with that of the *Scale of Perfection*. I didn't include the *Scale of Perfection* for lack of time.

Aitken: On survival rate I am reminded that in the late 16th century in Scotland you have a fair number of booksellers' wills, which are extant. They give the numbers of copies of books, many of them known but some unknown, both Latin and vernacular, in the stocks of the booksellers. Usually you find that only one or even no copy of these books survives and the numbers are usually of the order of a thousand or more. Out of a thousand copies, no copy survives. I think that from my memory of the *Testament of Cresseid*, there were something like 1,400 copies and we have one.[4]

Robert Lewis: I was thinking that it would be nice if Ian Doyle or Richard Beadle would gather all this information about surviving manuscripts and put it together and write it up. There are a few other things one would throw into the pot like the *Ayenbite of Inwit*[5] and the *Ormulum*,[6] for instance, which are single manuscripts. We have the original, yet there are no copies. But what does that tell us? The

---

[3] Note that this statement is based on a mass of collaborative work on the *Scale of Perfection* done, mainly in the 1960s, by Angus McIntosh and the late Professor Alan Bliss. This material is now housed in the Library of University College, Dublin. Its findings will no doubt be added to by Bliss's editorial successor and ultimately be published. — Eds.

[4] On checking I find that at his death in 1599 this particular printer/bookseller had 545 'Testamentis of Cresseid at iiij d. the pece'. But his 1593 print of Cresseid survives as a unique copy. In 1602 Robert Smyth had 1638 'Cressedis', of which none survives. Similar figures apply to other works and other Edinburgh printer/booksellers about this time. See D. Fox (ed.) 1981 *The Poems of Robert Henryson*, Clarendon Press: Oxford, pp. xciv and xcix–c and, for the texts of the wills, D. Laing (ed.) 1836 *The Bannatyne Miscellany* II, Bannatyne Club: Edinburgh, pp. 187–296. — A.J. Aitken.

[5] British Library, Arundel 57 items (1), (2).

[6] Bodleian Library, Bodley Junius 1.

same kind of thing that the 1493 book tells us, or something different? If one could somehow get this information together I think it would be very useful for all of us.

Doyle: Yes, scales of survival and surmises about the reasons. The *Gawain* manuscript[7] is another example containing single surviving texts.

Richard Hamer: Could I add a bit on the question of scribes who can be identified with more than one manuscript? Clearly there were a lot of professional scribes around once the book trade got started and some of them lived a long time and wrote a lot. For example, much of the extent of Ricardus Franciscus's activity has been recorded by Kathleen Scott; and quite a few manuscripts by him are known in English, French and Latin, in verse and prose.[8] Another one, Harley 4775, has been known for some time to be a close copy of Douce 372, but was only relatively recently identified as by Ricardus. Not long ago a sheet of another copy of this work, *Gilte Legende*, came to light in a bundle of stuff bought by T. Takamiya, and this sheet seems almost certain to have come from the exemplar used by the writers of Egerton 876.[9] Jeremy Griffiths spotted that this sheet was in the hand of a scribe who also wrote a copy of Nicholas Love, which was then in the possession of Charles Traylen, the Guildford bookseller. I cite these examples to show how randomly the dribs and drabs of information about the scribes come together, and doubtless when more photographs of hands in London book trade productions are published a lot more will emerge to enhance the general picture.

Alexander Fenton: Still on this question of distribution, I am struck by the parallel with a book I was reading lately, Margaret Spufford, *Small Books and Pleasant Histories* [Methuen: London, 1981]. She speaks about the chapbook distribution, with London as a centre, and in fact there were people who actually bought the material in London, traders and so on, who then rambled all over the country. These were secular people rather than religious. But the point really that I would like to raise is how actually were the manuscripts distributed? It has been touched on. But were there also secular distributors of some of these

---

[7] British Library, Cotton Nero A x.

[8] K.L. Scott 1968 A mid-fifteenth century English illuminating shop and its customers. *Journal of the Warburg and Courtauld Institutes* xxxi: 170.

[9] Takamiya MS 45.17.

early manuscripts? And even if they were of a religious nature why should they only have been for religious consumption through parish priests?

Doyle: The situation is very different after printing. One of the things which the Middle English *Atlas* and the related works help to underline, if not reveal, is the variable quantity and quality of regional production of manuscripts. It shows the relationship between the production of manuscripts and the spelling of assignable regions, whether or not their scribes did the writing in those places, which is the big caveat one has to make. But also, I think, it underlines very much how it is only at the end of the 14th century that the metropolitan production of vernacular manuscripts becomes a significant factor, a highly significant factor, and probably a commercial one. That fits in with documentary evidence but only from about 1400; and indeed it is certainly not dominant for quite a while afterwards. The book trade was organised in places like the Universities at Oxford and Cambridge and in London on a bespoke basis. You would go and order a copy if you couldn't find one second-hand. The book trade did not itself take a great deal of initiative in laying out money on speculative copies which it might have to sell on the spot and certainly did not risk distributing throughout the country. It is pretty clear this didn't happen before the necessity of large-scale distribution was forced by printing and the economies of printing and the numbers in a printing. Once you got printing and once a publisher had a lot of copies on his hands he had to get them distributed and therefore he had to find means of distributing them throughout the country as well as in the metropolis. There were general fairs, and books were sold at them at certain places — Stourbridge outside Cambridge and St Giles' Fair in Oxford, and so on. But I think it is very doubtful that there were chapmen to the same extent after the invention of printing. Clearly people who went in for entertainment, such as the minstrels, might I suppose have done a certain amount of writing and selling of small items. But I discount there being any large-scale distribution in that way. The dissemination was either organised by the author and his colleagues or by the professional interest of the people who wanted the books — either by copying themselves or by going and finding someone who would do the copying for them. It's very much individual initiative rather than a commercial enterprise.

Graham Caie: When the gilds of scriveners were organised towards the second half of the 14th century, to what extent did this have an effect on standardisation? You mentioned before that the patron possibly could have an influence. Could you go to your scrivener and say: 'I would like a copy of this, but please put it in my own dialect'? How did it work?

Doyle: One can only speculate there. The copyist might well have grasped the type of language which might be acceptable to a particular patron. Jeremy Smith has a very good case in what we call scribe D, who shows signs of having had a West Midland upbringing but is operating mostly or entirely in the metropolitan area as a professional paid scribe. He makes multiple copies of certain works, Gower in particular, and his spelling betrays both some local background — West Midland — and also the influence of the text he copied repeatedly — Gower.

Jeremy Smith: It's another example of hypercorrection. Scribe D is a fascinating fellow. He was identified by Ian Doyle and Malcolm Parkes back in 1978[10] and he copied something like eight Gowers — a large number — and some Trevisas and *Piers Plowman*s and a couple of very early Chaucers. What is interesting about him is that we could tell where he came from originally. He had come from somewhere in north Worcestershire. And then he moved to London. When he got there, being a north Worcestershire man was an uneasy thing to be. Of course, there were people who stayed in north Worcestershire and who continued to copy very peculiar sorts of north Worcestershire texts. And there is a Gower of the same date, for instance, which is very strong Herefordshire. When scribe D arrived in London he felt uneasy about his language so he tried to purge out his West-Midlandisms. It is actually possible to make a cline of his texts because there is so much material that you can rank them. There are early texts in his production which have a fair number of south-west-Midlandisms but they peter out. And this does seem to correlate with what is known about ownership and what is known as I understand it about the increasing lavishness of books. But when he was in London, scribe D got into the habit of copying Gowers. The trouble with Gower

---

10 A.I. Doyle and M.B. Parkes 1978 The production of copies of the *Canterbury Tales* and *Confessio Amantis* in the early fifteenth century. In: M.B. Parkes and A.G. Watson (eds.) *Mediaeval Scribes, Manuscripts and Libraries: Essays presented to N.R. Ker*. Scolar Press: London.

is that Gower's language is a very strange mixture. It generally wouldn't be out of place in many southern texts but there are features in it which show a mixture of Suffolk and Kentish. Some of these just seem like archaic London forms, but they were obviously felt to be appropriate to Gowers. And throughout the 15th century people kept on copying Gower-type spellings, for instance, ‹oghene› for 'own', and ‹-end› endings of the present participle. Gower has these and the people said, 'Oh, well, you've got to have them in a Gower', and so wrote them down. Scribe D learnt these and then when he went on to copy Chaucer he put them in there too because he obviously regarded this as the appropriate thing to do.

Matti Rissanen: I think, Jeremy, that you have just described beautifully a man with weak ties, haven't you? I welcome this idea that combines philology and linguistics. As for Farman, I think that is very interesting too. It might be that Farman lived in a period of weak ties, of dissolving ties in general. Then of course one could not tell whether it was simply that he was copying so much that he was exposed to texts with a variety of spelling; or that other people around him spoke so as to mix their *a*'s and *e*'s and *i*'s; or whether it was simply that the letter ‹æ› had lost the 'one sound one letter' principle and that was why he was using it for a variety of purposes. So perhaps in this case it was rather that that period in the history of English was indeed typically what James and Lesley Milroy would term a time of general weak ties.

Smith: That's a very good point. There are two things which one could learn from that. One thing that's puzzling about Farman is that he is writing in the 10th century and I've always been taught that that is very early to have a standardised *Schriftsprache*; Professor Gneuss would know much more about that. The second point perhaps connects up with the map of ‹þ› and ‹y›. Farman has a lot of ‹þ›s in his text and Michael Samuels says that he feels that there is a distribution of ‹þ› and ‹ð› in the Anglo-Saxon dialects which is really quite intriguing. He says that Farman seems to put in a lot more ‹þ›s than you would expect in a Mercian text. I don't think it's anything to do with sound. I think it's graphetic.

Derek Britton: I have a point which I would like to put to Jack Aitken or Harry Watson. Are there not rather more than he supposes of hypercorrect or hybrid forms like ‹quhois› for 'whose'? That is not just a one-off form in *Sir Lancelot*; you get that same spelling, I think, in William Dunbar's *Thistle and the Rose*. Could it not be a hybridisation? I was wondering, Jack, since you've got a labial there in 'who', could it not in fact be a genuine Scots form with the ‹oi› representing a vowel rounded through the labial preceding?

Aitken: I don't think so, unless it's part of a general trend.

Britton: You get [twɔː] out of [twɑː].

Aitken: *Sir Lancelot* is at the end of a cline of what I call anglicisation in Scots. It is the most extremely anglicised piece in Scots but it is not unique in that there is a whole range of poems starting with the poems of Robert Henryson at one end and taking in the *Kingis Quair* and the work of Gavin Douglas towards the other end. One of the first features is the subsitution of *o* for Scots *a*, particularly in rhyme, because it was the most obvious thing to do, and it is a deliberate anglicisation. It's an attempt to imitate the language of Chaucer. It's handy because it gives you a choice of rhymes, so you get an extra rhyme option.

Smith: That choice of alternative forms is a good point because you get it in *Gawain and the Green Knight* and in *Pearl*: 'More and more and ȝet wel mare'.[11] So there are *a* and *o* rhymes; there's obviously a choice.

Caie: Now, let me draw some threads together. The main theme has been the need for an integrated interdisciplinary approach to Middle English manuscripts and the investigation of textual sources, starting with Richard Beadle's paper on the production and dissemination of copies of late Middle English literary texts — their codicological environment.

Ian Doyle demonstrated the application of the Middle English *Atlas* in the process leading to identification of the work of an individual scribe in a number of codices and associations and habits of spelling with particular places or areas. He pointed out the need for a comprehensive taxonomy of the cursive anglicana scripts. I think one of the main aims of this meeting should be to identify future areas of this kind in which we can continue research.

---

[11] *Pearl*, line 145.

Jeremy Smith concluded with a plea for an integration of philology and linguistics and called on the help of modern textual criticism, sociology and indeed, anthropology to shed light on the circumstances surrounding a given text. I suppose one might pull it all together by using E.M. Forster's 'only connect' theory: the interconnectedness of layers of language and of language with extralinguistic events.

* * * * * *

Michael Benskin could not be present at the discussion recorded above. He supplies the following contribution:

From what Dr Doyle has said, it seems that my account of the Middle English confusion of 'þ' and 'y' was less clear than it should have been. When I set out what I believed (and still believe) to be the mechanics of that confusion, I did not mean to imply that every Middle English scribe who failed to distinguish these letters must, in the course of fixing his style of handwriting, have gone through the same mechanical process of bringing about their confusion. If that were so, then there should be no regional coherence at all between the local origins of the types of written language in which the confusion of 'þ' and 'y' appears. That coherence is, as Dr Doyle has affirmed, evidence that the usage was stable; and it can hardly have been perpetuated without being taught. In this connexion, it is worth noting the chronological range of the manuscripts from which the 'þ'/'y' map was compiled: it is at least a hundred and twenty years. Had regional practice not been settled during that period, frequent interruptions ought to appear in the distributions on the map; whereas what we find is not a chequerboard pattern, but solid blocs.

Since the 'þ'/'y' map was compiled (1978), I have examined many more manuscripts and some thousands of documents; the documents are mostly from the mid-fifteenth to the early-sixteenth centuries, and few of them are in local language uncontaminated by the emerging written standard. Even so, I have found nothing to invalidate the published account; in Essex there has emerged a small additional outcrop of early-fourteenth-century ‹y› for 'þ', and elsewhere some of the local detail can be refined; but so far that is all. Recent investigation of writings from the Salisbury area adds to the indications that the confusion of 'þ' and 'y', 'a development that became regular in northern Middle English, had begun, independently and probably sporadically, in early Middle English of southern England and the West Midlands; but in these areas it was checked in favour of the traditional system, and had all but disappeared by later Middle English times'.[12]

It may be worth restating my view that the confusion of '*þ*' and '*y*' in Anglicana scripts is a habit transferred from the writing of textura: the typically recurved-tail ‹y› of Anglicana looks nothing like a ‹þ›, yet throughout the North, it is the regular symbol for both historical '*y*' and '*þ*'.[13] This again points to a scribal tradition, codified behaviour taught by one generation to the next. In so far as the confusion of these letters in Anglicana became a regional trait, its transfer from textura must have been deliberate; otherwise, we should find it only sporadically in that script, as a practice individual or even idiosyncratic. Indeed, a revised version of the '*þ*'/'*y*' map ought to take account of the mode of script in which the confusion is attested; were it restricted to Anglicana, the regional pattern would be even more sharply defined.

---

[12] See M. Benskin 1982 The letters ‹þ› and ‹y› in later Middle English, and some related matters. *Journal of the Society of Arhcivists* 7: 13–30 (p. 25).
[13] Ibid., p. 25.

K   Historical Dialectology and Literary Text Traditions

Anthonij Dees

1. Introduction

French historical linguistics is hampered by some fundamental weaknesses, as I discovered during my work on the French demonstratives.

It is a well known fact that the French language has developed a system of demonstratives which, compared to the English, Dutch or German systems, is highly original. This development is puzzling, because the deictic forms inherited from Latin seem normal and perfectly orthodox:

near	remote	near	remote
ceste feme	*cele feme*	'this woman'	'that woman'
cestes femes	*celes femes*	'these women'	'those women'

Later French generalised a quite different solution:

near	remote
cette femme-ci	*cette femme-là*
ces femmes-ci	*ces femmes-là*

How can it be explained that an important linguistic category is subject to drastic changes in one language, but not in others? The traditional answers, which — in terms of analogy and so on — insist on the naturalness of the French evolution, fail to explain the divergent developments in different languages.

In my search for the specific conditions which could explain the aberrant French behaviour, I made some astonishing observations. The date of the first symptoms of the evolution being, in my view, of crucial interest, I saw that in specialised studies and current handbooks the date of the beginning of the change varied between the 12th and the 16th centuries, each of the intervening centuries having found its defenders. It seemed to me that this state of affairs concerning an observational fact was totally unacceptable. In trying to elaborate a less impressionistic dating, I discovered the real problem for this kind of investigation: a vast documentation of several hundreds of literary texts was an absolute minimum to really observe, with the usual statistical precautions, a sudden restructuring of the demonstrative system, a restructuring which, for Paris for instance, could be dated just after the middle of the 14th century.

During my research I discovered a second fundamental weakness in the available descriptions. Systematic dialectal variation, extremely important for the understanding of what happened in Old French, had been completely overlooked by previous research. These short-comings in the description of dialectal aspects of the demonstratives could be repaired by compiling a documentation of about 2,000 charters of known regional provenance (and of known date).

On the basis of this rather vast documentation I was able to propose an interpretation of the history of the demonstratives in medieval French which I am still prepared to defend as in essence correct. Note that in this interpretation I intuitively applied a precise criterion to control the correctness of a causal linguistic explanation, i.e. the criterion of temporal and spatial contiguity of cause and effect. In later studies this criterion has been repeatedly applied, for instance to demonstrate the doubtful character of analogy in causal argumentations.

As a result of my investigation into the evolution of the demonstratives I was obliged to conclude that knowledge of important aspects of Old French was lacking to an astonishing degree. This conclusion implied among other things — as I stated in 1971 — that the traditional view, shared by philologists and linguists working on Old French, namely that a type of common written Old French of Parisian origin was eliminating the older dialects during the 12th and the 13th century, was probably an important strategic error in matters of linguistic description.

After the publication of my thesis *Étude sur l'évolution des démonstratifs en ancien et en moyen français*, we decided — Pieter van Reenen having joined me in the meantime — to start a kind of Old French Dialect project, unaware of the fact that in Edinburgh a similar project had been undertaken long before. In order to avoid the errors of the past, we defined the following three principles for our project:

1. a dialectological investigation should be based on the best available witnesses, i.e. documents of known origin and of known date like charters (which we proposed to call primary witnesses, as opposed to derivative witnesses, such as numerous literary texts, the origin of which has been reconstructed by philologists on the basis of the available linguistic arguments);

2. the network of geographical points should in principle be as dense as possible, in order to avoid the inevitable deformation of reality which consists in forcing discovered isoglosses to coincide with arbitrarily imposed dialect boundaries;

3. considering the fact that medieval speech communities cannot possibly have been homogeneous, it was essential that frequencies of occurrence of regional phenomena should be estimated with maximal precision, a requirement which makes it possible to avoid idealised descriptions in terms of presence or absence of characteristics, i.e. in terms of 0% or 100%.

A first result of the Old French Dialect project was the publication, in 1980, of the *Atlas des formes et des constructions des chartes françaises du 13e siècle*. Strategically more important, maybe, was the creation, on the one hand, of a computerised data-base, consisting of about one million words that had resulted from the analysis of the 3,300 13th-century charters, and on the other hand of a new type of description of regional aspects.

Concerning the data-base, in research on particular problems it has rendered many services as the most reliable source of information on dialectal aspects of Old French. As for the new type of description, it replaces the traditional verbal descriptions and takes the form of a 87 x 270 cell matrix — the 87 rows representing 87 geographical points such as Paris or Nancy, and the 270 lines the first 270 linguistic phenomena described in the *Atlas* — filled with percentages corresponding to the estimated frequencies of the phenomena on the different geographical points.

One of the most interesting uses to be made of the matrix is the localisation of literary texts of unknown origin. The principle of the localisation is the calculation of the degree of correlation between the frequencies of the localisation criteria found in a literary text and those observed at each of the 87 geographical points entered in the matrix. The localisation program has been frequently tested, for instance on hundreds of charters of known origin of the 14th century, and the outcome is almost always very satisfying in the sense that the computer selects exactly the given geographical point. Localisation of some 200 literary texts (or long fragments of texts) resulted in a considerable extension of our data-base and in the publication, in 1987, of the 500 maps of our *Atlas des formes linguistiques des textes littéraires de l'ancien français*.

2 . Historical Dialectology and Literary Text Traditions

We now come to the subject of historical dialectology and literary text traditions. I shall discuss here three important aspects of philological work, namely the reconstruction of the relationships between the different versions of a literary text, the determination of the first regional origin of the text tradition and some provisional remarks on the translation process which was necessary to adapt the primitive version to new dialectal environments.

2.1 *The Stemmatological Problem*

Philologists are and should be interested in the relationships between the several — often widely divergent — versions of a given text, one of the main questions being the distance that separates later versions from the original form of the text. Traditionally, results obtained by investigations into this problem are presented in the form of a derivational tree and the main technique of analysis is the technique of the common error. The basic idea is that, if two or more versions have in common an evident error, this observation justifies the conclusion that these versions constitute a separate subfamily. By repeated application of this technique it should be possible to determine the whole net of relationships between original and derived versions of the text.

As I have repeatedly stated since 1975,[1] this technique of the common errors is in most cases insufficient to solve correctly the stemmatological problem, one of the main reasons being the enormous amount of possible solutions for even small numbers of versions:

Number of versions	Number of possible trees
2	3
3	22
4	262
5	4,336
6	91,984
7	2,381,408
8	72,800,928

Some 15 years ago I published the first results of a new approach to the stemmatological problem, an approach based on explicit calculation(s) and characterisation of all the possible trees for small numbers of versions. Fortunately, meanwhile, on the other side, I was able to define an algorithm to enumerate in a systematic way the possible trees for at least relatively small numbers of versions. Let me illustrate this algorithm for the case of four versions. All possible trees for four versions can be derived by distinguishing three successive levels of analysis.

2.1.1 *The Level of the Underlying Structures*

For the case of four versions there are exactly two underlying structures:

___
[1] See the relevant works cited on pp. xix–xxii of Reenen and Reenen-Stein 1988. — Eds.

The difference between (1) and (2) is that in the first structure no dichotomy in reading of the type AB/CD is possible, whereas in the second structure this kind of contrast is legitimate.

2.1.2 *The Level of Intermediarity*

On this level the philologist studies the question whether one or more versions are intermediary, i.e. lose their branch to become a node. Thus, if version 2 has the behaviour of an intermediary version, the resulting structure will be:

(3)

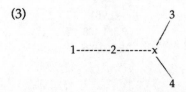

2.1.3 *The Level of Orientation*

The last operation is the choice of an adequate orientation to justify the observed behaviour of the versions. Each of the points of (3), the extant versions 1, 2, 3, 4, or x, or a point between these versions, qualifies as the top of a genealogical tree of the orthodox type, as for instance:

(4)   (5)

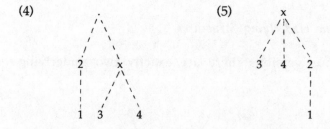

In this orientation phase one must consider arguments relative to questions of anteriority/posteriority. Arguments traditionally invoked in this matter are well known: evident errors, inconsistencies and so on. Besides these arguments, which sometimes leave the impression of arbitrary decisions, I shall presently propose a line of reasoning which takes into account linguistic, mainly dialectal considerations.

An additional problem in stemmatological reconstructions is the often observed fact of changes in relationships in one and the same text. These changes (probably due to division of labour in the process of reproduction of manuscripts) imply that several successive genealogical trees must be constructed for the different parts of the text. Sophisticated computer analysis is necessary to disentangle these complexities. Thanks to active collaboration with mathematicians and informaticians progress has been made in this field, as a thesis on the case of the *Perceval* tradition will make clear in the near future.[2]

2.2 *Determination of the First Regional Provenance of the Text*

In a dialectal situation it is normal that certain rhymes are possible in some regions, but excluded in others. The possibility or the impossibility of a given rhyme depends of course on the pronunciation norms that characterise a given region. If it were possible to obtain more precise indications about regional differences in pronunciation, this knowledge could serve to predict rhyme behaviour of literary texts created in a given dialect. A long-term enterprise aiming at a reconstruction of regionally differentiated pronunciation is now under way. The essence of the reconstruction procedure is global trust in the spellings of Old French words, combined with a check on the correctness of restituted pronunciations by analysis of rhymes found in texts of known regional origin. Sufficient insight has already been acquired to make hypotheses about the origin of a number of texts.

2.3 *Adaptation of Texts to New Dialectal Environments*

The adaptation of literary texts to new dialectal environments must have been one of the daily preoccupations of the medieval copyist. Two problems were essential in this perspective: on the one hand unfamiliar spellings and, on the other hand, rhymes that were unacceptable in the new environment. Recent work in this field has already resulted in interesting observations, for instance that copyists

---

2 Now published: see van Mulken 1993.

replace spellings more easily in the interior of verses than in rhyme position. We begin to understand certain problems encountered by the copyist in cases where the dialectal provenance of the original text and that of a later version could be determined.

Insight into this kind of problem will eventually result, we hope, in an alternative solution for the problem of choosing the correct orientation for a given underlying structure. If the traditional reasoning based on common errors could be replaced by an elaborated argumentation invoking a whole process of linguistic adaptation, the reconstruction of the text tradition would in our opinion greatly be improved.

This kind of linguistic reasoning can best be based on explicit expectations in matters of interdialectal translations. As such we propose the following set:

1. a literary text is born at a given point in time and in a given dialect and will reflect in its linguistic form the characteristics of that particular time and that particular dialect;

2. especially in the first period of Old French literature, the text is characterised by assonance (identity of the last tonic vowel of the line of verse) or by rhyme (identity of the last tonic vowel of the line of verse and of the consonants following that vowel);

3. the text is diffused by making new copies of either the original text or of later copies, the totality of these versions constituting the textual tradition of that text (almost inevitably a certain number of the versions, original or derived, will have disappeared since the period of reproduction of the text);

4. the original form of the text will essentially show the following characteristics:

    • an (almost) absolute degree of identity between the vowels in assonance or vowel + consonant in rhyme;

    • a high degree of consistency in representing vowels and consonants by written symbols and hence a high degree of regularity on the level of spelling;

5. in case the reproduction takes place at a later moment or at a different point in the dialectal space, the copyist will normally try to adapt the linguistic forms of his model to the norms of his own dialectal and temporal environment;

6. as a result of this adaptation the adapted version of the text will normally reflect conflicts at the levels of identity of word endings in rhyme or assonance position and of consistency in the spelling system.

References

Dees A. 1971 *Étude sur l'évolution des démonstratifs en ancien et en moyen français.* Wolters-Noordhoff: Groningen

Dees A., Reenen P.Th. van and De Vries J.A. 1980 *Atlas des formes et des constructions des chartes françaises du 13e Siécle.* Beihefte zur Zeitschrift für romanische Philologie 178: Tübingen

Dees A., Dekker M., Huber O. and Reenen-Stein K. van 1987 *Atlas des formes linguistiques des textes littéraires de l'ancien français.* Beihefte zur Zeitschrift für romanische Philologie 212: Tübingen

Mulken M. van 1993 *The Manuscript Tradition of the* Perceval *of Chrétien de Troyes.* Doctoral Thesis: Free University of Amsterdam

Reenen P. van, Reenen-Stein K. van (eds.) 1988 *Distributions spatiales et temporelles, constellations des manuscrits: Études de variation linguistique offertes `a Anthonij Dees `a l'occasion de son 60me anniversaire.* Benjamins: Amsterdam

Anthonij Dees   KEYNOTE ADDRESS

Discussion

chaired by *Angus McIntosh*

A.J. Aitken: I was interested in your discussion on reconstruction. I noticed you made no mention of modern dialects as one of the tools of reconstruction.

Anthonij Dees: I'm a little bit careful about modern dialects. It results from a practice we have of research in French where modern dialects have been used to reconstruct medieval dialects. I think this is a very dangerous operation and in my articles I have condemned this procedure. What I favour more is some way of linking modern and medieval dialects. I think the right procedure is to reconstruct the medieval situation as carefully as you can and then compare it to modern situations. And what do you observe? Certain phenomena remain unchanged in distribution between the 13th century and the 20th century. Other phenomena have changed or disappeared. So I think the first step, the careful reconstruction of the medieval situation, cannot be omitted. For the rest — since my resources are limited — it would be for me a project of high priority to proceed to a comparison of the medieval findings with the marvellous modern French dialect atlas we have. It's astonishing that this should not have begun. Until now it has been essential for us to reconstruct what has happened in medieval French over a period of four or five centuries. We know virtually nothing about the dialectal situation for the 17th and 18th centuries, but we have the means to reconstruct it. So I fully agree with you when you say that you should make comparisons with modern situtations — of course, it is an absolute necessity. I should like the same sort of thing to be done also for the French situation. I see the need, but I have no time to do anything in that direction at the moment.

Aitken: The 200,000 pairs of rhymes that you have, how are these organised and how do you present them? I've had in mind myself for a while a project for Older Scots. This is to study most or all of the poetry in rhyme in OSc, organising the rhymes in each poem in what I call rhyming sets. Now, these rhyming sets would in fact mirror what we have in the modern phonological Scots dialect atlas. In other words they would be organised by vowel and their following consonant.

Dees: I completely agree with you. This is my finding. I can tell you there are about 300 possible endings of words — if it is that that you mean — which are considered as extremely important for the reconstruction of the pronunciation.

Aitken: That is what I mean. My idea is to do this for each text, or for some discrete portion of text, so that each text has its own rhyme profile which is actually exactly mirroring the modern dialect phonological atlas in its arrangement. And in principle I think from that, you should be able to follow changes — mergers for instance — through the lexicon over time. You should be able to identify localities for particular texts, and so on, much as you can do for the modern phonological atlas.

Dees: I think I agree in general with you. Myself I would not base it on individual texts but on groups of texts from certain regions. That is the starting point. I see no reason why two texts belonging to the same region should have different behaviours in rhyme, so I start with determining what are the possible rhymes in a given region. And that region can very well be represented by four or five texts. I know several texts of the Picardian region, for instance. But I think in general we have had very much the same idea.

George Jack: One of the points that is discussed in traditional textual criticism is the way in which a scribe may correct the text back to the original form. The text has originally been correct. It has gone through an intermediate manuscript which has introduced an error. A scribe then copies from that and using that exemplar recognises there has been an error. He is a kind of textual critic himself and restores the original reading. In that situation, how can one discriminate between what is, as it were an original exemplar — an original manuscript — which is not in error and one into which error has been introduced and then removed? Now, it seems to me that the same kind of process may take place if one is looking at the situation where rhymes or assonances are involved. Is it possible to distinguish between a case where a text shows a pattern of correct rhymes or assonances and is broadly correct in some percentage of cases because it is close to the original and has undergone a small degree of change and another case which shows the same proportion of correctness but where there has been a preceding stage in which there was a greater degree of 'error' which a scribe has then corrected?

Dees: Let me say to start with that I am aware of about 20 different hypotheses all trying to explain why things observed do not correspond to the reconstructed tree. Well, in my talk I have tried to make clear that our stemmatological analyses are insufficient to correctly solve very complex realities. So, in my view, it is a question of high priority to refine our methods of analysis. If the tree we have in mind is not the correct one — which is, I can tell you, nearly always the case — the contradictions and inconsistencies are simply due to the fact that our analysis was inadequate. Wrong trees inevitably produce apparent contamination. Having discovered this important source of contamination, I am somewhat sceptical about all kinds of explanations philologists have imagined. So, in this particular case, I must ask you if you have really observed this behaviour of the text going back to the original after a change has intervened?

Jack: I'll answer that question indirectly for a moment. In traditional textual criticism it is often thought that one phenomenon that may lead to this is contamination and another is scribal self-correction. A scribe recognises that something is incorrect and corrects it, alters it. Now, I'm not in a position here and now to cite a particular example, but it seems to me that a scribe who is copying a text and is aware that that text is a rhyming text is quite likely in some cases to restore correct rhymes. It is clear that scribes do not necessarily just copy down what is in front of them; in some cases they recognise errors and change them.

Dees: You express yourself in terms of what we can *imagine* could have happened. In my talk I omitted one very important factor — contamination. My point is: why should every medieval text be contaminated? That was exactly why I started my investigations. That is not what is normal. It is mathematically speaking impossible, as I

discovered. I have in mind a very important factor: philologists have
observed that there are changes of relationship: in the beginning of a
long text — the *Perceval*, for instance — you have other types of
relationships than in the middle of the text or again at the end of the
text.   All great philologists have observed that. What is, I think, a
natural conclusion is that you never can be satisfied with one
genealogical tree. If you observe three stages you should have three
genealogical trees. That was my hypothesis and I'm still very satisfied
with it.   It obliges you to seek the limits between where this one
genealogical tree stops and where there is another tree. That's the kind
of work we are doing and we are successful in doing it. So this whole
question of contamination is an illusion, I think, once you have the
possibility of expressing yourself in terms of successive genealogical
trees.

There is a second remark to be made about this perspective. I
mentioned the observations of all great philologists on this issue. The
French philologist and palaeographer Micha made the prediction,
given the way manuscripts were reproduced, that there should be
confusions. What is curious is that the link has never been made
between the two ideas. There should be changes of relationship and
they are observable. My astonishment is that we have not concluded
that different genealogical trees are necessary to explain the situation.
That is the line I work on and I have no doubts whatsoever that this is
correct. We find very clearly different genealogical trees. We can see
where the validity of the first tree stops and the second tree begins.
This must correspond to the way medieval manuscripts, as a class,
were reproduced in the past.

Ian Doyle: Manly and Rickert in editing the Canterbury Tales identified
repeatedly switches of descent at particular points, but only in a very
limited number of cases. Only a very small number of cases, if any,
coincided with actual physical divisions in the surviving copies.

Dees: Yes. But there is a past for the manuscript — what has happened
to the text before what appears in the surviving manuscript.

Doyle: Yes.

Richard Beadle: One of the ways to reach the truth of the matter is to
examine closely cases where we not only have a scribal copy but also
the exemplar from which it was taken. There must be examples of that

in the body of French material that you've looked at. There are a few examples in Middle English, one of which I referred to in my paper this morning, the Glasgow Hunterian copy of the *Canterbury Tales* said to be directly derived in part from a manuscript in Cambridge University Library.[1] In that case the scribe of the Glasgow copy can definitely be shown to correct errors that he recognised in Cambridge, notably in the rhymes, but whether he got the corrections out of his head, or by consulting another copy, we can't say. I think we need to go into this in a systematic way, to look at a lot of exemplars and a lot of extant copies. Then we would be able to make much more confident statements.

Dees: I'm very much interested by what was said this morning concerning one copyist who can be very precisely observed. This is very valuable. This is what should be done. But I'm somewhat hostile — more than you think acceptable, maybe — to the many theories that there have been.

Derek Britton: My experience in working with the *Prick of Conscience* by and large supports Professor Dees's viewpoint rather than George Jack's. Scribes with authorial, or even editorial, pretentions must have existed, but they were very rare birds. Again, you find changing textual relationships, but they nearly always occur in chunks. You don't get interlinear mixed traditions. I think there's one case which you overlooked, where you can get interlinear contamination. Suppose someone has a copy of a manuscript; another copy of that same text comes into his hands; someone writes in the readings from this other text; the next scribe copies that text; and then you've got all hell let loose in terms of genetic transmission, haven't you?

Dees: I know this happens. This is one of the 20 varieties of peculiarity that have been observed. I know it happens in the Greek and Latin traditions. This is how contamination in general is explained, but it is impossible. You can't explain every case of contamination by marginal annotations. You see what is happening here? There has been contamination; we have tried to explain it; but we cannot find the factor that explains that contamination. Our imagination works and works and we come up with 20 factors of the type you cite. But none is sufficient to explain the whole situation, I think. Such phenomena as

---

[1] See paper II.1, p. 74 and cf., for another example, Introduction, p. 6 (Laing 1989b).

you have described do occur incidentally, but they do not make a general pattern.

Panel III

LANGUAGES IN CONTACT

III.1   Codes and Cultures

Angus McIntosh

I have to start with a confession, which is that as late as last night I knew exactly what I was going to say this afternoon. But in the course of the morning's deliberations and after maturer reflection I find that a good number of the things that I'd planned to say have either been anticipated or made already somewhat out of date; so I am wrestling with a diachronic problem — a chronic diachronic problem. The result of my discomfiture is that I now want to make just two, or at most three, small points which seem to me to be of relevance under the heading of my suggested title 'Codes and Cultures'. The intention of this catch-phrase was to bring out as well as I could the relationship between various forms of language — in this case I'm thinking of medieval English with a side glance at parallels — the relationship between 'English' in a purely linguistic sense and the environment and social and other conditions that pertained at the time when particular forms of that language were used.

I find I am more inclined to question certain basic assumptions than I would have been 20 or 30 years ago. One of the things that always gives me pause now has to do with people's tendency to assume that a language operates somehow on its own. So we speak of it almost as if it talked by itself to itself and we persons whose lips are moving or whose hands are pushing pens and so forth are mere incidental and irrelevant accompaniments to this more refined activity that somehow goes on beyond our own control.

Perhaps I can best illustrate this rather naive difficulty from another discipline: think of me, if you will, as professing the subject of comparative gastronomy. I want to suggest that in this role (which would give me ample opportunities of making agreeable tests in expensive restaurants) it would seem odd if this time instead of speaking of 'languages in contact', I were to speak of 'eating habits in contact'; just as if in yet another persona I were to go on, again quite professionally of course, about 'courtship customs in contact', where — incidentally — it would be illuminatingly evident that it isn't the customs that are in contact but what we might call the customers. I've been very much reminded in a host of different ways, including by what we've talked about this morning, that in all this buzz and hum (as it has been called), in all the things that come up when you put your little bucket down into the pool,[1] we are continually and quite normally confronted with situations in which language is in a sense merely incidental to a much wider range of activities.

To get that, as it were, under one's belt is to be able to think about language, whether it be dialect or whatever it may be, in a way that affirms and establishes the contacts that are implicit in so many of our own deliberations. I mean, for example, on the one hand with sociolinguistics and through that to sociology and on the other hand with psycholinguistics and through that to psychology. I like to think that in some ways the sort of deliberations we have had this morning help to redress the balance which is so commonly missing at the moment because so many people *do* seem to speak of instances of language or of *a* language as if they were little creatures that had a life of their own. And if we do redress this balance it makes much more natural, and I think more productive, such deliberations as we've had about the way manuscripts travel — in the area of written language — and also the whole problem of what we rather dangerously call 'languages in contact'. I won't say more now about that but will mention a somewhat similar thing which I think relevant to what we are here to discuss: the kind of difficulties that arise simply by our using such phrases as '*the* language' or '*a* language'. What we have here are situations where we encounter all kinds of small deviations from some pseudo-entity which we persist in thinking of as a sort of sacred norm.

For example, we take a medieval text like the *Prick of Conscience* and we seem determined to look on it as being, in its original form, a linguistically perfect entity which in one way or another gradually gets mucked about with by copiers or reciters or whoever. But then one has to reconsider and think of these very persons as being native users of English and reasonably competent scribes. If one of them perpetrates the sort of language that survives in, shall we say, a

---

[1] Smith's paper, II.3 (pp. 99–100), above.

somewhat garbled West Midland version of the poem, then we tend to say that that scribe 'writ no language' (as Ben Jonson said about Shakespeare), or else that his text is an interesting and rather suspect amalgam of somewhat odd and scarcely predictable things. As if any example of the language, whether of Chaucer's time or of what we're speaking now today in this room, wasn't a strange mixture of all sorts of things that any Anglo-Saxon would have been astonished at the sight of, or at the hearing of. This clinging to the notion of *a* language, this tendency that we always seem to have to try, by fostering it, to make things neat and tidy, this runs relentlessly through many deliberations about the interaction of codes and cultures, because we like to think of something being a norm and then to insist that deviations from it truly *are* deviations: not alternative phenomena, but 'real' deviations.

It would seem to me wiser to take the notion of language, or of *a* language, and try to rid it of this postulated abstract monolithic solidarity and instead to regard everything to do with it as in a state of flux. This would partly consist of what I would call a *diatopic* state of flux, or at least state of variation. Then, if we choose to look at things in a chronological way and think of there being a continual state of flux or development or change on the *diachronic* level, we finish up with a picture containing no single entity whatever, but a sort of flow of something more like a river and not just a river running in one dimension, but a river running so to speak in two dimensions. That is where geography and time come in, jointly, and of course there is far more to flux than just these two things.

I believe that it is helpful to keep in mind at all times that we have as a primary concern this phenomenon of *linguistic behaviour*. If this is 'rule governed', as we are frequently exhorted to believe, we should nevertheless avoid the trap of concluding that language, or *a* language, makes *its own* rules, any more than tennis does or plainsong or common law: codes neither generate themselves nor control their own tangled evolution. Fully to accept the implications of this for our own discipline would be to bring it more realistically into line with other branches of human science. Fundamentally, what we mean by 'languages in contact' is 'users of language in contact' and to insist upon this is much more than a mere terminological quibble and has far from trivial consequences.

III.2 The Celtic Languages: some Current and some Neglected Questions

William Gillies

In the following presentation I shall attempt to capture something of the flavour of Celtic studies, more particularly with reference to the medieval Celtic languages and to questions of language contact. After a soupçon of orientation — some brief remarks on the disposition of our material — I shall proceed via the 'current' and 'neglected' questions of my title, which are intended to capture something of the quality of life in Celtic studies at present, to some even briefer concluding remarks on the limitations and potential of the Celtic languages for the sorts of study championed by the present Colloquium.

1. Celtic Languages and Language Contact

Thinking of language contact in the British Isles in the Middle Ages, we may justly conclude that the number of linguistic frontiers (and hence of potential investigations in the context of the present discussion) is quite formidable. From the Celticist's point of view we have, on the Goedelic or Gaelic side, the several and various contacts which occurred between the Gaelic speakers of Ireland, Scotland and the Isle of Man, and speakers of varieties of Old and Middle English on the other; and similarly those occurring between Goedelic dialects and Scandinavian. On the Brythonic or British side we have to reckon with a similarly complex set of relationships involving differing phases and types of contact between speakers of the Old or Middle stages of English dialects and speakers of corresponding stages in the evolution of Welsh, Cumbric and Cornish. (From the Celticist's point of view it would be natural to add here, despite geographical considerations, the Breton–French interface; and I duly mention it, though not to pursue it on the present occasion.)

Even if we were to confine ourselves to circumstances of *Sprachkontakt* involving the Celtic languages alone, there would be no shortage of cases to study. For there were enough linguistic frontiers within the 'Celtic Fringe'. In what was later to become Scotland there were of necessity Goedelic–Brythonic contacts, as the Gaelic-speaking subjects of the Dalriadic kings of the Scots infiltrated and colonised Pictland and Strathclyde. For the Irish there were notable contacts across the Irish Sea to Wales and Cornwall in the sub-Roman and proto-historical period, in addition to the Norse presence in Ireland from the 9th century, and the Anglo–Norman presence from the 12th century. The Isle of Man, as one might guess from its location in the centre of the Irish Sea area, enjoyed a complex linguistic history in which Brythonic and Goedelic phases alternated with Norse and English.

Incidentally, I take it that these differing combinations of linguistic neighbourliness played their part in the processes of differentiation and divergence which led to the emergence of the separate Goedelic and Brythonic languages of modern times: Scottish Gaelic, Irish and Manx; and Welsh, Cornish and Breton. Once these languages had duly 'emerged', of course, there was fresh potential for languages to be in contact with one another, and it is possible to talk in terms of contact between Irish and Scottish Gaelic, or between Irish and Manx, or Scottish Gaelic and Manx; and so within the Brythonic group of Celtic languages.

One should also mention a set of contacts which existed on a rather different plane: those involving Latin and Insular Celtic languages from Roman times onwards. This type of contact may have been most prolonged and intimate on the Brythonic side, whence my old teacher Kenneth Jackson used occasionally to refer to Welsh as 'the forgotten Romance language'; but it was not confined to the Brythonic languages. Equally, it was not confined to the Roman period; for Latin was a permanent fixture throughout the Middle Ages in all the Celtic realms.

Not all of these contact situations have left us sufficient evidence to enable us to draw meaningful conclusions about the linguistic relations involved. In the cases of Cumbric and Pictish the direct linguistic testimony is almost nonexistent; and the same can be said of the bilingual situation that must have existed between Gaelic and English (or proto-Scots) in eastern and southern parts of Scotland in the Middle Ages. In cases like these we have to make what sense we can of scattered clues in the later languages plus the indirect testimony of place-names and the like.

Even in situations where there is a substantial body of literature for us to work on, it is possible to complain about the quality of the evidence. For instance, the relatively abundant materials we possess in Old Irish (7th–9th century) contain an exasperating *absence* of variation; what has survived is a deliberately and successfully homogenised literary language. And after an apparently chaotic period of linguistic innovation in the Middle Irish period (9th–11th century) the shutters close down again in the Classical Early Modern period (12th–16th century), when we know perfectly well that the Gaelic vernacular dialects were widely and increasingly differentiated, but the literary language was tied to an artificial standard — a vernacular equivalent to the lingua franca. Much the same is true, one may add, in the case of Medieval Welsh: the signs of regionally based differentiation are pretty meagre, and the literary language had clearly evolved along a trajectory that minimised dialectal differences.

However, where Celtic speakers have (1) left a plentiful written record (or at least where texts have survived in substantial numbers until modern times), and (2) absorbed an intrusive element (as with the Norse immigrants to Gaelic Scotland) or conquered or settled in an alien territory (as with the British immigrants to Britanny), we can start to conduct research into language contact in the normal way. Thus, for example, the French element in Breton is studied in Piette (1973); the Scandinavian element in Irish in Marstrander (1915); and the English and Latin elements in Welsh are studied, respectively, by Parry-Williams (1923) and Lewis (1943). These and similar works have carved out relatively manageable territories to explore, and have, by and large, adopted procedures and techniques which are no different from those deployed in similar circumstances outside the Celtic area. More ambitious by far was Kenneth Jackson's *Language and History in Early Britain* (1953), which attempted to draw together the whole range of linguistic evidence available for the Brythonic lanugages, together with all that could be gleaned from the testimony of British Latin, Anglo–Saxon and Irish, as a means to constructing a comprehensive history of the phonology of the Brythonic languages, from 1st-century Romano–British through to Middle Welsh, Cornish and Breton. But Jackson has been the only large-scale practitioner of this sort of philology in the Celtic field in the second half of the 20th century. (Cf. also Jackson 1967). The nearest comparable work on the Goedelic side,

Thomas F. O'Rahilly's *Irish Dialects Past and Present* (1932), is much more modest in its scope.

If I were obliged to choose a single adjective with which to characterise the state of play in medieval Celtic dialectology, that word would have to be one that recurs all too frequently in Celtic contexts: 'patchy'. Despite some intensive work in certain areas, others remain seriously neglected; some fundamental tools of the trade have yet to be fashioned; and we lag behind our neighbouring disciplines in the development of appropriate techniques to extract information indirectly, where (as all too often happens) direct testimony is hard to come by.

2. 'Some Current and some Neglected Questions'

2.1 *Nativists versus Europeanists*

Over the last decade we have seen a strong challenge to the orthodoxy that prevailed in my own student days, which talked of an archaic, peripheral Celtic world, flourishing especially in Ireland, untouched by the homogenising influences of the Roman Empire, and preserving in oral tradition an unadulterated Indo-European inheritance of law, institutions and religion which continued to flourish side by side with the Christian, literate tradition, and came to be written down as Early Irish literature. (I exaggerate, but not enormously.) Nowadays scholars are much more keen to stress Celtic participation in the wider world of medieval Europe and of Christendom. Where my teachers saw early Irish secular schools descended from druidic schools, operating independently of the monastic schools, my colleagues of today tend to see no such dichotomy, and berate those who do. (See, for example, McCone 1990.)

In the context of this debate, the circumstances of language contact between Latin and Irish have received increased exposure, from both traditional and innovative angles. We have seen important refinements in our understanding of the distribution and stratification of Latin loanwords in Irish (McManus 1983). Fresh attention has been paid to the emergence and development of 'written–oral' and thence purely written vernacular styles for narrative and lyric purposes (Tristram 1989). The teaching of Latin and the linguistic study of Latin and Irish have likewise been profitably studied (Ahlqvist 1983). All sorts of questions relating to Latin–Irish diglossia and bilingualism and literacy call out for further research: e.g. the apparently free-and-easy language switching that goes on in various types of early text, or the strong tendency for the phrase (as stress unit) to function as the 'word' in scribal terms.

2.2 *'Who Taught What to Whom?'*

A particularly important aspect of the previous point, but also one which has developed independently and in its own right, concerns the process whereby the Latin alphabet was adapted to meet the phonological needs of Early Irish and Welsh (and Cornish and Breton). Here the view expressed in *Language and History in Early Britain* was that the Irish learned to write Irish on the basis of literacy in Latin which they had gained from Britons who spoke a conservative brand of Latin with a British accent. Considerable discussion has taken place, and a recent study has concluded that the hypothesis of British intermediacy is not a necessary one (Harvey 1992). These discussions have also coincided with a flurry of views as to the dating of the beginnings of literacy in Irish, and re-assessments of the *ogham* inscriptions as symbols of a contingent sort of literacy. Archaeological advances have also provided food for thought, e.g. in the form of evidence for Roman contacts with Ireland, Romano–British expatriates settling in Ireland, and Christian communities during the Roman period. Maybe we shall be suggesting that the Irish taught the Welsh to write before too long! (On these questions see also: Carney 1975; McManus1986; Harvey 1987a and 1987b.)

2.3 *The Need for an Overview*

Who is going to do for the 1990s what Kenneth Jackson's *Language and History* did for the previous 40 years? One reason why Jackson's work surpassed that of the previous scholars (such as Morris-Jones, Förster and Ekwall) was that he came to it at the end of a cycle of discovery, stabilisation and consolidation in Germanic, Celtic and Romance philology. Another was his mastery of the sources in all the languages involved, and of the intellectual and administrative skills required to avoid circularity in the ordering and dating of Brythonic sound changes by reference to forms preserved in Latin, Anglo–Saxon and Irish sources. At the time of its publication it was justly regarded as the 'state of the art'. Since the early 1950s, however, new materials have been discovered, new interpretations have found favour, and in some cases whole new fields have been developed in all the disciplines on which Jackson drew. *Language and History* has survived frontal assault (Gratwick 1982; McManus 1984) but the individual bases on which it rests have been so buffeted that a complete overhaul is needed. But who, at this stage in the game could take over the work of interdisciplinary synthesis that was almost out of reach even in the 1950s? The 'neglected question' here is not an absence of work in the field as a whole: there is plenty of that (cf. Evans 1990). It is the large work of synthesis, in the manner of *Language and History*, which we lack. Maybe teamwork is called for. Surely it would have to be inter-disciplinary in its make-up. Maybe, then, instead of pressing the whole edifice into the service of one of the constituent languages the field of explicit inquiry should be widened to include not only Welsh but also Irish, not only Celtic but also the Germanic languages (and Insular Latin), together with questions of literacy and orthography pertaining to each. McManus (1984: 186) would appear to be of the same view: 'One hopes that the solution will be found in the (amicable) co-operation of Celtic, Germanic, Classical and Romance scholars alike'. At all events, the conclusions which could be drawn from such a study are so valuable, and the applications for which they could be needed are so varied, that this task must be regarded as an extremely important one.

2.4 *Common Gaelic*

For my last 'talking point' and second 'neglected question' I have chosen the question of the differentiation of the Gaelic languages, Irish, Scottish Gaelic and Manx Gaelic, from their ancestor, 'Common Gaelic'. When one thinks of the settlement patterns involved in the Gaelic colonisation of Pictland (7th–9th century?) and Strathclyde and Lothian (9th–11th century?), and in the Norse colonisation of the Hebrides and Western sea-board (9th–11th century?), it is hard to imagine that these would not have left their mark in the Gaelic speech of colonists and colonised — by comparison, say, with the Gaelic of the Gaels living in Ireland. Yet the present orthodoxy (Jackson 1953) maintains that there was no divergence between Scottish and Manx on the one hand ('Eastern Gaelic') and Irish ('Western Gaelic') until the end of the 'Middle Irish' period, i.e. till the centuries after ca. 1200.

Nor is this simply a matter of a priori speculation. We have known for years that Scottish Gaelic retains hiatus in vowel sequences where Irish was monophthongising by the late Old Irish period. A series of syntactic features in which Scottish Gaelic agrees with Welsh against Irish has been pointed out over the years, and a certain number of Brythonic loanwords in Scottish Gaelic but not in Irish have been known for long enough. Again, though more controversially, the particular sort of pre-aspiration found in Lewis Gaelic, together with certain aspects of Lewis intonation, have been compared with similar phenomena in Norwegian dialects. Equally, we have become more conscious of the fact that the homogeneity of written Old Irish was more a matter of convention than of uniformity of speech; and that the Scottish Gaelic dialects of the Hebrides and west central Highlands have been subject to reinforcement by Irish and high-register pan-Gaelic influences during the Early Modern period (12th–16th century); and that the most characteristically Scottish dialectal features were all in place in the Gaelic of Perthshire by the time of the Book of the Dean of Lismore (early 16th century). All these points tend to reinforce one's belief that the idea of a unified Gaelic language until the 13th century is at best an oversimplification.

In other words, the question of 'Common Gaelic' is worth re-opening. Ideally, this should take place not in isolation but as part of a wider review of the whole history of the Goedelic languages. In my view we should be re-examining the evidence for dialectalism and variation in Old Irish itself. We should review the welter of forms that confront us in Middle Irish, not just asking whether our texts can be put into a single chronological sequence (which they mostly cannot), but whether they exhibit characteristics such as 'higher/lower'; progressive/conservative; northerly/southerly; and so forth, in conjunction with the 'early/late' criterion. For the Early Modern period we should look again at the alternatives prescribed by the Irish Grammatical Tracts, and analyse the non-standard forms which crop up (against the odds, as it were) in datable, locatable manuscripts and texts. At the same time we should seek fresh dating criteria (e.g. using Gaelic onomastic evidence with greater sophistication than hitherto) and re-appraise known categories of evidence (e.g. loanwords). If we can cultivate a readiness to recognise the dynamic quality of the language (or languages), as spoken by real speakers who were sometimes monoglot, sometimes bilingual or trilingual; who were sometimes careful and sometimes careless speakers; sometimes learners and sometimes native speakers of the language; who habitually employed whole bundles of speech registers in the course of their daily existence; and who had frequent contact with neighbours who spoke the same language but in a recognisably different way; if we can inject this sort of open-mindedness into our study, I believe we shall find the Gaelic languages full of interesting and sometimes surprising treasures which have not yet been fully discovered.

3. Conclusions: Celtic and non-Celtic Languages

The Celtic languages have not always been exploited as they deserve to be by non-Celticists. I think Celticists are on the whole better at appreciating and allowing for the non-Celtic element in their material; though there has always been a species whom we may term the 'Celtomane', to whom everything he meets is Celtic. But non-Celticists seem, in linguistic as in literary studies, to veer unpredictably between over-use of 'Celtic' as a default category for anything that lacks a ready explanation, and embarrassment about admitting Celtic paternity for phenomena that clearly are Celtic. When this happens in Britain there are sometimes ideological reasons for underplaying the Celtic element, of course. A recent study which identified literally hundreds of Gaelic words in the *Scottish National Dictionary* was prompted by the frequently heard (rhetorical) question 'Why is there no Gaelic in (Scottish) English?' (McClure 1986). No doubt the unwarranted question will continue to be heard. Clearly, this sort of prejudice is unsatisfactory, but it can be very difficult to eradicate.

Finally, I would repeat that the Celtic group of languages in the Middle Ages could stand more intensive study than they have so far received. The unique patterning of relationships between them and the unique scatter of evidence they provide should be of interest to linguists in general, and I believe the findings and problems of Celtic scholars can be particularly instructive to workers in the neighbouring field of what used to be called Germanic philology; the converse is certainly true. A fortiori, I believe that the network of corridors that link the Germanic languages and the Celtic, over a very long period, require us in our own best scholarly interests to break down barriers wherever possible. I am conscious that one of the reasons why it is hard, even for Celticists, to get at the Celtic evidence is the comparatively primitive state of Celtic Studies. But the last 20 years have seen considerable improvements in a number of key areas; maybe one day we shall catch up with Classics and English in the matter of making our texts and languages accessible to the wider scholarly world!

References

Ahlqvist A. 1983 *The Early Irish Linguist*. Societas Scientiarum Fennica: Helsinki

Carney J. 1975 The invention of the Ogam cipher. *Eriu* **26**: 53–65

Evans D.E. 1990 Insular Celtic and the emergence of the Welsh language. In: Bammesberger A., Wollmann A. (eds.) *Britain 400–600: Language and History*. Carl Winter: Heidelberg, pp. 149–78

Gratwick A. 1982 *Latinitas brittanica*: was British Latin archaic? In: Brooks N. (ed.) *Latin and the Vernacular Languages in Early Medieval Britain*. Leicester University Press: Leicester, pp. 1–80

Hamp E.P. 1975 Social gradience in British spoken Latin. *Brittania* **6**: 150–61

Harvey A. 1987a The Ogam inscriptions and their geminate symbols. *Eriu* **38**: 45–72

Harvey A. 1987b Early literacy in Ireland: the evidence from Ogam. *Cambridge Medieval Celtic Studies* **14**: 1–16

Harvey A. 1992 Latin, literacy and the Celtic vernaculars around the year AD 500. In: Byrne C.J., Harry M., O Siadhail P. (eds.) *Celtic Languages and Celtic Peoples*. Halifax, NS, pp. 11–26

Jackson K.H. 1953 *Language and History in Early Britain*. Edinburgh University Press: Edinburgh

Jackson K.H. 1967 *A Historical Phonology of Breton*. Dublin Institute for Advanced Studies: Dublin

Lewis H. 1943. *Yr elfen Ladin yn yr iaith Gymraeg*. Gwasg Prifysgol Cymru: Cardiff

McClure J.D. 1986 What Scots owes to Gaelic. *Scottish Language* **5** (Proceedings of the First International Conference on the Languages of Scotland — University of Aberdeen 26–29 July 1985), pp. 85–98

McCone K. 1990 *Pagan Past and Christian Present in Early Irish Literature*. An Sagart: Maynooth

McManus D. 1983 A chronology of the Latin loan-words in Irish. *Eriu* **34**: 21–71

McManus D. 1984 *Linguarum diversitas*: Latin and the vernaculars in early medieval Britain. *Peritia* **3**: 151–88

McManus D. 1986 Ogam: archaizing, orthography and the authenticity of the manuscript key to the alphabet. *Eriu* **37**: 1–32

Marstrander C.J.S. 1915 *Bidrag til der norske sprogs historie i Irland*. Videnskapsselskapets Skrifter: Kristiania

O'Rahilly T.F. 1932 *Irish Dialects Past and Present*. Browne and Nolan: Dublin

Parry-Williams T.H. 1923 *The English Element in Welsh*. Cymmrodorion Record Series 10: London

Piette J.F.R. 1973 *French Loanwords in Middle Breton*. University of Wales Press: Cardiff

Tristram H.L.C. 1989 Early modes of Insular expression. In: O Corráin D., Breatnach L., McCone K. (eds.) *Sages, Saints and Storytellers*. An Sagart: Maynooth, pp. 449–62

III.3   Language Contact in Early Medieval England: Latin and Old English

Helmut Gneuss

Since the early 17th century, historians and antiquarians have shown an interest in the relations between the Anglo-Saxons and their neighbours, before and after the migration from the Continent, and in how these relations are mirrored in the Old English language. A scientific study of language contact in early England could only begin, however, after the methods of historical linguistics had been established in the 19th century, when the modern languages became the subject of intensive research. As far as the influence of Latin on Old English is concerned, the seminal work on which most of our present-day handbooks still rely was published in the space of 25 years, from 1888 to 1914, and is thus contemporary with the appearance of most of the *Oxford English Dictionary* (which had reached the entry *speech* in 1913). It is the work of Alois Pogatscher (1888), Walter William Skeat (1887 [1892]: ch. xxi), Friedrich Kluge (1913 [1891]: 9–30), H.S. MacGillivray (1902) and Otto Funke (1914).

Have the results of their work stood the test of time, or do we have to revise or rewrite the history of lexical borrowing from Latin into Old English in the light of more recent research? In my view, much of what the earlier scholars have to tell us remains sound and valid (like so much of the philological work produced a hundred years ago), and this seems especially true of the etymological sections in the entries for early Latin loanwords in the *OED*. Nevertheless, English philology and related disciplines have not stood still since then; some issues have become clearer, others appear more complicated now, and a great deal of important evidence has come to light. When we deal with language contact in Anglo-Saxon England (and during the prehistory of Old English), we shall have to take into account three important aspects: (1) history and archaeology, (2) historical linguistics and (3) manuscript evidence.

1. History and Archaeology

The study of Anglo-Saxon history and archaeology has significantly advanced in the course of the 20th century. The work done in these fields needs to be considered when we try to picture the conditions under which language contact took place in Britain in the centuries before the Norman Conquest. A few examples will suffice.

Professor Kenneth Jackson in his magisterial *Language and History in Early Britain* (1953) tells us about the relations of Britons and Saxons that

> The whole picture is, at any rate, totally incompatible with the old theory of the complete extermination of the British inhabitants.
>
> (Jackson 1953: 246)

How can we relate this to the handful of genuine Celtic loans in Old English (cf. Förster 1921 on this subject)? Myres (1986 [1989]) appears to be certain that Saxon settlement occurred on a considerable scale (in England) in the 4th century. Could this affect our views of the history of individual Latin loanwords in Old English? Sawyer (1958) assumes that there was no Scandinavian colonisation on a massive scale in England, and that consequently there was only a comparatively small number of Norse speakers. How does this tally with what we know about the impact of Norse on Old (and early Middle) English?[1] Other examples might be adduced; I am thinking in particular of our steadily increasing knowledge of Anglo–French relations in the later 10th and in the 11th century.

2. Progress in Historical Linguistics

Great steps forward have been made in historical linguistics. Let me mention the ever-growing number of investigations concerned with linguistic interference and bilingualism; also, the interest in semantic borrowing and loan-formations as well as in structural interference (i.e. interference in phonology, morphology and syntax). Far more

---

[1] For this and later work by P.H. Sawyer, cf. Fellows-Jensen (1975, 1991).

important for our purpose here was the appearance of the *Microfiche Concordance of Old English* (Healey and Venezky 1980) and of a work (preceded by earlier publications) that seems to have been widely ignored in English philology, *Germania Romana* by Theodor Frings (first edn. 1932) which — based on a large number of Latin loanwords in the Germanic north-west, and on their history in the Romance languages — has established beyond any doubt an *Einheitsgebiet* (a common sphere of Latin use and influence) comprising Gaul, Britain, the Netherlands and the lower Rhine area as far south as Cologne and Trier (Frings and Müller 1966–68 [1932]). Also important for our subject could be the more recent claims made by Roger Wright (1982), who believes that the 'classical' pronunciation of Latin in the Romance-speaking countries was an invention of the Carolingian Renaissance, and that before then the only way of pronouncing Latin was determined by the local vernacular; but Wright's theory appears to have remained highly controversial.

3. Manuscript Evidence

Apart from the study of certain place-names, whatever we know about Latin influence on Old English depends on manuscript evidence. It is only since 1957 that we have in Neil Ker's great *Catalogue of Manuscripts Containing Anglo-Saxon* a full inventory of all Old English texts (except charters) and glosses, published or not, and a safe guide to the date and provenance of these texts and their copies. Ker's book, together with editions of Old English texts published after the days of Pogatscher, Skeat and Kluge will provide us with a securer foundation for the study of loans than was available to our late 19th-century predecessors. As an example, I may here mention the French loanwords that entered the English language up to the Norman Conquest. More than 40 words have been suggested by various authors as falling into this category, but on closer inspection it turns out that only half a dozen of these can legitimately be counted as pre-Conquest French loans; as to the rest, they are either from Latin or appear in manuscripts that must be considered post-Conquest. Moreover, the earliest occurrence of the only word of the group that (together with its word-family) is at all frequent, OE *pryde*, has had to be post-dated for half a century because of a misreading in a 10th-century manuscript.

3.1 *Early Treatments of Latin Loanwords*

Of the early treatments of Latin loanwords in Old English, that by Alois Pogatscher was no doubt the most thorough work and the one that became and remained most influential. Pogatscher distinguished between 'popular' and 'learned' words on the basis of phonological criteria: popular loanwords were adopted with their spoken, Vulgar Latin form and were then subject to the sound changes of Old English; learned loanwords were taken over with their 'classical' Latin spelling, with no changes in the quality of their sounds (as opposed to quantity and accent). This distinction is linked with what I shall call Pogatscher's three-period model (similar to one proposed somewhat earlier by Henry Sweet) which places Latin loanwords in Old English in a chronological sequence:

1.   Continental loanwords, borrowed until ca. 450 AD (popular);

2.   Early insular loanwords
        taken over from the spoken Latin of Romanised Celts in
        Britain ca. 450–600 AD (also popular);

3.   Later loanwords, after ca. 600 (learned or popular).

Again, phonological criteria — but not only these — are employed in order to differentiate these three strata. There is not time to discuss even superficially the complex problems involved in this model; Pogatscher's assumption of the survival of spoken Latin in Celtic Britain (soon to be opposed by Joseph Loth) is among the most controversial issues (Loth 1892). Nevertheless, the model became the basis for nearly all later treatments of the field, including those by Karl Luick and Mary S. Serjeantson, until our own days (Luick 1914–40; Serjeantson 1935). Before 1990 I notice only two dissenting voices, those of Kenneth Jackson (who saw the difficulty of clearly separating the three strata on phonological grounds) and of Alistair Campbell in his *Old English Grammar*, who wisely decided not to distinguish between words of the first and second period (Jackson 1953; Campbell 1959: ch. x). A thorough investigation of the issue was long overdue; it has now been carried out — very successfully, I think — in a PhD thesis by Alfred Wollmann, in which the author convincingly demonstrates that the assumption of a kind of linguistic borderline about the middle of the 5th century is untenable (Wollmann 1990; see Figure 1, p. 157).

3.2 *Borrowings Direct from Greek*

Allow me to try to lay another ghost in loanword studies, that of words borrowed direct from Greek. Thanks to the work of Bernhard Bischoff, and others, of which I will only refer to a recent article by Michael Lapidge (Lapidge 1988), we now have a fairly clear idea of the knowledge and teaching of Greek in Anglo-Saxon England. As far as Greek loanwords are concerned, we may distinguish — i.e. in traditional scholarship — two groups:

1.   those words that were transmitted by way of Latin,[2] and

2.   those that are said to have reached the Germanic peoples directly.

The first comprises a substantial number of items in Mary S. Serjeantson's lists of Latin loans in Old English; whether they were all actually in use in late Latin has to my knowledge never been examined in detail. The second group consists of a small number of words — above all *biscop, engel, deofol, cirice* — which according to Friedrich Kluge were imported to southern Germany by Gothic missionaries travelling up the Danube (*Donaumission*) and then spread from there northwards (Kluge 1909). Although historians and philologists have written a great deal about and against this hypothesis, these Greek words linger on as a specially treated group in our handbooks. Again, I can only briefly offer some comments. There seem to be no serious phonological or historical problems in explaining *biscop, engel* and *deofol* as early loanwords from Latin as spoken in Gaul. The word for 'church' is a different case, as it is not found in the Romance languages, but Frings and others have traced its origin in West Germanic to the Trier region and ultimately to southern France. Similarly, Old English semantic loans have been explained as continuing a Gothic and High German tradition, as e.g. OE *dyppan, dēpan* 'baptise', an explanation

---

2 Examples are OE *antefn, butere, disc, martir, mynster, pistol, ymen.*

that ignores the textual transmission of these words. For *dyppan*, *dēpan* in the sense of 'baptise' are rare words in 10th-century interlinear glosses and not the Anglo-Saxon standard terms for the concept. Also, it seems hard to believe that an Anglo-Saxon translator or glossator would have been unable to ascertain the original meaning of Greek and Latin *baptizo*.

It is well-known that lexical borrowing — not only in Old English — comprises loanwords (and 'foreign' words) as well as loan-formations and semantic loans. The identification of the relevant vocabulary and the classification according to the various types and subtypes is not always unproblematic; thus, the etymology of not a few items usually or occasionally listed as loanwords is doubtful.

3.4 *Dialectal Distribution of Loanwords*

In a colloquium devoted predominantly to historical dialectology one might also expect a word about the dialectal distribution of loanwords. Owing to the work of earlier scholars like Joseph Wright, but in particular to two magnificent scholarly works of our time, the *Survey of English Dialects* and the *Linguistic Atlas of Late Mediaeval English*, we know a great deal about the geographical distribution of Scandinavian loanwords in Britain, but it seems next to impossible to speak of the distribution of Latin loanwords in Old English, or to give rational explanations why a word occurs only in a particular text, place or area. There is one exception, however: when we can show that a particular 'school' deliberately chose — or rejected — a lexical loan for some concept. What this line of enquiry has to offer has been demonstrated in a recent study by Walter Hofstetter of the vocabulary that was evidently taught by Æthelwold of Winchester in the second half of the 10th century and was employed by his pupils, especially Ælfric (Hofstetter 1987). Here we find that OE *cirice* was almost never used in the sense of 'the Church', 'the community of the faithful' (the translation word for *ecclesia* in this sense being *gelaðung*), while the preferred word for 'martyr' was either *cypere* (apparently a semantic loan) or the loanword *martir*; but *martir* soon became dominant (as can be seen in Ælfric's works), whereas a third Old English term — *þrowere* — was not used at all by the Winchester School. An investigation of the occurrence of loanwords in Old English texts, based on the full evidence of the *Microfiche Concordance* (Healey and

Venezky 1980), may help us to learn more about the use and transmission of such words.

In this brief paper I have only been able to outline a few important facts and problems of my subject. I am dealing in greater detail, supported by the appropriate documentation, with language contact and lexical borrowing in Old English in Gneuss (1994 forthcoming). To date the most comprehensive treatment of the field is Kastovsky (1992).

References

Campbell A. 1959 *Old English Grammar*. Clarendon Press: Oxford

Fellows-Jensen G. 1975 The Vikings in England: a review. *Anglo-Saxon England* 4: 181–206

Fellows-Jensen G. 1991 Of Danes —and Thanes — and Domesday Book. In: Wood I., Lund N. (eds.) *People and Places in Northern Europe 500–1600: Essays in Honour of Peter Hayes Sawyer*. The Boydell Press: Woodbridge, pp. 107–21

Förster M. 1921 Keltisches Wortgut im Englischen. Eine sprachliche Untersuchung. In: *Texte und Untersuchungen zur englischen Kulturgeschichte: Festgabe für Felix Liebermann*. Niemeyer: Halle, pp. 119–242

Frings Th., Müller G. 1966–68 [1932] *Germania Romana*, 2 vols. Niemeyer: Halle

Funke O. 1914 *Die gelehrten lateinischen Lehn- und Fremdwörter in der altenglischen Literatur von der Mitte des X. Jahrhunderts bis um das Jahr 1066*. Niemeyer: Halle

Gnuess H. 1994 (forthcoming) *Anglicae linguae interpretatio*: language contact, lexical borrowing and glossing in Anglo-Saxon England. *Proceedings of the British Academy* 82: 107–48

Healey A.Di P., Venezky R.L. 1980 *A Microfiche Concordance to Old English*. Dictionary of Old English: Toronto

Hofstetter W. 1987 *Winchester und der spätaltenglische Sprachgebrauch: Untersuchungen zur geographischen und zeitlichen Verbreitung altenglischer Synonyme*. Fink: Munich

Jackson K.H. 1953 *Language and History in Early Britain. A Chronological Survey of the Brittonic Languages First to Twelfth Century A.D.* Edinburgh University Press: Edinburgh

Kastovsky D. 1992 Semantics and vocabulary. In: Hogg R.M. (ed.) *The Cambridge History of the English Language*, vol. 1: *The Beginnings to 1066*. Cambridge University Press: Cambridge, pp. 290–408

Ker N.R. 1957 *Catalogue of Manuscripts Containing Anglo-Saxon*. Clarendon Press: Oxford

Kluge F. 1909 Gotische Lehnworte im Althochdeutschen. *PBB* 35: 124–60

Kluge F. 1913 [1891]*Urgermanisch: Vorgeschichte der altgermanischen Dialekte*, 3rd edn. Trübner: Strassburg; 1st edn. in Paul H. (ed.) 1891 *Grundriss der Germanischen Philologie*, pp. 305–20 and 783–85

Lapidge M. 1988 The study of Greek at the School of Canterbury in the seventh century. In: Herren M.W. (ed.) *The Sacred Nectar of the Greeks: the Study of Greek in the West in the Early Middle Ages*. King's College: London, pp. 169–94

Loth J. 1892 *Les mots latin dans les langues brittoniques*. Paris

Luick K. 1914–40 *Historische Grammatik der englischen Sprache*. Tauchnitz: Leipzig

MacGillivray H.S. 1902 *The Influence of Christianity on the Vocabulary of Old English*. Niemeyer: Halle

Myres J.N.L. 1986 [1989] *The English Settlements. The Oxford History of England*, IB. Oxford University Press: Oxford; rev. 1989

Pogatscher A. 1888 *Zur Lautlehre der griechischen, lateinischen und romanischen Lehnworte im Altenglischen*. Trübner: Strassburg

Sawyer P.H. 1958 The density of the Danish settlement in England. *University of Birmingham Historical Journal* 6: 1–17

Serjeantson M.S. 1935 *A History of Foreign Words in English*. Routledge: London

Skeat W.W. 1887 [1892] *Principles of English Etymology. First Series*. Clarendon Press: Oxford; 2nd edn. 1892

Wollmann A. 1990 *Untersuchungen zu den frühen lateinischen Lehnwörtern im Altenglischen: Phonologie und Datierung*. Fink: Munich

Wright R. 1982 *Late Latin and Early Romance in Spain and Carolingian France*. Francis Cairns: Liverpool

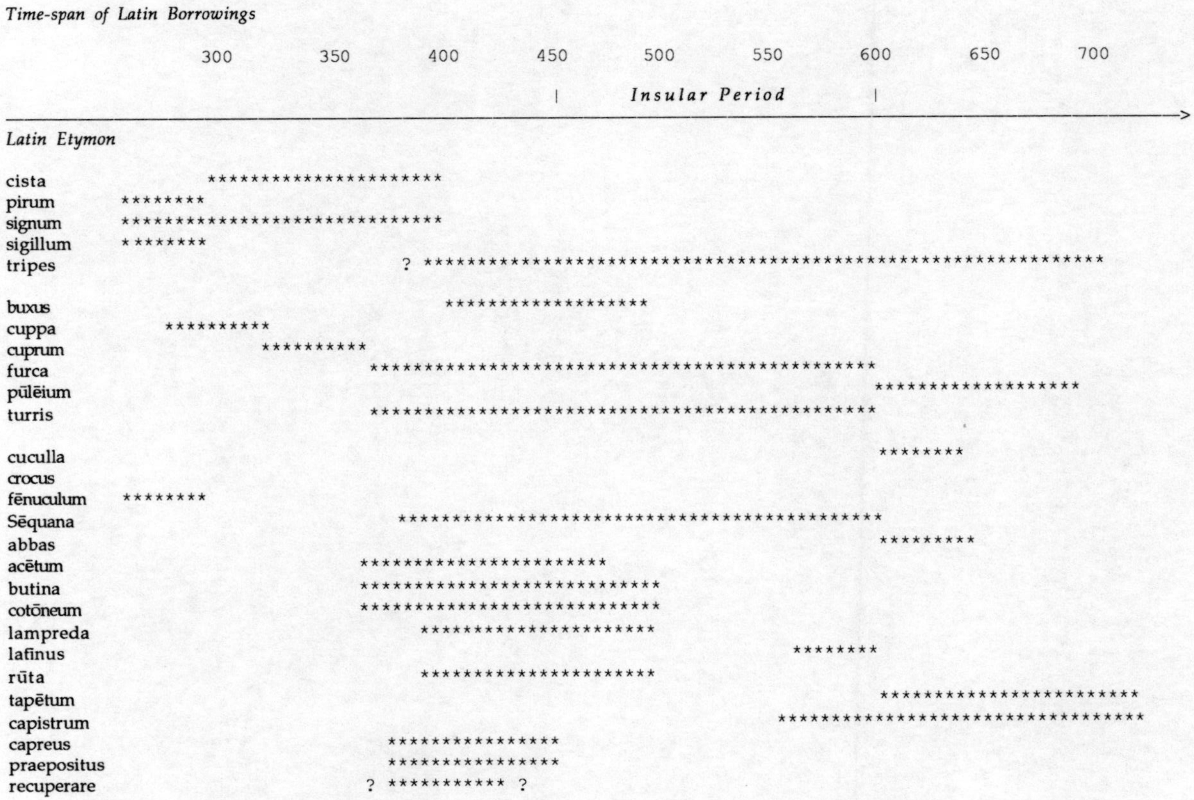

Figure 1: Time-span of Latin borrowings into Old English (from Wollmann 1990: 671, with the kind permission of the author).

Panel III LANGUAGES IN CONTACT

Discussion

chaired by *Alexander Fenton*

Jeremy Smith: I have a question for Professor McIntosh. The thing I liked about your paper was when you talked about little deviations leading to big results, the way in which small change can build up to produce a large change. This, of course, fits in with evolutionary theory.

Angus McIntosh: And also with modern chaos theory.

Smith: Indeed, and that was the parallel that leapt into my mind. The obvious example that came to me was the development of the Old English sound changes — how they work differently in the different dialects. You can work out the whole series of West Saxon–Anglian dialect deviations from a very few variant forms from the very beginning of the whole series. The rest of the sequence follows in order after that. And it seems to me that this emphasis on small change, order coming out of chaos, which Michael Halliday has also drawn attention to, is a very valuable insight and one that is worth building into our theories of language change.

McIntosh: Normally, when we speak of languages in contact, we perhaps think of the one communicating something to the other: like French influencing English. But when we come to examine this at the micro level, it is useful to think of dialects as merely one end of a continuum where the entities in question are much closer to one another. Certain 'forces' are pulling one dialect apart from the other, partly because of the inherent tendency for languages, if not in contact, to diverge. But, at the same time, there is a very powerful factor which, within the constraints of the sociological situation, keeps things held together. It is the combination of these two opposite tendencies that strikes me as being extraordinarily interesting and extraordinarily difficult to keep apart and to handle within one and the same environment.

Smith: Yes, because you're dealing constantly with interaction between user and system, system and user; and of course, the system comprises the users.

Robert Lewis: I have a question for Helmut Gneuss. You talked about 40 Latin words or 40 French loans, or 40 possible genuine French loans. Could you say something about how it was determined that they were French and weren't in fact in most cases Latin? What kind of criteria were used to make that judgement after they were called French originally?

Helmut Gneuss: Most of the so-called French pre-Conquest loans that have to be discarded came in the later 11th or the 12th century. At any rate they only occur in post-Conquest manuscripts, particularly the Peterborough Chronicle. And there are very few genuine French pre-Conquest loans. One is the word *sot*(*t*). There's a variant with a long *o*, which could be from French. The variant with short *o* followed by a double *t* is supposed to be a Latin form. Flasdieck has discussed this in an article in *Anglia*.[1] A second word is *castel*, which in fact occurs once before the Norman Conquest in the sense of 'fortification', and refers to a fortification belonging to one of the French friends of Edward the Confessor. *Castel* appears quite frequently in the West Saxon Gospels. It never refers to a fortification, but to a small town or a village. The West Saxon Gospels being rather earlier (although we can't date them exactly), there is no good reason to assume that the word is from French when you might as well derive it from *castellum*. There are one or two more examples. You'll find a long list of these words by Kluge,[2] repeated by Skeat in an issue of *The Academy*.[3] What we have is one occurrence of 'castle', four occurrences of 'juggler' — they seem to be French forms — and then 'pride', 'proud'; the word 'cowl' is fairly frequent, which must have to do with the Fleury influence on the

---

[1] H.M. Flasdieck 1951 Studien zur Laut- und Wortgeschichte. *Anglia* 70: 240–71.

[2] F. Kluge 1895 Ne. *Proud – Pride. Englische Studien* 21: 334–35.

[3] W.W. Skeat 1895 English words borrowed from French before the Conquest. *The Academy*, Sept 28, 1895: p. 252.

Benedictine habit.[4] There are one or two that are doubtful — they occur only once — and all the rest are not French, or are later.

Margaret Laing: I'm in the process of compiling a list[5] of all the 12th- and 13th-century manuscripts which contain writings in English. I'm trying to make it as comprehensive as I can and to include glosses such as those Tony Hunt has been working on.[6] With glosses you have no context other than a single word. It's sometimes very difficult to say any more than that they are 'vernacular'. For instance, unless they are labelled *Gallice* or *Anglice*, at what point do you decide whether the word is English or whether it's still thought of as French? I'd value any comments on my predicament. Probably, in many cases, it cannot be decided. They were words that were known to both English and French speakers in England and 'vernacular' is the best word to describe these.

Gneuss: Well, Tony Hunt's book deals with a different field. He is dealing with a later period, where you can expect French words which you wouldn't normally expect so early in Anglo-Saxon England. And Tony Hunt deals mainly with scattered glosses, which we could also call lexical or vocabulary glosses. At the end of my talk I was referring to what Neil Ker used to call continuous glosses. We can now show that they were written largely by intelligent people (I am talking not about the copying scribe but the original glossator), because we have the syntactical glosses and cases where people use psalter commentaries. It's hard to believe that somebody who can understand the psalter commentary by Cassiodorus or Augustine should not be able to write a decent Old English gloss. But with regard to your question, the point is simply to try to determine on phonological grounds whether a word is, or could be, French, or a loanword from French or a loanword from Latin. There are, however, a number of loanwords whose etymology is still uncertain. We don't even know whether they are Germanic or Latin.

Gillis Kristensson: I've very often been faced with the lexicographical problem of whether one should look upon a French or a Latin word

---

[4] OE *castel, iugelere, prut, pryte, cule.*

[5] Now published: M. Laing 1993 *Catalogue of Sources for a Linguistic Atlas of Early Medieval English*. D.S. Brewer: Cambridge.

[6] T. Hunt 1991 *Teaching and Learning Latin in Thirteenth-Century England*, 3 vols. D.S. Brewer: Cambridge.

that occurs in a manuscript as native or as just the work of a scribe who is very good at Latin or French. For instance, there are in the Middle Ages so many official documents that teemed with French loanwords, but the question is always, is this what only a Norman scribe took down, or was it a word that you could count upon as being current in at least some circles in England? And the same is true with Latin. It is a problem for the *Middle English Dictionary*. In Sweden we have dealt a lot with problems of this kind and generally we have had to be very careful about both French and Latin loanwords.

Gneuss: The decision is very often difficult. It depends on the social stratum of those who use the word. And this is why I've always felt that Funke's[7] attempt to distinguish between foreign words and loanwords on the basis of inflexional endings doesn't really work, because if there is a distinction it is according to whether the word is familiar or not. I suppose all that we can do is see in which texts these words occur, and count their frequency and also see whether the word has survived. It's quite clear that we still use some of the earliest loanwords, *mile* and *street*, and so on, so apparently these were in common use.

Pieter van Reenen: I also have a question for Professor Gneuss. I do not know exactly how to interpret your handout [see Figure 1, p. 157]. How is it possible that a word like *tripes* is introduced before 400 and it's still introduced in 700? It looks like taking up smoking — you can do it every week.

Gneuss: The handout gives the gist of Wollmann's 700-page book.[8] His dates are based on several phonological criteria. I admit I couldn't explain all these 'stars' here. But in this particular case, I think the point is that it's Old English *trefet*, and he assumes that the voicing of intervocalic voiceless stops in Romance occurred not before the 5th century, and some people even make it go on into the 7th century. Now, you have in *trefet* the lowering of /i/ in open syllables to /e/, and so you could put this word in the early period because the /i/ to /e/ lowering is supposed to be earlier than the /u/ to /o/ lowering.

---

7   O. Funke 1914 *Die gelehrten lateinischen Lehn- und Fremdwörter in der alt-englischen Literatur von der Mitte des X. Jahrhunderts bis um das Jahr 1066*. Niemeyer: Halle, p. 44

8   A. Wollmann 1990 *Untersuchungen zu den frühen lateinischen Lehnwörtern im Altenglischen: Phonologie und Datierung*. Fink: Munich.

But you then have the problem of the intervocalic consonant, and this is, of course, why he dates *trefet* so late as opposed to the other words. And there are similar explanations for all these. Wollmann's book is highly technical and rather complicated, but I think convincing. Above all what becomes quite clear is that strict borderlines don't work. We don't know enough about Vulgar Latin to be able to date the introduction of loanwords so exactly.

Derek Britton: You didn't mention syntactic influence of Latin on English. Do you think we can dismiss it because it had no impact on English as a living language, only in translation?

Gneuss: Not at all. When you look at the index to Bruce Mitchell's *Old English Syntax*, there are about 200 references to what is called Latin influence. Now, in a number of these cases he just mentions that it might be a Latinism. But he has several other cases where he points out that Latin influence is probable or even certain. And there is earlier work on this: I don't know whether you know the thesis by Manfred Scheler[9] which deals mainly with the absolute participle.

Britton: But the influence is only seen in translations from Latin? It never occurs independently of any Latin source?

Gneuss: Yes, it does occur. For instance, if I may quote the text of the West Saxon Gospels — which I consider is quite a good prose version of the Gospels — you do find absolute participles there. I recall one: *þinre dura belocene* for *clauso ostio tuo*, 'the doors being closed'.[10] Here we have a Latin source, but the absolute construction is found in a text in good idiomatic Old English prose. Absolute constructions do however occur independently of Latin models, as Bruce Mitchell has shown.[11] Its use here means, of course, that it is already in common use.

Terry Hoad: Professor Gneuss mentioned in passing the apparent paradox that estimates of the size of the Celtic survival in earlier Anglo-Saxon England have increased, whereas we have next to

---

[9] M. Scheler 1961 *Altenglische Lehnsyntax: Die syntakischen Latinismen im Altenglischen.* Dissertation: Berlin.

[10] Matthew 6.6.

[11] B. Mitchell 1985 *Old English Syntax.* Oxford University Press: Oxford, §§ 3804–3831, especially 3829.

nothing in the way of loanwords. This is contrary to what we see with the Normans. I wonder if he has any further thoughts about that or whether it was really put up as a topic for further investigation?

Gneuss: I'm not a Celticist so I ought not to say anything about it. I only found one reasoned attempt at explaining this: by Wolfgang Meid in one of the Eichstätt conference volumes.[12] He suggests that originally there were far more Celtic loanwords in Anglo-Saxon, especially in northern Britain, but they were given up later under some sort of pressure. It's not very convincing; it's connected with Henry Lewis's speculation on how far Latin was spoken and used in Celtic Britain.

William Gillies: Place-name scholars such as Kenneth Cameron have made suggestions (for example based on *walh-*) concerning the nature of social interaction, or rather non-interaction/segregation, of Britons and Angles in the heartlands of Anglo-Saxon England. This may help to explain how scholars can give more generous estimates of Celtic survival but without being able to point to a great deal of linguistic evidence for that survival. However, the interaction may have been greater, or more linguistically fruitful, than we can at present demonstrate.

In support of Professor Meid's position we may note first that linguistic promiscuity does seem to be normal in cases where we can obtain close-range evidence. We may take as a parallel the case of the Gaelic element in Scots. Here too one encounters a persistent view that the Gaelic presence is minimal. Yet McClure was able to come up with fistfuls, literally hundreds of Gaelic loans, respectably authenticated in the main Scots dictionaries, for purposes of a recent paper.[13] We may note that many of these loans were very localised or specialised (rural, domestic, trade, craft, etc.), and others were stigmatised (e.g. in comic or humorous literature). There was, hence, a bias against their gaining acceptance into 'general' Scots speech. This is part of the sociolinguistics of Scots. The main point is that where we

---

12 W. Meid 1990 Englisch und sein britischer Hintergrund. In: A. Bammesberger and A. Wollmann (eds.) *Britain 400–600: Language and History*. Carl Winter: Heidelberg, pp. 97–119 [113–14].

13 J.D. McClure 1986 What Scots owes to Gaelic. *Scottish Language* 5 (Proceedings of the First International Conference on the Languages of Scotland — University of Aberdeen 26–29 July 1985), pp. 85–98.

can make a close-up inspection we find evidence that numbers of Gaelic words made a transient or fleeting entry into the Scots language.

We may also observe that a good number of Gaelic words, more than are customarily acknowledged, did win their way through to 'general' Scots usage — against the odds, as it were. When these occur in dictionaries they tend to be given the tag 'etymology unknown', or to appear decked out with elaborate but unnecessary Romance or Germanic derivations.

Was the linguistic interface between Gaelic and Scots between (say) the 14th and 17th centuries so different from that which existed between Brythonic and Germanic speakers in England between (say) the 7th and 10th centuries? Though one would not want to press this too far, the raids and feuds, the shifting alliances and abiding enmities that spanned the Highland–Lowland line in the later period bear comparison in certain respects with the Welsh–English frontier in the ealier period. I would submit that these were both perfectly normal *Sprachkontakt* situations.

Again, the later history of English shows the same tension between a centrally based linguistic imperialism that would militate against the survival of peripheral forms, and a facility for importing numbers of items from the periphery and giving them metropolitan accreditation. It would seem as though similar forces may also have been at work within the language in the earlier period.

A further parallel exists, in the form of under-reporting of Celtic loanwords in the English lexicographical tradition. This is a case that needs to be argued patiently and in detail, since the field has in the past been tarnished by sub-scientific and 'lunatic fringe' interventions. Nevertheless, it is clear to me that for a mixture of reasons (primarily ignorance and ideological bias) there are words and phrases which could be added to the list of recognised Celtic loans in English, but which currently appear as 'of uncertain origin' or similar.

The upshot of this is that there are both general and particular reasons for taking Professor Meid's scenario seriously. The real answer, of course, is to re-examine our materials more minutely than before, using all the resources and tools currently available. This has been done recently by Patrick Sims-Williams for the Hwicce and Magonsaetan in the West Midlands, to splendid effect.[14] When he talks about the relations between the British and English communities

---

[14] P. Sims-Williams 1990 *Religion and Literature in Western England, 600–800*. D.S. Brewer: Cambridge.

in his chosen area we have to abandon old generalisations and take note.

Smith: On the same point: we know from the Galloway place-names, for instance, that the Norse and Celtic languages, and indeed languages descending from Anglo-Saxon, are all interacting in most interesting and intriguing ways. I was reading the other day in Nicolaisen's book about the ordering of place-name evidence.[15]   Place-names like *Kirkcudbright*, which have a Germanic element put into a Celtic word-formation structure, seem to me to show that the intimacy of the relationship must have been very profound.

Gillies: That's right.   You're thinking of things like *Glenstockdale* or *Glenormiston*, where you can see the strata being built up.

Smith: Yes. Or *Maibothelbeg* and *Maibothelmor*.

Matti Rissanen: I have another reference to the question of loan syntax in Old English. A Finnish scholar called Matti Kilpiö[16] has recently published a very good study on passives in Bede and Alfred's *Pastoral Care*. He suggests that in the passive there was Latin influence on Old English distribution and use of the agent prepositions.

Can I ask Professor Gneuss, have you been able to use, or has any of your students used, the Toronto *Dictionary of Old English* corpus for loanword studies? Are there any new insights to be got from that excellent corpus, from either the microfiche concordance or the computer tape? Either is useful.

Gneuss: We use the microfiche concordance of course. Wollman's dissertation, as far as the evidence is concerned, is based not only on the microfiche concordance but also on all the variant readings. The microfiche concordance records all the variant readings of the interlinear psalters because they differ a great deal, but not, for instance, the variant readings of Ælfric's *Homilies*. The first volume of the new edition has not yet appeared; for the second volume (which is out), and for some other texts, the *DOE* has a collection of variant

---

15 W.F.H. Nicolaisen 1976 *Scottish Place-Names*. Batsford: London.
16 Matti Kilpiö 1989 *Passive Constructions in Old English Translations from Latin with special reference to the OE Bede and the* Pastoral Care. Mémoires de la Société Néophilologique de Helsinki 49.

readings now, for the lexicographical work on the spot, but these readings have not yet gone into the microfiche concordance.

Fenton: Is a Scots word in a Latin text a foreign word?

Keith Williamson: Regarding cases where one finds a mixture of Celtic and Latin words in running text, this seems to occur in other places. I was reading the introduction to the *Südwestdeutscher Sprachatlas*, which deals with 14th-century medieval German texts, in particular the *Urbare* which are inventories of what people own in particular lands. One often finds cases where originally the rolls were in Latin and then they start to appear with German words in them. First, there's a mixture in the inflexional forms, with a Latin form on a German word. Then one gets examples which tend towards a very mixed language — fifty-fifty Latin and German. The end of the process is the production of these documents in the vernacular. In 13th-century Scottish Latin texts vernacular Scots words appear among the Latin. This is something that would be worth investigating properly: the extent to which Latin texts incorporate the vernacular and the whole linguistic structure where Latin and vernacular terms are intermixed.

Gillies: That was very much my point, and in the Irish context it's a stage in a dynamic process. It's not static. It's a move towards the use of the vernacular for such purposes as annals and chronicles and homilies. It's the adolescence of the vernacular as a medium for writing.

Fenton: I don't think it's a secret that the Celtic Congress is to be held in Edinburgh in 1995, and a lot of these questions will I'm sure be aired more than thoroughly on that occasion.

Gillies: This is very much part of our intention.

Fenton: In summary I think that one or two points need to be made. Professor McIntosh's idea that languages don't really exist solely in themselves is an important one that we should think about, and also the difficulties in talking of *a* or *the* language. It's even more complicated by the fact that any single individual talking to some other individual will vary his language, even within a very quick space of time, for example the pronunciation of 'Gaelic' as [geːlɪk], [gaːlɪk] or [gəilɪk] shows how readily that can be done. As far as Celtic is concerned, it is worth remarking the degree to which the Celtic-speaking areas had a certain degree of cohesion with strong links also across the sea. I think a recent book on the Irish Sea[17] has a great deal of relevance, in cultural terms, to the kind of linguistic material that we've been discussing. So, I would make a plea for looking at the cultural side and not only at the linguistic side. The concept of differing vernaculars and the plainly homogeneous quality of manuscript Old Irish that Willie Gillies mentioned is quite striking. It seems to me to be somewhat different from the ways in which people look at the Germanic languages. These kinds of difference between different groups of languages need to be examined in greater detail.

Professor Gneuss discussed a set of approaches, using archaeology and periodisation in order to interpret the sequences of loanwords. That's obviously an ongoing process in which lexicography is very important, as are atlases that show distributions in time and space. But I always like to try to get in social milieu as well, because these three units are also the three legs on which ethnologists run — like Manxmen, I suppose. It all simply reinforces my belief that a solid partnership between *Wörter und Sachen* is absolutely essential for my kind of work as an ethnologist and for linguists' work in general. When I was a lexicographer, working on the *Scottish National Dictionary*, I found that the only way I could really be sure of defining words properly was to get to know the cultural background. And in a way that's what turned me into being an ethnologist. So now the pendulum is swinging back again.

---

17   M. McCaughan and J. Appleby (eds.) 1989 *The Irish Sea: Aspects of Maritime History*. Institute of Irish Studies, Queen's University, Belfast / Ulster Folk and Transport Museum: Belfast.

Panel I Revisited

Descriptions of Dialect and Areal Distributions

Michael Benskin

This paper begins with some perhaps simple-minded observations on the way in which it is customary to talk about regional dialect; for it has long seemed to me that the conventional modes of description and analysis are bedevilled by certain categorial confusions.

For example, it is customary to talk about such things as 'the Norfolk dialect'. This is in its way unobjectionable, until scholars start agonising about where the boundaries of 'the Norfolk dialect' are to be set. This ought really to be no problem at all. The boundary of 'the Norfolk dialect' is the administrative county boundary of Norfolk, and that is that. Scholarly agonisings, of course, reflect the fact that dialectally Norfolk is not all of a piece: within the county there is marked regional variation. Similarly, features characteristic in Norfolk usage may be found across the county boundary, in other parts of the country as well: 'characteristically' does not entail 'exclusively', though many have written as if it does. Consider Map 1 (p. 170), which represents the regional distributions of certain forms found commonly in the writings of Norfolk scribes from the later 14th and 15th centuries. It will be seen that, even in respect of these few 'Norfolk characteristics', Norfolk is dialectally rather complex. Not one of these characteristics is found over the whole county, and neither is any of them confined to it. Clearly, were we to plot the distributions of a few more 'Norfolk characteristics', the pattern within the county would become quite extraordinarily complex, and the bad sense of talking about 'the Norfolk dialect' ought by then to be obvious.

Yet scholars continue to talk not only about 'the Norfolk dialect', but about things like *'the* East Anglian dialect' and *'the* West Midland

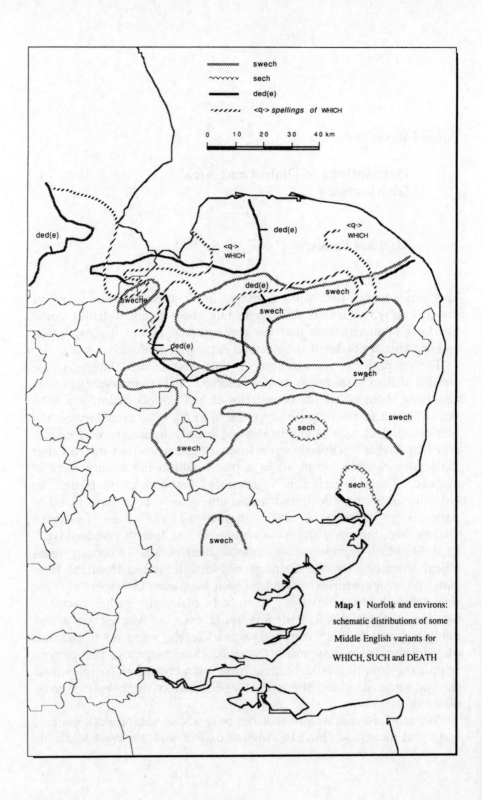

Map 1 Norfolk and environs: schematic distributions of some Middle English variants for WHICH, SUCH and DEATH

dialect' as well. For these also, they try to determine boundaries; some claim rather to discover them. The boundaries of the regional entities to which these dialects may be supposed to correspond, are not like the county boundary of Norfolk, but are in themselves somewhat negotiable; even when the criteria are exclusively topographical, for example, geographers may quite reasonably differ among themselves as to where, in detail, the regional boundaries should be drawn. Regional dialects are no more discrete entities than are the geographer's natural regions. The boundary between 'the East Anglian dialect' and 'the East Midland dialect' shifts west or east according as we focus on the domain of one East Anglian form or another. For some forms, it would be more or less the same as the administrative boundaries of Norfolk and Suffolk with Cambridgeshire; for others, it would lie well within Cambridgeshire or even as far west as Huntingdonshire; and for others still, it would exclude the language of the western parts of Norfolk and Suffolk altogether from 'the East Anglian dialect'. In other words, to talk about 'the East Anglian dialect' as if it were a thing discretely bounded, makes even less sense than to talk about 'the Norfolk dialect' in such a way: 'the Norfolk dialect' can always be defined as whatever sorts of English are contained within the administrative county of Norfolk, however much it may offend our linguistic proprieties to do so.

The dilemma inherent in this mode of thinking is sometimes evaded by adopting a single feature to define a large regional complex, which complex we may then expect to be tacitly regarded as monolithic. Suppose, then, that 'the West Midland dialect' is presented as that type (and only that type) of Midland English having o as the reflex of WGmc $\breve{a}$: then, to establish the isogloss (or isograph) for that o is by definition to determine the boundary of 'the West Midland dialect'. But is anything useful being said by fixing the label 'West Midland Dialect' on to the area so enclosed? —anything more, that is, than would have been said by labelling it 'Midland domain of o derived from WGmc $\breve{a}$'? To take a single feature as indexical for a whole complex is useful only if the members of the complex it defines have more in common with each other than they have with anything outside, and here that is not the case. Why is o derived from WGmc $\breve{a}$ a more important characteristic than (say) s instead of $þ$ or *th* for the ending of the 3sg. present indicative? Or than n instead of $þ$ in the pres. indic. pl.? Or than *mony* for 'many', or *vch* for 'each'? And so the list could go on.

The traditional preoccupation with dialect boundaries is understandable even so. Once a dialect is abstracted from the continuum to which it belongs, once it is regarded as a thing in its own right, then it is natural to define it; and rigorous definition becomes all too easily an exercise in essentialism, and an end in itself. Since for regional dialects the terms of reference are geographical, 'defining the dialect' becomes a quest for areal boundaries. The mistake lies in thinking of dialect as a thing at all. Instead of 'once a dialect is abstracted', read 'once an abstraction is made from a dialectal continuum'; for 'defining the dialect', read 'justifying that abstraction from the continuum as opposed to some other'. Rather, therefore, we should think in terms of dialectal continua within the county or the region as well: hence 'the Norfolk dialects' or 'the East Anglian dialects'. If, as a result of investigation, it should appear that the dialect material for some given county is homogeneous and distinctive, then the fact in itself would be of interest; but there is no ground whatever for building such an assumption into the investigation at its very start.

Perhaps all this seems very obvious, but it has not been obvious to most writers on Old English dialects. The standard description is in terms of political groupings, that is, of the early Anglo-Saxon kingdoms: Northumbrian, Kentish, Mercian, and West Saxon. Here, notice, 'East Anglian' is not recognised at all, but tacitly subsumed under 'Mercian':[1] what pass for dialect boundaries are for the most part political boundaries, in so far as even these can be confidently drawn.

Within this framework, an Old English dialectal feature is identified as, let us say, 'Anglian'. The grounds for recognising it as 'Anglian' are: (i) that it is regular in those writings for which there is good, extra-linguistic evidence of origin within what politically appears to have been Anglian territory; and (ii) that it is not characteristic in writings known to be from outside this territory. Suppose now that the same dialect feature turns up in a work recognised as emanating from the kingdom of Wessex, which work displays most of the linguistic features conventionally associated with Wessex: well, that is evidence of contamination, of a corrupt mixture of 'West Saxon' with 'Anglian' — or, with appeal to proximity and political history, of the intrusion of a 'Mercian scribal form'. The

---

[1] See the map of the Mercian kingdom in Stenton 1947: 200 and further, Stenton 1918.

more such forms identified in a predominantly 'West Saxon' text, the heavier is the alleged overlay of Mercian scribal tradition.

In some cases, that may well be the correct interpretation. I do not wish to deny that scriptoria in some parts of the country, at different times, variously influenced the writing and spelling systems of others. But if we start with the assumption — axiom, even — that there were just these four dialects, then we exclude at the outset the possibility of discovering what would, I think, be regarded as a norm by anyone who has worked with atlases of the regional dialects of the present day: that is, that the areal transition between one dialect type and another is graded, not discrete. Our assumption would also commit us, as a corollary, to accounting for any co-occurrence of the forms characteristic of The Four Dialects, as an unnatural assemblage that betokens no more than the influence of one scribal tradition on another; and it is at least possible that that is not always right.

'Characteristically Anglian, therefore exclusively Anglian. If it appears in a West Saxon text, then the text shows Anglian influence.' The 'therefore' is of course a *non sequitur*, but such is the chain of thought that underlies many a pronouncement on the dialectal character of mediaeval texts. Could it be, rather, that the language of some of those texts long regarded as 'essentially West Saxon but overlain with Mercian', is a genuinely local form of language, that it belongs to some part of the polity of Wessex in which features characteristically (but not exclusively) Anglian combined with other features characteristically (but not exclusively) West Saxon, as ordinary local dialects? The West Saxon texts themselves, after all, show that the language of Wessex cannot have been monolithic. It seems to be widely accepted that literary Late West Saxon cannot, in detail, be descended from literary Early West Saxon, but how often is this recognised as evidence for *regional* diversity? The language of Ælfric looks back to some variety of West Saxon co-aeval with Ælfred's, but not identical with it; and whatever the hazards of manuscript production and survival, there is no ground for thinking that, sometime before Ælfric's day, the Ælfredian variety had become extinct.

II

I turn now to consider certain aspects of spatial distributions, though I shall later come back to dialect boundaries and what ought to appear on our maps.

In 1980, Roger Lass wrote at length against the way that linguists often 'base major claims on arguments so weak, shoddy or confused that they would surely not pass muster outside the hermeneutic confines of the subject' (Lass 1980: x). Like him, I believe that arguments of a kind shown in other disciplines to be invalid on the grounds of logic or method, ought not to be accepted merely because the subject happens to be linguistics. In general, it is fair to say that the humanities are not statistically well informed. When people in the humanities count things — and increasingly, as computer-based corpora are developed, they count rather a lot — they interpret their collections on the basis of, well, percentages. Of statistics, most seem entirely innocent. I do not wish to suggest that statistical analysis offers some general panacea, an instant solution for all our problems; I do think that arguments on the basis of quantitative distributions ought to be properly grounded. No-one, I maintain, should persuade us — or seek to persuade us — that on the basis of quantitative distributions this or that is the case, without first having applied the ordinary statistical procedures that biologists or social scientists would have to apply to similar data, had they any hope of being taken seriously at all. People in the humanities often give the impression of seeing statistical analysis as a threat. Sometimes they convey an unspoken feeling that if we were to use statistics, we should no longer be allowed to believe those things we really want to believe. It is understandable, but it betokens a pretty poor estimation of their subject. Rather, they should consider that some of the things they would like to believe, but are afraid to say so in public, might look a lot more respectable after a proper statistical analysis. Particularly is this so when small samples are at issue, as with historical materials is often and perforce the case; yet people having not the slightest knowledge of well-explored techniques for evaluating such samples, authoritatively dismiss this or that degree of attestation as 'too small to be significant'.

So far, ignorance is culpable. Statistical handbooks are legion, and the scholar who baulks at learning to use them may consult the rabbis. The relevant statistical procedures are in principle there for the asking: if students of the humanities wish to handle quantitative data rigorously, they do not in general need to devise new techniques. For the analysis of regional distributions, by contrast, that is, for the formal analysis of certain types of distribution over space, established procedures are far to seek. There seem to be no standard routines at all for assessing the likelihood that superficially similar patterns are indeed of related origin, or that they are independent of one another. This is a problem which confronts, among others, epidemiologists as well as linguistic geographers.

Regional dialect maps are made not merely as ends in themselves, but as research tools: it is a commonplace that geographical distributions may of themselves throw light on the origins and evolution of words and forms, and sometimes of grammatical or even syntactic sub-systems. Arguments from spatial distribution, however, though they have been deployed confidently enough since the very beginnings of dialect mapping, seem never to have been thought about as a class. The linguistic geographer makes a visual comparison between the regional distributions of, let us say, two dialectal forms, and then asserts that because these distributions are so similar, there must be some causal relation between them. The contrast with what is expected of arguments from non-spatial distributions is very striking: although in the humanities the handling of quantitative data, and of statistical correlation generally, falls far short of what is demanded as a minimum in the natural or social sciences, organised comparison of a sort is at least conventional. Areal distributions, by contrast, are normally left to speak for themselves. To a surprising degree, this is true for other kinds of geography as well.

At this point, it may appear that some familiar presentations of medical statistics have been overlooked. An obvious case arises from the claim that British nuclear power stations cause leukaemia. Incidences of leukaemia in populations living beside British nuclear power stations have been compared with the incidence of leukaemia in the British population overall; and they have been compared also with incidences of leukaemia in British local populations far removed from such places. For present purposes, there is no need to enter the argument as to how these figures should be interpreted, or what other variables may be relevant to the case; rather, the facts of spatial distribution have been analysed statistically, and it may appear that the techniques employed ought to apply to the analysis of areal distributions in general. That they do not, reflects the almost trivial extent to which these data are in fact areal. The crux of the matter is the effects of long-term exposure, the proximity of individuals to one of a few places clearly identified; there is no suggestion that individuals, except through genetic inheritance, can be infected by others. Accordingly, the relevant correlations can be assessed without any statistical concept of area: atomic power stations can be regarded as points in an array, and so also the populations in which the incidence of leukaemia is examined.

It is possible, albeit cumbersome, to apply the same type of analysis to the geographical patterns of a large-scale dialect survey. Each survey point can be treated as a column in an array; the particular combination of features attested there can be entered into the column row by row; and the features can be correlated in turn, one by one or in combinations, with the co-occurrences of features attested at all the other survey points.[2] Without any concept of area, it is possible to make statements like 'feature x occurs only with feature y', 'feature y occurs frequently without feature x', 'feature p never occurs with feature q', and so on. Correlations of this type are especially useful for the recognition and analysis of systems, but they fail to reflect the properties of adjacency and areal cohesion between the particular survey points at which they are attested. These properties may bear directly on an understanding of the phenomena mapped.

Suppose, to take a hypothetical example from medical geography, that a disease is found to be rife in the populations at half the survey points on the map. Suppose also that the population at any given survey point is in regular physical contact with those at the neighbouring survey points, but not with any of those beyond. Then, if the distribution of the infected populations is like that of the black squares on a chess board, and the distribution of the unaffected populations is like that of the white, there will be prima facie reason for thinking that the disease is not contagious. In these circumstances, the cause of the disease may be narrowed down if not firmly established by isolating the shared conditions that set the diseased populations apart from the healthy ones. If, by contrast, the distribution were such that most of the infected populations had as their neighbours only other infected populations, then, other things being equal, it would appear that the disease was contagious. Especially would this be so if, in subsequent mappings, newly infected populations appeared only in the near neighbourhood of those previously infected. The example is simplistic, and it need not be laboured: the obvious and essential contrast is between (i) diffusion through contact, and (ii) independent convergence, and the different types of areal distribution that may be associated with them.

---

[2] Professor Dees's paper in the present volume reports the use of a similar technique in the analysis of dialect material from 13th-century France (see pp. 117–25). For a small-scale graphic example, see Benskin 1988: 16–19.

The use of dialect maps has long been familiar in the historical analysis of discrete forms. The products of geographical variation apparent at any one period may reflect what within a single variety of the language are successive historical stages.[3] In this there is nothing very controversial. Similarly, the regional distributions of various linguistic features have been compared with distributions of a non-linguistic sort, as well as with each other: it is, indeed, normal practice to argue from the facts of areal distribution to historical conclusions. Such practice bears closer examination.

Shown on pp. 178–79 are two dialect maps of late mediaeval England, on which appear what Professor M.L. Samuels has dubbed 'The Great Scandinavian Belt' (Samuels 1985).[4] This belt extends between Cumbria and the Yorkshire coast, corresponding roughly to the old Scandinavian kingdom of York; various of the Norse-derived features whose distributions constitute the belt, are found also in the Danelaw as well as in minor areas of Scandinavian settlement. On Map 2 appears the recorded distribution of *efter* (in contrast to *after*) for 'after', which for the most part reflects Scandinavian England: compare OE *æfter*, ON *eptir*. In some areas, however, *efter* is very unlikely to be of Norse origin. In Kent it arises as merely one instance of a sound change whereby OE *æ* generally became *e*. Similarly, in parts of the West Midlands *efter* reflects a native sound change, the pan-Mercian second fronting; but here, particularly in north Hereford-shire and south Shropshire, *efter* may not always be independent of Norse speech (see Dobson 1976: 118–21). Notice how, in this brief summary, areal distributions are interpreted by reference to prior knowledge that does not depend on the map: for example, we already have reasons for thinking that Kentish *efter* is independent of Middle English *efter* in that form's main area of attestation. Consider now the distribution of ME *at* as an infinitive marker (Map 3). It is confined to Scandinavian England, but it is not recorded throughout that area; in some parts, *to*, or the much less common *til*, appears in its place. As an infinitive marker, ME *at* can only be of Norse origin: I do not think that any philologist has supposed it to be native English. The belief that it is of Norse origin is not invalidated by the

---

[3] Some of the best-known examples are from the Romance languages: see, for a review, chapter III of R. Posner's (1970) revised edition of Iordan-Orr *An Introduction to Romance Linguistics*, esp. pp. 154–79. For some Middle English examples, see Samuels 1965 and McIntosh 1983.

[4] For the belt as it appears in the modern dialects, see Kolb 1965. The maps are taken from *A Linguistic Atlas of Late Mediaeval English*, vol. I, no. 180 & no. 688.

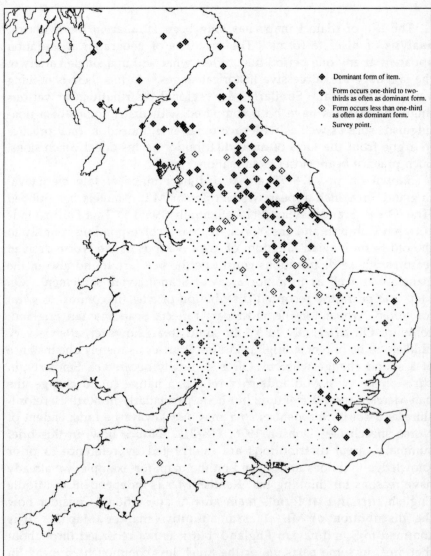

◆ Dominant form of item.

⬦ Form occurs one-third to two-thirds as often as dominant form.

◇ Form occurs less than one-third as often as dominant form.

· Survey point.

Map 2 AFTER: Middle English forms with *e* as the root vowel.

(Re-creation of Dotmap 180 in *A Linguistic Atlas of Late Mediaeval English*, vol. 1, p. 349.)

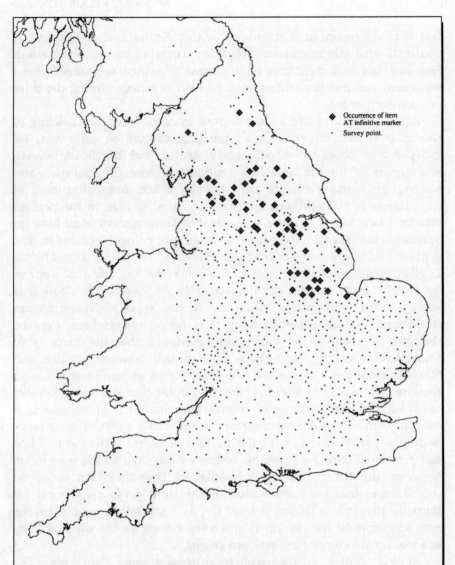

Map 3 Middle English AT as infinitive marker.

fact that its recorded distribution within Scandinavian England is confined and discontinuous, that the correlation is only partial: Scandinavian settlement may be described as a cause necessary but not sufficient, and the distribution may be held to reflect varying densities of such settlement.

What procedures are to be adopted in cases when our reading of the map is not informed, and perhaps cannot be informed, by independent observation? Nobody denies that the Scandinavian settlements of the 9th and 10th centuries altered the English vocabulary; the Norse elements are naturally much more prominent in the dialects of the northern and eastern counties than in the present standard language. There is considerable disagreement as to how far Scandinavian speech may have affected phonology, accidence and syntax; and there are variously problematic forms in later Middle English, when texts from most of Scandinavian England first appear, for which Norse origins might reasonably be sought. To show that such a form is found in and only in the areas of Scandinavian settlement, and that within them it is found everywhere, may be thought by itself to be very good evidence that the form is of Scandinavian origin, or perhaps that contact between English and Norse speakers is a necessary condition for its appearance; it would remain, of course, to identify the particular Scandinavian element borrowed, or the patterns of interference that had given rise to a contact form. Consider by contrast a form whose range of occurrence is only a partial match with the pattern of Norse settlement. How different must these two areas be before we can say that the association between the form and the presence of Scandinavians is of no significance, that the distribution of the form gives no ground for thinking that it is of Norse origin? Or, as a statistician would prefer, how similar must the two distributions be before we can say that there is a significant correlation between them?

At this point it may be well to anticipate some objections. The foregoing examples involve on the one hand the distributions of words or sounds, and on the other hand, those of populations. It may perhaps be urged that in comparing them, mathematical rigour is or ought to be precluded by the different kinds of evidence on which our knowledge of them rests; this knowledge is in any case imperfect, we cannot count the Scandinavian-speaking heads, we must reckon with the hazards of survival implicit in the historical record, and we have quite properly varying degrees of confidence in such sources as do survive. The case could be developed, and rehearsed at length, but there may be no need for it to be so; for the premises may be admitted readily enough, and I wish to reject only the conclusion. I do not for one moment imagine that it would be useful to treat correlations of this kind in exclusively mathematical terms, and it is of course the case that much of what concerns us here simply cannot be quantified. That ought not, however, to commit us to the view that comparisons cannot be *informed* by mathematical principle, that the only possible procedure is ad hoc visual comparison, and that any one observer's judgment as to correlation is as good as any other's. To reject mathematical techniques altogether is to license a methodological shambles.

Take, for example, the way that people sometimes invoke Old Norse as the explanation for this or that puzzling development in mediaeval or modern English. I have heard conference performances in which it seemed that almost any isogloss running in roughly the same direction and within thirty or forty miles of the Danelaw boundary, was of itself sufficient proof that the form it delimited was of Scandinavian origin. A possible philological connexion had been proposed, and the map now proved that it was right. In face of such proof, we remain, perhaps, politely unconvinced; but at what point and according to what principles can we justify our refusal to accept it?

Comparisons involving dialectal forms and dark-age populations are not, of course, the best ground on which to persuade the sceptic of the need for systematic correlation or of the relevance of statistical procedures. When, however, the distributions in question are those of one well-recorded dialectal feature against another, it is hard to see that any reasonable objection could be sustained; and from a purely quantitative point of view, much of the available material for the middle ages is in fact rather good. Why, in any case, should we not attach formal confidence measures to our sources, and so gauge the reliability of the correlations we derive from them? In a text which contains a hundred examples of the word 'man', all spelled ‹man›, the absence of ‹mon› is telling; in a text containing only one instance of the word, the absence of ‹mon› may be mere chance. The techniques for assessing such distributions have long been available, and in the age of the personal computer, their application is hardly laborious. On what grounds are they ignored? Why does even the software supplied with computer-based textual corpora, whether mediaeval or modern, so rarely acknowledge their existence?

For the formal comparison of areal distributions, as I have said, there seem to be no recognised procedures; such, at any rate, is the view of the statisticians and geographers I have consulted. Nevertheless, it is not hard to think of ways in which appropriate techniques might be developed. For example, an arbitrary grid could be imposed on the map, and distributions compared according to the particular squares of the grid that they occupy. Adjacency, which in mathematical terms is a very slippery notion, could be defined in terms of squares having one or more sets of x,y coordinates in common. The survey points could be indexed by the grid squares to which they belong, so that interruptions in a distribution could be recognised by a comparison of indices. As it happens, something very like this was done late in the making of *A Linguistic Atlas of Late Mediaeval English*, when a version of the 'fit'-technique was developed as a computer program. There are, obviously, quite different ways of tackling the problem. One could calculate, for example, the centre of gravity of a distribution, record the distances from the centre to each of the constituent points, and then combine these measures into a single coefficient. Such a coefficient would characterise the distribution as a whole; the comparison of different distributions could then proceed as a comparison of their coefficients. (Additionally or alternatively, coefficients based on the pairwise distances between all points might be taken into account.) It remains to be seen how far measures of this kind could capture the essential properties of a distribution, if indeed they could express them adequately at all; mathematically, the problem is of some interest, and I hope to have a graduate student working at it before long.

III

I return now to the topic with which I began, namely the typology of regional dialects. Allow, in spite of what I have said, that it may be reasonable to ask questions like 'What are they?', and 'Where are the boundaries between them?' Even today, it is nothing unusual for an authority to decide on the criteria for such a classification before any distributional analysis is attempted, if, indeed, it is attempted at all; and this procedure, I maintain, is fundamentally mistaken.

For example, some eighteen months ago, a famous dialectologist — he is famous for being so — presented to an international colloquium a purported analysis of the present-day English regiolects. The classification was arrived at on the basis of seven pre-selected isophones. Each isophone was presented in turn on a separate map, and the separate maps were then placed one on top of another to make a single map. From this composite map, and as a kind of conjuring trick, the alleged regiolects automatically emerged. These, the audience was told, were the regional divisions that now matter, regardless of how things may have been in the past. Here is The South-Eastern Regiolect, with London at its core, and here is The West-Midland One, spreading outwards from Birmingham, and so on. Well, it is true that the map of England was so divided into several large sectors, and perhaps we should share the conviction that it must be right on the grounds that it conforms to the speaker's intuitions. The obvious question, of course, is what happens if we add an eighth isophone, or a ninth, or a twenty-seventh; or do we need even so many as seven?

Consider now an example relating to early Middle English. In 1981, Dr G.P. Cubbin published a detailed analysis of the onomastic material in a range of Latin documents relating to Lancashire (Cubbin 1981). The spoken language assumed to be encoded by the vernacular spellings was the object of investigation, and of overriding concern were the Middle English reflexes of Old English [y(:)]. If such a reflex were spelled ‹i› or ‹y›, then the spoken form was assumed to have [i(:)]; if spelled ‹u›, then the spoken form had [u(:)]. A chief aim was to establish whether southern Lancashire was a 'u-county' or an 'i-county': one or the other, note, for if both spellings were used in the same text, then that was evidence of 'confusion on the part of the scribes' (p. 70). Unreliable sources were naturally to be excluded, and (p. 71)

> it is most expedient to begin by examining the documents which attest i-forms in the search for those which are apparently reliable.

That is, documents attesting only u-forms were beyond suspicion, but documents showing any i-forms were unreliable unless otherwise proven. There is an accordingly hollow ring to the assurance that (p. 74)

> It cannot be stressed too strongly that the object of examining these forms in these sources is not to prove that they are wrong. It is to raise doubts about them. We may be dealing with a very complex set of dialect boundaries, or we may be dealing with confused scribes.

No doubts were to be raised about any of the u-forms, though for reasons unexplained. Various potential sources were then weighed and found wanting; and though some of them were rightly discarded on the grounds that they are inherently likely to be the work of outsiders,[5] the acid test of a document's reliability was whether it included the offending *i*-forms. The centre-piece of the article, however, was held to be of entirely different stuff: the Coucher Book of Whalley Abbey attests *u*-forms over three hundred times in about twelve hundred pages, and so 'finally establishes the whole of South Lancashire as a solid *u*-county' (p. 89). In other words, the investigator knew in advance what the pattern ought to be, and in so far as he found it in the Coucher Book, the Coucher Book was a first-rate source. In these circumstances, it may be asked why he troubled to analyse it at all: the Coucher Book could tell him nothing he did not already know, and it could not alter his view as to what was right. Dr Cubbin's paper is not without value, and the documents noticed are worth detailed investigation; but for present purposes, it affords a rather depressing sidelight on what may pass as scholarly method.[6]

Indeed, 'On pushing carts with horses' would be an apt title for a review of much that has been written in historical and areal linguistics. One of its prize exhibits might well be the 'dialect area' conceived of as an entity that somehow transcends geographical space. 'The whole valley is in a single dialect area, but now it is all in the West Midland area': what is the ontological status of an area in which

---

[5] Even so, some of Dr Cubbin's comments on the diplomatic give pause. For example, to say of the *Calendar of Inquisitions* that it 'may also have been copied in London, and even if it is original, its place of compilation is not clear' (p. 80) implies that it is a single document and mediaeval; whereas, it is a modern work that presents in summary form the contents of some thousands of mediaeval documents. These documents are records of local inquisitions ordered by the Crown, which were locally drawn up and then returned into the Chancery. The originals are extant at the Public Record Office.

[6] It later emerges that the Coucher Book does not, after all, show *u*-forms to the complete exclusion of *i*-forms (p. 90):

> There are only about 30 or 40 cases of *i*, it is true, as opposed to hundreds of *u*, but these exceptions fall into what appears to be a small number of extremely significant groups.

(The tally, 'about 30 or 40', is curiously vague in view of the great importance claimed for the Whalley material, and especially so in view of the author's remarks on scholars who fail to count.) The *i*-forms do appear to pattern coherently, and it is possible that the local and chronological variations were as Dr Cubbin represents them. It is accordingly hard to see why other sources containing *i*-forms were dismissed out of hand, instead of being subjected to similarly close analysis. It may be added that the analysis even of the Coucher Book is far from satisfactory: except incidentally, neither the hands of the Coucher Book nor the individual documents copied into it are distinguished. For some further comment, see Kristensson 1987: xi–xiii.

a valley or an administrative county is sometimes to be found and sometimes not? It may be objected, of course, that this is merely a manner of speaking, a way of saying that, for some of its feature the dialect of this area is of West Midland type, whereas for others, it is not. Where is the harm in that? Well, not least that these dialect types, whatever the outcome, remain the unalterable basis for description; and how far is it reasonable to insist on them as the basis for classification, when, by hypothesis, whole counties have yet to be surveyed? So we return to The Four Dialects of Old English, political boundaries as opposed to linguistic ones, reflecting in their apparent neatness a sparsity of manuscript sources, and not even all these taken properly into account.

In establishing a regional classification, if regional classification we must have, would it not be better to map the distributions of forms one by one, see how they turn out, and then derive our classification from what we discover? Implicit in any linguistic atlas is an enormous number of overlapping distributions. For taxonomic purposes, some will be useless, chequerboard distributions admitting no geographical cohesion at all; and perhaps many will be so. There will be others, however, that divide the map into cohesive blocs; and of these, some will be more or less the same, some will enclose other blocs, some will be mutually exclusive, and between some there will be partial overlap. How many themes are to be discerned behind all these variations? How many basic patterns need be recognised in order to classify the distributions that appear on the maps?

Formal procedures for establishing typologies in this way seem not to have been developed, though various types of areal analysis based on numerical taxonomy are now well established.[7] (Numerical

---

[7] It is no doubt invidious to cite so few examples, but the following, and the references they contain, may be useful:

Computer Methods in Dialectology, being a special issue of the *Journal of English Linguistics* 22.1 (April 1989), ed. W.A. Kretzschmar, Jr., E.W. Schneider and E. Johnson.

Goebl H. 1981 Eléments d'analyses dialectométrique (avec application à l'AIS), *Revue de linguistique romane* 45 (nos. 179–180), pp. 349–420. Société de linguistique romane: Strasbourg.

Goebl H. 1982 Atlas, matrices et similarités: petit aperçu dialectométrique, *Computers and the Humanities* 16: 69–84.

Goebl H. 1984 *Dialektometrische Studien*. Niemeyer: Tübingen.

Huber O., Reenen-Stein K. van 1988 Correlations et groupements dans l'*Atlas des formes et constructions des chartes françaises du XIIIe siècle*, pp. 93–101 of the Dees Festschrift (Reenen and Reenen–Stein 1988), in which appear several other papers touching on these matters.

taxonomy is based on quantified similarities and dissimilarities, measured pairwise between all the objects to be classified. Typically, it treats the objects as points, and aggregates their (dis)similarities as distances between them.) It may be that the procedures suggested here would not, in practice, lead to results materially different from those obtainable by existing methods of computation; but their premisses are not the same, and I think that they are worth serious investigation. (Points and distances are not a transform of areas and overlaps, of inclusions and exclusions.)[8] The essential feature, however, and common to both types of analysis, is that any areal classification would be derived, and it would be derived from the whole corpus of attested variation. It would not be, as all too often it has been, something presupposed and built into the operation at the start, a schema that in large measure precludes the very kind of discovery that is the supposed end in view.

Postscript

A year after the Edinburgh Colloquium was held, and while this paper was in press, there was published an article that is a landmark in the study of Old English dialects: Dr Peter Kitson's 'Geographical variation in Old English prepositions and the location of Ælfric's and other literary dialects', *English Studies* **74** (1993), 1–50. Since preaching is seldom so convincing as demonstration, it may appear that much of what I have written is now superfluous; I should be delighted were it to be so.

References

Benskin M. 1988 The numerical classification of languages, and dialect maps for the past. In: Reenen and Reenen-Stein 1988, pp. 13–38
Cubbin G.P. 1981 Dialect and scribal usage in medieval Lancashire: a new approach to local documents. *Transactions of the Philological Society*: 67–117
Dobson E.J. 1976 *The Origins of Ancrene Wisse*. Oxford University Press: London

---

Reenen P. Th. van 1989 Isoglosses and gradual differences across dialects in Medieval French. In: Schouten M.E.H. van and Reenen P.Th. van (eds.) *New Methods in Dialectology*. Foris: Dordrecht, pp. 135–54.
Thomas A.R. 1980 *Areal Analysis of Dialect by Computer: a Welsh example*. University of Wales Press: Cardiff.

[8] See Benskin 1988.

Kitson P. 1993 Geographical variation in Old English prepositions and the location of Ælfric's and other literary dialects. *English Studies* 74: 1–50

Kolb E. 1965 Skandinavisches in den nordenglischen Dialekten. *Anglia* 83: 127–53

Kristensson G. 1987 *A Survey of Middle English Dialects 1290–1350. The West Midland Counties.* Skrifta utgivna av Vetenskapssocieteten i Lund 18. Lund University Press: Lund

Laing M. (ed.) 1989 *Middle English Dialectology. Essays on some principles and problems.* Aberdeen University Press: Aberdeen

Lass R. 1980 *On Explaining Language Change.* Cambridge University Press: Cambridge

McIntosh A. 1983 Present indicative plural forms in the later Middle English of the North Midlands. In: Gray D. and Stanley E.G. (eds.) 1983 *Middle English Studies presented to Norman Davis.* Oxford University Press: Oxford, pp. 235–44; repr. in Laing M. 1989, pp. 116–22

Posner R. 1970 revised edition of Iordan-Orr *An Introduction to Romance Linguistics.* Basil Blackwell: Oxford

Reenen P.Th. van and Reenen-Stein K. van (eds.) 1988 *Distributions spatiales et temporelles, constellations des manuscrits. Etudes de variation linguistique offertes à Anthonij Dees à l'occasion de son 60me anniversaire.* Benjamins: Amsterdam & Philadelphia

Samuels M.L. 1965 The role of functional selection in the history of English. *Transactions of the Philological Society*: 15–40; repr. in Lass R. (ed.) 1969 *Approaches to English Historical Linguistics.* Holt Rinehart & Winston: New York, pp. 404–18

Samuels M.L. 1985 The Great Scandinavian Belt. In: Eaton R. et al. (eds.) 1985 *Papers from the 4th International Conference on English Historical Linguistics* Amsterdam studies in the theory and history of linguistic science, ser. IV, vol. 41. Benjamins: Amsterdam & Philadelphia, pp. 269–81; repr. in Laing M. 1989, pp. 106–15

Stenton F.M. 1918 The supremacy of the Mercian kings. *English Historical Review* 33: 432–52; repr. in Stenton D.M. (ed.) 1970 *Preparatory to Anglo-Saxon England.* Clarendon Press: Oxford, pp. 48–66

Stenton F.M. 1947 *Anglo-Saxon England*, 2nd edn. Clarendon Press: Oxford

TAXONOMY AND TYPOLOGY IN
         MEDIEVAL DIALECT STUDIES

         Michael Benskin's Paper

         Discussion

         chaired by *Matti Rissanen*

A.J. Aitken: The description of the errors of dialectologists, which
Michael has given, pretty well fits what we do in modern Scots
dialectology. We still operate with the districts and boundaries set out
by James Murray in 1873.[1] Murray actually knew a lot about Southern
Scots — which, incidentally, is one of the more homogeneous groups
of dialects. He knew a little, but not very much, about Scots in the rest
of Scotland. Nevertheless, he drew dialect boundaries and he gave
them names and by and large these are still what we use, for instance,
in the *Concise Scots Dictionary*. Now, I see no harm in this. The
terminology provided by Murray is useful for broad descriptions and
we all need these sometimes. Actually, you used a number, I noticed,
Michael. I heard you talking about Kentish dialect. But, of course, we
want to go on refining them on proper dialectological grounds, based
on criteria which we discover later and plot on maps.

Michael Benskin: I was *pointing* at Kent.

Gillis Kristensson: I think we must agree with Michael in the general
principle, because what we want to map is any item that shows a
difference between one area and another. Any such item is worthy of
being plotted on the map. And when we have all those maps, we have
the basis for discovering the dialects. But we can't get away from the
fact that all Middle English dialects are developments of Old English

---

1 J.A.H. Murray 1873 The Dialect of the Southern Counties of Scotland. *Transactions
of the Philological Society 1870–2*: 1–251.

dialects. When we try, and perhaps succeed, in delimiting the different dialect areas, we must also look at the background of their development and the cultural–political environment of the Middle English dialects. Because I think the forms have a background in the real life of that time.

Benskin: I agree. But the problem is that what we know about Old English dialects is pretty sketchy, as I think anybody would admit. There are so many gaps. And I'm not sure that the gaps need be as big as they are. If you start with the idea that any Anglo-Saxon manuscript showing a mixture of forms, which we recognise as being characteristically West Saxon on the one hand or characteristically Anglian on the other, must be corrupt, must be a mixture, and therefore is not worth further consideration for dialect mapping, then we limit even more the material that is available. My complaint is that we simply don't know enough about Old English dialects — and I don't think we're ever going to — to make them the *foundation* for a description of Middle English.

Kristensson: Couldn't we go the other way round — examine the Middle English dialects and let them shed light on Old English dialects?

Benskin: It seems to me an eminently sensible thing to do, and one of the things I find rather surprising is the way that in writing Old English grammars, for example, precious little attention is ever paid to Middle English texts. People will always look at the AB language in connexion with the *Vespasian Psalter* gloss, but that's all. I looked just recently at Richard Hogg's new book on Old English phonology[2] and I must say that it offers some improvement: he is alive at least to the fact that West Saxon is heterogeneous. But it does seem to me that people have taken a long time to wake up to that fact. You perhaps remember Wrenn's paper on standard Old English:[3] the cultural background he sketches for Wessex and his account of the settlements and peoples. I should have thought this would predispose us to think that West Saxon was likely to be extremely heterogeneous. Yet, nothing of this appears in the mainstream scholarship now.

---

[2] R. Hogg 1992 *A Grammar of Old English. Vol. I: Phonology.* Blackwell: Oxford.

[3] C.L. Wrenn Standard Old English *Transactions of the Philological Society* 1933: 65–88; repr. in C.L. Wrenn 1967 *Word and Symbol: Studies in English Language* (English Language Series). Longmans, Green & Co.: London.

Terry Hoad: Concerning statistics, I think it would be wonderful if we were able to have some rigorous and systematic method of assessing the similarities of distributions. But when you put up the maps, you talked in particular about the likelihood of a feature being explained by Scandinavian influence. It seemed to me that no amount of statistical correlation is ever going to demonstrate the causes of the occurrence of a particular feature. Even if you had a complete match of half a dozen features which were certainly Scandinavian in origin and one or two which were less clearly so, you would have no proof of common origin.

Pieter van Reenen: Your maps are just a systematic way of representing data. That's OK; it's the best way to do it. Nothing remarkable about that. But then you have a theory and this theory says something about political boundaries and Scandinavian influence. You look at these maps again and you say, 'The lower maps fit nicely because I can explain the things in the South' — no problem. 'The upper right map is OK as well because I can connect this linguistically.' But then there is another map and now you say, 'I definitely cannot connect this in a linguistic way with the Scandinavian influence theory'. Whether there are many data or not is not important, I would just say, 'Your theory is not right — well, not completely right — and you have to think over your theory again and try something else'. That would be my approach. What's your answer to that?

Benskin: My answer to that is, I go along with you entirely. If you are arguing on the basis of distribution and even if you have a 100 per cent fit, you still have to find a mechanism. But how close a correlation do you have to have between the distribution of some linguistic form whose origin you seek to explain and some other distribution — which may be that of Scandinavian settlement, or may be the distribution of some other form — before you can reasonably claim that there is a common origin, or that they are in some way related?

van Reenen: I just try to avoid this problem by presenting it in some other way and having another theory which might be better.

Benskin: I'm concerned rather with that range of phenomena in Middle English which are not explained: for example, the ⟨q⟩ spellings in words like 'which', 'where' and 'when', and so on — ‹qu›, ‹qw›, etc. for OE ‹hw›. You find it wherever there is Norse settlement. You can't explain it as an import, of course, it turns up far too late and in the wrong sort of Norse for it to be of directly Norse origin. But if you find some form that you can't explain and statistically its correlation with, for example, Scandinavian settlement is impressive, you should at least consider the possibility of Norse origins — not necessarily origins within Norse itself, but origins, perhaps, as a contact phenomenon. And I think in fact the ‹q› spellings could very well be explained as a contact phenomenon. Rather than solving your problem, it may indicate that there is a connexion worth exploring: there may very well be a significant link between two distributions. But to come back to one of Dr Kristensson's points, one of our problems with the Old English dialects is our lack of knowledge. You can find many distributions which look as if they may be of Scandinavian origin in England, but which I don't think are Scandinavian at all, in terms of mechanisms or linguistic affiliation. Rather, our Scandinavian-looking distribution reflects our ignorance of the dialects outside Wessex, outside the southern part of the country.

Anthonij Dees: I should like to come back to the notion of dialects. I think you demonstrated the weaknesses of this notion, but I had the impression you had some regrets. I don't have that kind of regret for the French situation. I have abandoned the notion of dialect, which is extremely dangerous in its applications. So why shouldn't we express ourselves in terms of geographical points with numbers? That would be better, I think, and would avoid all kinds of misunderstandings. For instance, I give you one example of the error that results from applying the notion of 'dialects': I don't remember a single edition of a text where you don't see as a comment that the language is a mixture. In French tradition there is always a dialect mixture — of Picardian and Waloonian or Picardian and Parisian. This is very characteristic of the use of the word 'dialect'. You have an idealised dialect and that is where the difficulty begins. You don't find it in reality, of course because it's an idealised entity you have created. So that is why we in Amsterdam express ourselves in terms of a matrix of features and geographical points. There is no need then to invoke notions that are not real.

Benskin: *Je ne regrette rien.* I'm sorry if I gave that impression.

Hans Frede Nielsen: Concerning the maps, my main worry is, how much qualitative analysis do you have to do to them before you can expose them to statistical analysis? If you take, for example, the top left map, how much interference is there, how much noise is in the channel? Do you have to work this out in each case? What about the *at* map, does *at* replace *to* in other functions? You have to ask a lot of questions about these maps before you can expose them to statistical analysis. And then the question is, how much statistical material do you need in order to come up with something? That is a lot of work, and it's not an easy matter.

* * * * * *

The discussion was at this point brought to a close because time was short. In answer to Hans Frede Nielsen's questions in the final contribution, Michael Benskin writes as follows:

Benskin: The idea that a statistical treatment is vitiated by data that are incomplete or otherwise less than perfect, is to misunderstand what a great deal of statistics is about. It is precisely because our data are inadequate that we need principled ways of deciding what conclusions can reasonably be drawn from them, and — this is the crucial point — what confidence we can place in those conclusions.[4] Why should we expect discursive and unprincipled evaluations of quantitative data to advance our understanding if the subject-matter falls within the humanities, when we accept that such procedures have no place at all in that more reliable body of knowledge we call 'science'?

* * * * * *

After the Colloquium, Anthonij Dees and Michael Benskin talked further about matters arising from the latter's paper. A version of that discussion is here provided by Michael Benskin:

Benskin: I seem to have given you the wrong impression yesterday: I have no wish to cling on to the idea of dialect areas for their own sake, and for myself much prefer to think in terms of a dialect continuum.

---

4 For a classic account, see R.A. Fisher 1935 *The Design of Experiments*. Oliver and Boyd: London and Edinburgh.

Dees: That is my own position. I gave up long ago the idea that dialect divisions of that kind are at all useful. I think we agree on this.

Benskin: Even so, the way that patterns of distribution recur is of some interest. If we allow that dialectal similarities reflect social networks, then the closer the dialectal similarities, the more cohesive we may expect the corresponding network to be. Would you accept the idea that dialect is indexical (or may be), that it may reflect social groupings for which we have otherwise inadequate means of identification, or no means at all?

Dees: I think there is a difference here between the motives of Anglicists and Romance scholars. You are much concerned with settlement history, and for this, dialect maps have been important. If you classify, of course, you must analyse the patterns of distribution first. But I do not think that these regional classifications are important for understanding the system of the language.

Benskin: And in your own work, it is the system that has always concerned you?

Dees: Yes, that is so.

Panel IV

WORD GEOGRAPHY

IV.1 Word Geography: Previous Approaches and Achievements

Terry Hoad

What I would like to do is to remind you of some of the main work done in the field of Middle English word geography in the past, and to offer a few remarks about how this work can most effectively be built upon.

As has been frequently remarked on by scholars over a longish period of time, the history of word-geographical studies in Middle English has been a disappointing one. In 1937 Rolf Kaiser, in the preface to the book which has remained virtually the only large-scale attempt to establish some of the geographical boundaries of word uses in Middle English, declared that 'up to now word geography has been a stepchild of English philology'.[1] (Kaiser was speaking, of course, with reference to all periods of English.) Little had changed 45 years later, when Michael Benskin and Margaret Laing commented that 'the study of M.E. word geography remains ... in a thoroughly rudimentary state' (Benskin and Laing 1981: 106); and Anne Hudson almost simultaneously noted that 'in the investigation of Middle English dialects the field of vocabulary has been a neglected area' (Hudson 1983: 74).

In what work there has been, we have been offered two principal paradigms. The first is that represented most fully by the work of Kaiser. Kaiser, as is well-known, based his investigation on an examination of the points at which the more southerly version of *Cursor Mundi* replaced words used in the northerly, and presumably more original, version. The assumption behind such an examination is that it will catch the more southerly 'translator' revealing which words in his source he is unwilling to use. A further assumption is

---

[1] Kaiser (1937: v): 'Die Wortgeographie war bisher ein Stiefkind der anglistischen Philologie.'

that such unwillingness will tend to be due to the words not being current in his dialect.

Kaiser was alert to at least some of the possible traps. For example, he recognised the obvious point that one text alone will not yield conclusive evidence for the dialectal distribution of a given word. Sometimes a word in the northern version of *Cursor Mundi* that is replaced by the more southerly 'translator' will nevertheless be evidenced in other texts of known southern provenance. In such cases, the *Cursor Mundi* 'translator's' avoidance of the word cannot be seen simply as a matter of regional variation in vocabulary. He may have avoided it because, say, it seemed to him too old-fashioned, or because he just misunderstood.[2]

A more recent application of Kaiser's principles is to be found in Anne Hudson's analysis of the vocabulary changes in a south-to-north 'translation' of the standard Lollard sermon-cycle (Hudson 1983). She says of Kaiser's choice of the versions of *Cursor Mundi* as the basis for his work that

> it is difficult to challenge the theory that led to this decision: if a true comparison between dialects is to be made, there must be no chance that the discrepancies in vocabulary between two texts could be explicable on the basis of their differing interests. The easiest way to exclude factors of subject matter, register or audience is to use a single text, whose original provenance is known, and a derivative copy in another dialect.
>
> (Hudson 1983: 74)

Such studies reveal in the first place the lexical choices of individual authors and copyists, choices made in the particular conditions of their composing or copying. It may be that those choices reflect general regional habits of word use, and in so far as the results can be replicated in investigations of other texts extant in alternative versions, there will perhaps be reason for slightly more confidence that a dialectal division has been uncovered, rather than a more idiosyncratic set of preferences such as I mentioned a moment or two ago.

---

[2] Kaiser (1937: 16–17): 'Manches Wort, das nach dem blossen Handschriftenvergleich des C.M. als dialektgesichert gelten konnte, musste daraufhin fortgelassen werden; denn wenn ein Wort auch ständig von dem Abschreiber T geändert wird — etwa 'drightin', das von Ms. T niemals übernommen und nach genauer Zählung 221 mal ersetzt wird, — und es ist trotzdem aus einwandfreien Südtexten zu belegen — 'drightin' aus Shoreham, K. Alis., Arth. & Merl. etc., — so ist das betreffende Wort für eine geographische Bestimmung nicht zu verwerten. Ein Teil dieser Wörter wurde von Ms. T wahrscheinlich als überaltert empfunden und deshalb durch lebendigeres Sprachgut ersetzt, ein anderer infolge mangelnder Sachkenntnis missverstanden.'

The other main paradigm is that most clearly represented by those scholars associated with the work that has led to the *Linguistic Atlas of Late Mediaeval English,* and set forth in particular in articles written by Angus McIntosh. The starting-point in this case is not the comparison of a 'translated' text with its source (although the study of the practice of 'translation' of texts is of course a central concern of the scholars in question). It is rather the assembling of a very large body of data, from manuscripts the provenance of which has been established, on the basis of which data the occurrence of particular words can be observed, and here it is in the first place the quantity of material which offers grounds for believing that the patterns of distribution observed are to some extent reliable. The value of comparing parallel and dialectally distinct versions of a given text is also recognized in this approach to word-geographical questions. (See, for example, McIntosh 1978 [1989: 101].)

It is the very quantity of the material to be assembled which has so far prevented there being published more than a few illustrative examples of this mode of inquiry. As Angus McIntosh has repeatedly pointed out, what would be needed in order to carry out a more systematic investigation is the collaborative effort of a sizable number of scholars, together with financial support for the establishment of the necessary corpus of texts. (See, e.g., McIntosh 1973 [1989: 93–94]; McIntosh 1978 [1989: 102].)

There has tended not to be much explicit definition of the aims of 'word-geographical' studies in Middle English. Rather, it seems to have been generally assumed that the goal of identifying the patterns of distribution of words is one that is so self-explanatory as to need little further comment. Kaiser, after a few more general remarks, announced that 'the goal is the establishment of a list of words the occurrence of which — alongside other, more strictly grammatical criteria — will make possible the localisation of a text'.[3] For him, therefore, any theoretical issues raised by the topic of word geography itself are almost immediately passed over, the focus of attention being on the use to be made of the conclusions arrived at.

There has frequently been an at least implicit aim of identifying the distinctive words used in various geographical areas to refer to the 'same' concept. This is, of course, the task which most Modern English

---

[3] Kaiser (1937: 1): 'das Ziel ist ... die Aufstellung einer Liste von Wörten, durch deren Vorkommen die Lokalisierung eines Textes — neben den Mitteln der anderen, im engeren Sinn grammatischen Kriterien — ermöglicht wird.'

dialectologists have set themselves with regard to vocabulary. As Martyn Wakelin puts it:

> Word geography is concerned with the regional distribution of expressions for various notions, e.g. the ant, the pigsty, the stream, the pantry, chitterlings, freckles, fainting, prettiness, cold, a door being ajar, etc., and in the deductions, linguistic and non-linguistic, which can be made from examining such distributions.
>
> (Wakelin 1972 [1977]: 64)

As far as Middle English is concerned, a similar conception of the aims of word-geographical studies seems to lie behind such remarks as these (by Angus McIntosh):

> The implications ... for word geography are as follows. The information provided by the *Atlas* will make it possible for anyone to search a large number of now for the first time localised or localisable texts for their individual dialectal peculiarities. What, for example, are the facts about the medieval equivalents of the modern English word 'church'? Is it the case that the four forms *kirk, chirch, church,* and *cherch* (without going into further shades of formal distinction) each have reasonably well-defined areas of use, or are they scattered haphazardly about the map? ... Or we may want to know whether *stern* 'star' (ON *starn*) is adequately characterised by being described as the 'northern' equivalent of southern *sterre* (OE *steorra*).
>
> (McIntosh 1973 [1989: 87])

The underlying assumption seems to be that there is a system of 'meanings' shared by all speakers and realised by various systems of phonological (or orthographical) words, it being the task of the word geographer to determine the latter systems.

The system of 'meanings' is not always matched in each dialect by a system of words with an identical number of terms. For example, it is recognised that sometimes a given word will have in one dialect a wider range of meanings than it has in another. To quote McIntosh again,

> the noun *fare* in the sense 'gear', 'accoutrements', seems to be pretty strictly confined to the North and to parts of the North Midlands though it is used much more widely in other meanings.
>
> (McIntosh 1973 [1989: 91])

As will be seen, this conception of aims has been very closely tied in with the methodology of Middle English word-geographical investigations. It is capable of producing valuable results, and for a large part of the vocabulary of the language — in particular, for the more 'referential' words — it is no doubt an obvious starting-point. However, it would clearly be a mistake to work on the unspoken assumption that the lexical *structures* in various dialects are going to be the same, and that all that has to be ascertained is which phonological or orthographic words are used to represent which meanings.

Those who have ventured into the field of Middle English word geography have on the whole not been very precise as to what kinds of distinction between 'words' are relevant to their studies. Kaiser offers some indications of his practice. After noting other constraints dictated by the volume and complexity of his material, he informs his readers that

> for the same reason less significant variations in spelling were left out of account, particularly since what is important in this investigation is always the identity of the word-form as a concept and not orthographic differentiation. Neither, therefore, were any examples included where their avoidance resulted from a differing historical development in phonology. Variants which are explicable as the products of differing linguistic tendencies are similarly excluded. Among these I count the numerous contractions in the north: *ta* (*take*), *ma* (*make*), *tan, tas; bus* (*behoves*) etc.; and also the particular frequency of '*n-*' negation in the south: *nis* (*ne is*), *nere* (*ne were*), *nabbe, nadde, nolde*, etc.[4]

McIntosh, as we have seen, takes the variants *kirk, chirch, church* and *cherch* by way of illustration of a word-geographical distribution in Middle English. Benskin and Laing, discussing different levels of translation between dialects by medieval scribes, note the difficulty of deciding where the lines are to be drawn:

> It may of course be arguable whether a given item represents translation lexical rather than orthographic (e.g., *kirk ~ cherch* 'church'), orthographic rather than morphological (e.g. *moch ~ mekyll* 'much'), or morphological rather than lexical (e.g., *hi ~ þei* 'they'). In many cases, classification will depend upon the preferred view as to historical origins: thus, for example, *at*

---

4 Kaiser (1937: 14): 'Aus dem gleichen Grunde blieben weniger wichtige Unterschiede der Schreibung unberücksichtigt, zumal es ja in dieser Untersuchung immer auf das Bekanntsein des Wortkörpers als Begriff und nicht auf die orthographische Differenzierung ankommt. Deshalb wurden auch keine Belege aufgenommen, deren Vermeidung wegen einer verschiedene lautgeschichtlichen Entwicklung erfolgte. Ebenso sind auch Abweichungen nicht eingereiht, die sich aus verscheidenartigen Sprachtendenzen erklären. Hierzu rechne ich auch die zahlreichen Kontraktionen für den Norden: ta (take), ma (make), tan, tas; bus (behoves) etc.; wie auch etwa die besondere Häufigkeit der 'n-' Negation für den Süden: nis (ne is), nere (ne were), nabbe, nadde, nolde, etc.'

rel. part. may in the dialects of some areas be a reduced form of *þat* (cf. the construction *þat at* 'that which'), but in the Scandinavian parts of England it may be better accounted as a loanword; the contrast between *at* and *þat* may accordingly be regarded as either morphological or lexical, depending on the linguistic context.

(Benskin and Laing 1981: 94)

In terms of the assignation of words to dialect areas, Kaiser worked essentially with a division into North and South. As has since been pointed out more than once,[5] this is too crude a classification to be of much use in the localisation of texts. It reflects in a general way, however, a contrast of long-standing and considerable importance, and Kaiser's material is so far the most substantial contribution to the establishment of word-geographical patterns in Middle English.

The North–South division bears a clear relationship to the Anglian–West Saxon division that forms a basis for much of the work that has been done on Old English word geography. Thanks largely to the more manageable volume of data, much more has been achieved in the earlier period by way of determining the dialectal restrictions affecting Old English words. Scholars have hardly begun to work out the relationship between patterns of distribution of words in the Anglo-Saxon period and such patterns in the Middle English period.

One recent attempt to do so with reference to a particular group of Middle English texts is Janet Bately's examination of the vocabulary of the so-called 'Katherine Group' (Bately 1988). Bately's procedure is essentially to look for occurrences — in Katherine Group texts and also, for comparison, in other early Middle English texts from the Midlands — of the Middle English descendants of words which have been identified as characteristically Anglian in the Old English period. Her conclusions are that the Katherine Group is not strongly marked by the use of what had previously been distinctively Anglian words, and nor is this the result of the ousting of traditionally Anglian words through the adoption of 'the literary standard of the late West Saxon Winchester School' (Bately 1988: 64 and 66).

In her article Bately does not explicitly address the question of what the full geographical range of use of the previously Anglian words

---

5 For example, Borroff (1962: 38): 'The criterion of vocabulary developed by Kaiser proved of limited value in the determination of regional provenience. By the very nature of his material, he was committed to a broad division of England into 'North' and 'South', exclusive of an indeterminate Midland area — obviously a much less comprehensive and exact system than that afforded by the study of dialect differences.'

might have been in the early Middle English period. Her work nevertheless points the way to a kind of investigation which will be necessary for the fullest possible understanding of the word geography of Middle English.

This has been only a brief sketch of the current state of word-geographical research in Middle English, but I hope it will have succeeded in highlighting at least some of the main lines of previous research as well as indicating some potentially rewarding avenues for future work.

References

Bately J. 1988 On some aspects of the vocabulary of the West Midlands in the early Middle Ages: the language of the Katherine Group. In: Kennedy E.D., Waldron R., Wittig J.S. (eds.) *Medieval English Studies Presented to George Kane*. D.S. Brewer: Cambridge, pp. 55–77

Benskin M., Laing M. 1981 Translations and *Mischsprachen* in Middle English manuscripts. In: Benskin M., Samuels M.L. (eds.) *So Meny People Longages and Tonges: Philological essays in Scots and mediaeval English presented to Angus McIntosh*. Published by the editors: Edinburgh, pp. 55–106

Borroff M. 1962 *Sir Gawain and the Green Knight: A Stylistic and Metrical Study*. Yale Studies in English 152. New Haven and London

Hudson A. 1983 Observations on a northerner's vocabulary. In: Stanley E.G., Gray D. (eds.) *Five Hundred Years of Words and Sounds: A Festschrift for Eric Dobson*. D.S. Brewer: Cambridge, pp. 74–83

Kaiser R. 1937 *Zur Geographie des mittelenglischen Wortschatzes*. Palaestra 205. Leipzig

Laing M. 1989 (ed.) *Middle English Dialectology: Essays on some principles and problems*. Aberdeen University Press: Aberdeen

McIntosh A. 1973 [1989] Word geography in the lexicography of medieval English. *Annals of the New York Academy of Sciences* 211: 55–66; repr. in Laing M. 1989, pp. 86–97

McIntosh A. 1978 [1989] Middle English word-geography: its potential role in the study of the long-term impact of the Scandinavian settlements upon English. In: Anderson T., Sandred K.I. (eds.) *The Vikings: Proceedings of the Symposium of the Faculty of Arts of Uppsala University, June 6–9, 1977*. Uppsala, pp. 124–30; repr. in Laing M. 1989, pp. 98–105

Wakelin M. 1972 [1977] *English Dialects: An Introduction*. The Athlone Press: London; rev. edn. 1977

IV.2 Sources and Techniques for the Study of Middle English Word Geography

Robert E. Lewis

Nearly 20 years ago Angus McIntosh suggested that for an adequate study of Middle English word geography we would need approximately 10,000 words from each of 500 texts of the B-variety (that is, those in which the scribe has 'converted' his exemplar 'into his own kind of language'), chosen so that they would 'cover the whole country fairly evenly and fairly densely, so that no sizeable part of England is unrepresented', and for most texts to be 'of considerable length and ... offer ... a reasonable expectation of finding examples of a large number of common words in them' (McIntosh 1973 [1989: 92–93]). When put into a computer-concordanced format, the total number of words would be approximately 4,500,000. Some of this data could of course come from printed editions, but in order to achieve the proper density, many of the texts would have to be transcribed from the manuscripts or from photographic reproductions of them. So far as I know, no one has begun to collect the data in this systematic way; indeed, even the reduced version that McIntosh suggested a few years later — 'a set of only one hundred substantial dialectal texts selected on the basis of their providing between them an optimal spread of geographical coverage' McIntosh (1977 [1989: 102]) — has not been attempted.

However, what we do have is a great deal of Middle English data of the kind appropriate for the study of word geography, much of it collected during the years since McIntosh made his first suggestion, and my theme in these brief remarks is that while this data is not ideal, it is full enough and useful enough for us to make a start now on the long overdue study of Middle English word geography.

First of all, we have the *Linguistic Atlas of Late Mediaeval English*, in which a large number of texts have, for the first time been localised, giving us the necessary underpinnings for our study.

Second, we now have a number of Middle English texts in machine-readable format. Most of you will know about the Oxford Text Archive, which includes for the Middle English period such important texts as the *Speculum Vitae*, the *Prick of Conscience*, the *Siege of Jerusalem*, the Wycliffite sermons, and the works of the Katherine Group, and about the diachronic part of the Helsinki Corpus of English Texts, which contains Middle English extracts from all parts of the period and from the major dialect areas totalling approximately 600,000 words. These can now be supplemented by individual collections. For example, in our library at the University of Michigan we have in machine-readable format such dialectally useful things as the *Alliterative Morte Arthure*, all of the documents in John Fisher's *Anthology of Chancery English*, the Harley Lyrics, both texts of Layamon's *Brut*, the two manuscripts of the *Owl and the Nightingale*, volume I of the Paston Letters, and the two manuscripts of the northern *Octavian*. Other libraries and scholars no doubt have additional electronic texts that could be made available to interested researchers. Though this data is not being collected in the systematic way that would be most useful for word-geographical studies, it is precisely the kind we need, and more of it is becoming available each year.

Third, there are a number of concordances of Middle English texts now in print; when they are based on localised manuscripts, as many of them are (for example, the poems of the *Pearl* poet, the Towneley plays, some of the lyrics), they are nearly as useful for word-geographical studies as the texts in machine-readable format.

Fourth, we have a great deal of data, primarily printed but in a few cases unprinted, for some of those works 'of a popular nature' that exist in multiple versions and multiple manuscripts and that constitute the most convenient and often the most enlightening data for a study of word geography. Those of you who work in Middle English will know the kinds of texts I mean, so a few brief examples will suffice:

(a)   We now have published transcripts of six of the nine manuscripts of the *Cursor Mundi*, five in Morris's edition and the sixth in the nearly completed edition of the southern revision begun by Sarah Horrall, with substantive variants from the other southern manuscripts; the dozen or so main hands of eight of these nine manuscripts have been given approximate placings in the *Atlas*.

(b) The important Lincoln's Inn MS Hale 150, from Shropshire, is in parallel-text editions of *Arthur and Merlin* and *Kyng Alisaunder*, with variants from this manuscript in the editions of *Libeaus* and the *Siege of Troy*.

(c) We have full editions of two of the important early manuscripts of the South English Legendary that we can examine side by side, Corpus Christi Cambridge 145 from Berkshire and Hampshire, supplemented by Harley 2277 from Somerset, and Laud Miscellaneous 108 originally from Gloucestershire, and in addition for certain legends we can now compare these manuscripts with a north-east Midland revision in Cambridge University Library Additional 3039 (and three related manuscripts), and for another legend we have a Norfolk version in St John's Cambridge 28 (B.6) that can be compared with the fragmentary Laud text.

(d) And there are other texts and other editions of a similar kind: parallel-text editions of two localised manuscripts of the *Parlement of the Thre Ages*, and two of the *Awntyrs of Arthure*, for example; or the editions of *King Horn* in at least two localised manuscripts, or *Sir Orfeo* in three.

Some of the data on these popular texts is unpublished. For example, Derek Britton has full collations of the 18 northern manuscripts of the *Prick of Conscience*; I have some 40,000 words in my collations of the eight manuscripts of the *Stimulus Consciencie Minor*, based on the *Prick of Conscience*, six of which have been localised. Thomas Heffernan has collations of four manuscripts of the *Northern Homily Cycle*; I assume, having known him, that the late James Gordon has or had full collations of the 39 or more manuscripts of the *Speculum Vitae*; and Lister Matheson has collations of a number of manuscripts of the prose *Brut*.

With a few exceptions, this material is not in machine-readable format and it would be difficult to use it in its present form for a systematic study of word geography, but I want to emphasise that it is nearly all in parallel-text format, most of the manuscripts have been localised, and the material can easily be used for individual word-geographical studies.

Finally, there is the *Middle English Dictionary*, which is the largest repository of analysed lexical data available; it is nearly finished, with the last part of S published last month [March 1992] and the first of T to be published next year [1993], and with editing nearing the end of V. The parts from Q on are already in computer-readable form, and we are planning to have the earlier letters optically scanned so that the whole *MED* can be made available in this form. Since the letter G at least we have tried to give as full a representation of specific dialect texts as we can in the space we have, and beginning with the first volume of S, and especially in the second volume, I have begun to note when a word appears only in one dialect or in two related dialects.

When the *Atlas* appeared in 1986, I hoped that we would be able to make use of its dialect data, both to extend and to refine our own dialect lists, which are based primarily on the work of Moore, Meech and Whitehall and Oakden, and we began to put together a computerised tool that would allow easy interchange between the *MED* short titles and the geographical labels in the *Atlas*. We finally concluded, however, that we were so far along in our work that it would be both too time-consuming and too great a departure from past practice to make a complete change-over, and we suspended work on the computerised tool, though I hasten to add that we use the *Atlas* data to confirm, extend, or call into question the dialect labels that we do use.

Earlier this year, as I was beginning to think about the subject of this panel, I returned to this computerised tool and revised and added to it. I have given you a sample of it on the handout,[1] and one copy of the full (but still incomplete) version is circulating. It is arranged [Appendix 1] by library, manuscript, and hand or language according to the repository list in volume I of the *Atlas*, with all the relevant *MED* short titles listed under each individual entry, and with the geographical designation from the *Atlas* to the right of the entry. By a simple program the whole list can be alphabetised by *MED* short titles, with the geographical labels attached, or by geographical label with an alphabetised list of the relevant *MED* short titles underneath. Samples of these two permutations are also on the handout [Appendix 2 and 3].

I tried this tool out on a word I was reviewing last month, the verb *tharnen* meaning 'to lack, lose', derived from Old Norse. The word is in Kaiser's lists as a northern word, but we have additional evidence for it in our files, and I wanted to see if Kaiser's observation could be refined. The list of short titles is on the handout, with geographical labels to the right [Appendix 4]. Most of the labels are from the *Atlas*;

---

[1] Reproduced here on pp. 211–213 as an appendix.

the ones not there I have taken either from the *MED*'s lists and my own analysis (for the Rawlinson manuscript of the *Dialogue Between St Bernard and the Virgin*) or, for the early texts, from Margaret Laing's article in the Riddy anthology, *Regionalism in Late Medieval Manuscripts and Texts* (Laing 1991).

You will see from the localisations that the heartland of the word is the North, chiefly Yorkshire, including the West Riding, and that the area of familiarity extends, even at an early date, southward into Lincolnshire and west Norfolk, and perhaps as far as Peterborough (though I am reserving judgment on this for the moment, since the example in the *Peterborough Chronicle* is in the pre-1122 copied section and has a form that could indicate that it may be derived from an unattested Old English original). This general northern and north-east Midlands area, extending down to just below The Wash, is what one would expect of a word of Norse origin, but already that is a refinement of Kaiser's designation northern. And a more detailed look further adds to the geographical picture. Three texts appear from the localisations in the *Atlas* to be outside the general area: the *Avowing of King Arthur* from south Lancashire, the version of Rolle's *Psalter* in Laud Miscellaneous 286 from Derbyshire, and a Lollard interpolated version of this *Psalter* from Huntingdonshire. But the *Avowing* is based on the northern original, as the rhymes indicate, and the example of *tharnen* in the text is in rhyme position, suggesting that it was also in the northern original. The Derbyshire example may simply indicate a slight extension of the geographical area, since there are a number of examples already in texts from the West Riding of Yorkshire, or — since the original *Psalter* was presumably from Yorkshire — it may be from the original and was copied by the scribe whether or not he understood it. And finally, the Huntingdonshire example in the Lollard interpolated version of Rolle's *Psalter* turns out to be an erroneous form, *parve*, suggesting that the interpolator (or scribe) did not understand the more northerly word *tharne* and produced a corruption based on a verb from Old English with a similar meaning, *tharven* 'to need'.

To supplement the inquiry, I looked at the other categories of data that I mentioned a few minutes ago. The word is not in the *Atlas*, of course: it is too limited geographically. Nor does it appear in any of the concordances or electronic texts and databases available to me; in the Helsinki Corpus, which Matti Rissanen has kindly searched for me, the word appears in no new texts (only three examples from *Havelok* already known from the *MED* files). No new evidence is of some

interest here, for it means that the word is not used in the primarily
London or south-east Midlands documents in Fisher's *Anthology of
Chancery English*, not used in volume I of the Paston Letters from
Norfolk, and not used in such south-west and south-west Midlands
texts as the Harley Lyrics, Layamon's *Brut*, and the *Owl and the
Nightingale*.

Of works that exist in multiple versions and multiple manuscripts,
the *Cursor Mundi* has the word in the Vespasian, Göttingen and Edinburgh manuscripts from the West Riding, whereas the Fairfax
manuscript from Lancashire and the manuscripts of the southern
revision substitute *want(e*. The Longleat manuscript of the *Metrical
Paraphrase of the Old Testament*, from somewhere in the Midlands,
omits the word that appears in the Selden manuscript from the West
Riding, suggesting that the Longleat scribe did not know the word.
Derek Britton has very kindly checked his collations for the example
from the *Prick of Conscience*, and of eleven manuscripts running at
this point five have *wante*, four of which are northern Middle English
or south-west Yorkshire, which may suggest that even in the northern
area the word was only in restricted use. My collations for the
Stimulus Consciencie Minor contain one example of the word, in the
base manuscript, Additional 33995, from north-west Yorkshire (the
other northern manuscript, Wellesley 8, closely related to it, is
unfortunately not running at this point). The other four localisable
manuscripts, from the north central Midlands (Staffordshire, Derbyshire, and Leicestershire), substitute either *want* or *lese*.

Naturally, some further analysis of these examples would need to
be done before we could make a definitive statement about *tharnen*,
but you can see how the cumulative evidence from the various
sources available to us — printed, unprinted and electronic — can
produce a pretty clear picture of the geographical correlations of an
individual word, and, further, how studies such as this one, when
combined with other, similar studies, would begin to produce a larger
word-geographical picture. I am not suggesting that this is the ideal
way to go about the study of Middle English word geography: one
would still like to have the body of computer-concordanced data
gathered in a systematic way called for by McIntosh, and we should
continue to promote that idea with institutions and granting agencies,
but the data we have is serviceable, the amount of it is increasing each
year, especially the electronic variety, and the time to make a start is
right now.

Appendix

Samples of a Computer-generated Match of MED Source Texts with
Language Provenances given in *LALME*

1. Listed by Library and Manuscript

]London, British, Library, Arundel 286, Hand B   {Warwicks
a1425 <u>Benj.Minor</u> (Arun)
a1425 <u>Life Soul</u> (Arun)
a1425 <u>MChristi</u> (Arun)
a1425 <u>12 PTrib.(3)</u> (Arun)

]London, British Library, Arundel 327   {Suffolk
1447 Bokenham <u>Sts.Gloss</u> (Arun)
?a1500 Bokenham <u>Sts.Gloss</u> (Arun)

]London, British Library, Arundel 334   {Cheshire
?c1425 <u>Arun.Cook.Recipes</u> (Arun 334)

]London, British Library, Arundel 396   {Suffolk
?c1450 Cpgr.<u>St.Kath</u>. (Arun 396)

]London, British Library, Arundel 507   {Durham
a1425 <u>Ancr.Warning</u> (Arun)
a1425 <u>For as MMS</u> (Arun)
a1425 <u>HBk.GDei</u> (Arun)
a1425 <u>Medit.Pass.(1)</u> (Arun)
a1425 Rolle <u>EDormio</u> (Arun)
a1425 Rolle <u>FLiving</u> (Arun)
a1425 <u>Synful man loke vp</u> (Arun)
a1425 <u>When þe hee</u> (Arun)

]London, British Library, Cotton Appendix 7, Hand A   {Lincs
a1425 <u>Castle Love(4)</u> (CotApp)

]London, British Library, Cotton Caligula A.xi   {Gloucs
c1325(c1300) <u>Glo.Chron.A</u> (Clg)

]London, British Library, Cotton Claudius A.ii, Hands A-C   {Staffs
a1450 Mirk <u>Fest</u>. (Cld)
a1450(a1415) Mirk <u>Fest.Alk</u>. (Cld)
a1450(a1415) Mirk <u>Fest.Suppl</u>. (Cld)
a1450(a1415) Mirk <u>Fest.Win</u>. (Cld)

]London, British Library, Cotton Claudius A.ii, Hand D   {Salop
a1450 <u>Form Excom.(1)</u> (Cld)
a1450(a1425) Mirk <u>IPP</u> (Cld)

]London, British Library, Cotton Claudius E.iii   {Leics
a1500(v.d.) <u>Knighton Chron.Contin</u>. (Cld E.3)
?a1500 <u>Wycl.Eucharist(1)</u> (Cld)

2. Listed by Incipit

c1450 <u>A babel</u> (Sln)	Norfolk
1372 <u>A barge</u> (Adv)	Norfolk
c1430 <u>A celuy</u> (Cmb)	Cambs
a1500 <u>A chyld ys born(2)</u> (StJ-C)	Norfolk
a1500 <u>A ferly thing</u> (BodPoet)	Norfolk
c1475 <u>A hart harborowith</u> (Brm)	Norfolk
1372 <u>A iesu so</u> (Adv)	Norfolk
a1450 <u>A Lacrim.</u> (Bod)	Cambs
a1500 <u>A man þt will</u> (Cmb)	Derbys
c1450 <u>A man þt xuld</u> (Sln)	Norfolk
a1500 <u>A man was þe fyrst</u> (BodPoet)	Norfolk
a1300 <u>A Mayde Cristes</u> (Jes-O)	Herefords
c1450 <u>A newe song</u> (Sln)	Norfolk
a1500 <u>A patre unigenitus</u> (BodPoet)	Norfolk
a1450 <u>A pryncypal poynth</u> (Trin-C)	Norfolk
1372 <u>A schelde</u> (Adv)	Norfolk
a1450 <u>A solitari here</u> (Fst)	Norfolk
1372 <u>A sory buerech</u> (Adv)	Norfolk
c1430 <u>A soun</u> (Cmb)	Cambs
c1250 <u>A þeif</u> (Trin-C)	Worcs
a1400 <u>A tokne</u> (Hrl)	Warwicks
a1400 <u>A tresour</u> (Hrl)	Warwicks
c1250 *<u>A vidue</u> (Trin-C)	Worcs
c1325 <u>A wayle whyt</u> (Hrl)	Herefords
1591(?a1425) *<u>Abbey HG</u> (Corp-O 155)	Lincs
c1465 <u>Abbey HG</u> (Hrl 1704)	Leics
c1390 <u>Abbey HG</u> (Vrn)	Worcs
?a1550(?a1475) <u>Abbot & C.</u> (Hrl)	No dialect
a1500 <u>ABC Arist.</u> (Cmb)	Derbys
a1500 <u>ABC Arist.</u> (Hrl 1706)	Northants
c1450 <u>ABC Arist.</u> (Lamb)	Mixed: (Hunts S; Northants E; Beds N)
c1250 *<u>Abel wes looset</u> (Trin-C)	Worcs
?a1425 <u>Abyde gudmen</u> (Rwl)	Yorks NR
a1450 <u>Abyde I hope</u> (Trin-C)	Norfolk
c1330 <u>Adam & E.(1)</u> (Auch)	Middx
c1390(?a1325) <u>Adam & E.(2)</u> (Vrn)	Worcs
a1475 <u>Adam & E.(3)</u> (Hrl)	Surrey
a1425 <u>Adam & E.(3)</u> (Wht)	Soke / Ely NW (?)
a1425 <u>Adam & E.(4)</u> (Bod)	Herts
c1450 <u>Adam lay</u> (Sln)	Norfolk
c1450 <u>Adam our fader</u> (Sln)	Norfolk
a1500 <u>Add.Hymnal</u> (Add)	Leics
?a1450 <u>Add.Mir.Virg.</u> (Add)	Leics
a1475 <u>Add.12195 Accedence</u> (Add 12195)	Norfolk
c1400 <u>Aelred Inst.(1)</u> (Vrn)	Worcs
a1450 <u>Aelred Inst.(2)</u> (Bod)	Cambs
a1475 <u>Afore mete</u> (Rwl)	Oxon
a1500 <u>Agnus Castus</u> (Hrl)	Wilts
a1500 <u>Agnus Castus</u> (Ld)	Herefords
?a1450 <u>Agnus Castus</u> (Stockh)	Norfolk
a1425 <u>Al es bot</u> (Glb)	NME
a1300 <u>Al fram ehvuele</u> (Em)	Wilts
1372 <u>Al oure wele</u> (Adv)	Norfolk
a1400 <u>Al þe ioʒe</u> (Hrl)	Norfolk
a1500 <u>Alas howe schale</u> (Pen)	Wales

3. Listed under County Designation

Salop

a1425 <u>Arth. & M.</u> (LinI)
c1455 Chaucer <u>CT</u> (Rwl F.141)
a1500 <u>Clerk & H.</u> (Add)
?a1425 <u>Const.Masonry(1)</u> (Roy)
a1450 <u>Form Excom. (1)</u> (Cld)
c1425 Hilton <u>CPerf</u> (StJ-O)
a1425 <u>KAlex</u> (LinI)
a1425 <u>Libeaus</u> (LinI)
a1450(a1425) Mirk <u>IPP</u> (Cld)
c1450 <u>Peniarth Accedence(2)</u> (Pen)
c1450 <u>Peniarth Comparacio(2)</u> (Pen)
c1450 <u>Peniarth Informacio(2)</u> (Pen)
a1425 <u>Siege Troy(1)</u> (LinI)
c1450(?a1400) <u>SLChrist</u> (Add)
c1425 <u>Treat.10 Com.</u> (StJ-O)
1370-2 <u>Y am by-wylt</u> (Shrop)

4. Word Geography

MED Texts Containing *tharnen* v.

c1450(?c1425) <u>Avow.Arth.</u> (Ir)	Lancs
a1425 <u>Ben.Rule(1)</u> (Lnsd)	Yorks
?a1425(?a1350) Castleford <u>Chron.</u>(Göt)	Yorks
a1400(a1325) <u>Cursor</u> (Vsp)	WRY
a1400 <u>Cursor</u> (Göt)	WRY
a1400 <u>Cursor</u> (Phys-E)	WRY
?a1425 <u>Dial.Bern. & V. (1)</u> (Rwl)	NME
?c1400 <u>Dial.Bern. & V. (1)</u> (Tbr)	NME
(c1300) <u>Havelok</u> (Ld)	W Norfolk
c1450 <u>Interp.Rolle.Ps.</u> (Bod 288)	Hunts
c1425 <u>Mandev.(2)</u> (Eg)	NRY
c1450(a1425) <u>MOTest.</u> (Seld)	WRY
a1425(c1300) <u>NHom.(1) Alex.</u> (Ashm)	NME
a1425 <u>NHom.(1) Alex.</u> (Cmb)	NME
a1425 (?c1375) <u>NHom.(3) Leg.</u> (Hrl)	NME
c1400 <u>NHom.(3) Leg.</u> (Tbr)	NME
?c1200 <u>Orm.</u> (Jun)	S Lincs
a1425(a1400) <u>PConsc.</u> (Glb)	NME
a1121 <u>Peterb.Chron.</u> (Ld)	?Peterborough
a1425(c1340) Rolle <u>Psalter</u> (Ld 286), Hand G	Derbys
?c1400(c1340) Rolle <u>Psalter</u> (Sid)	Lincs
a1500(c1340) Rolle <u>Psalter</u> (UC 64)	Yorks
a1500(a1460) <u>Towneley Pl.</u> (Hnt)	WRY
c1450(?a1400) <u>Wars Alex.</u> (Ashm)	Durham
a1500 <u>Wars Alex.</u> (Dub)	Durham or Northumberland
a1450 <u>Yk.Pl.</u> (Add), Hand B	S of York

References

Kaiser R. 1937 *Zur Geographie des mittelenglischen Wortschatzes.* Palaestra 205: Leipzig

Laing M. (ed.) 1989 *Middle English Dialectology: Essays on some principles and problems.* Aberdeen University Press: Aberdeen

Laing M. 1991 Anchor texts and literary manuscripts in early Middle English. In: Riddy F. (ed.) *Regionalism in Late Medieval Manuscripts and Texts.* D.S. Brewer: Cambridge

McIntosh A. 1973 [1989] Word geography in the lexicography of medieval English. *Annals of the New York Academy of Sciences* **211**: 55–66; repr. in Laing M. 1989, pp. 86–97

McIntosh A. 1977 [1989] Middle English word geography: its potential role in the study of the long-term impact of the Scandinavian settlements on English. In: Andersson T., Sandred K.I. (eds.) 1978 *The Vikings, Proceedings of the Symposium of the Faculty of Arts of Uppsala Univeristy, June 6-9, 1977.* Uppsala, pp. 124-30; repr. in Laing M. 1989, pp. 98–105

McIntosh A., Samuels M.L., Benskin M. 1986 *A Linguistic Atlas of Late Mediaeval English,* 4 vols. Aberdeen University Press: Aberdeen

IV.3 Place-names and Word Geography: some Words of Warning

Gillian Fellows-Jensen

Place-names can make an important contribution to word geography. If a name has been recorded in a written source and the locality it denotes can be identified, the name will in most cases provide an exact localisation for the lexical material it contains. The exploitation of onomastic material is not entirely straightforward, however, and I want to draw attention briefly to some of the pitfalls that may be encountered. I shall begin with settlement names, firstly because these are mostly well documented in early sources and secondly because sufficient work has been done on them to make it possible to compile reasonably comprehensive distribution maps. Unfortunately, however, the situation is usually less clear-cut than might appear from such maps. Hugh Smith's map of the distribution of the Old English generic *worþ* and its derivatives *worþig* and *worþign*, for example, shows that *worþ* was used to denote 'an enclosure for habitation' in place-names in the greater part of England (Smith 1956: map 3). Its absence from the Lake District and the northern and eastern parts of Yorkshire and its comparative rarity in Lincolnshire and eastern Leicestershire are presumably to be accounted for by the fact that many English place-names in these areas were replaced by names of Scandinavian origin in the course of the Viking settlements. In two other areas, however, the absence of *worþ* is compensated for by the occurrence of derivative forms. In the South-west there are *worþig*-forms. In addition to the instances on the map, *worþig*-names also occur in eastern Cornwall (Smith 1956 ii: 276; Svensson 1987: 121). The significant fact to be remembered in connexion with this element is that in independent use the derivative *worþig* eventually came to replace *worþ*. The *worþig*-names in the South-west are thus probably to be explained as dating from the period after *worþig* had supplanted *worþ* in the language and hence as being younger than the *worþ*-names further to the east. Whereas *worþ* occurs in place-names recorded as early as the 7th century, *worþig* was clearly still being used to coin place-names in Devon after the Norman Conquest. It has also been noted that *worþig* was occasionally used erroneously by West Saxon scribes for place-names whose original forms were in *-worþ*, particularly in counties such as Gloucestershire and Dorset. It has also been suggested that scribal influence accounts for the occurrence of *worþig* in Tamworth in Staffordshire and **Norþworþig*, the English name of the town which the Danes renamed as Derby (Cameron 1959: 446). Noting that the earliest spellings for Tamworth are in Mercian charters (e.g. *in Tamouuorðie* [781] 11; S 120), Margaret Gelling has argued that **Tamworþig* and **Norþworþig* are to be looked upon as true local forms and that *worþig* developed a special meaning in the Midlands, akin to that of *burh* (Gelling et al. 1970: 82, 179). **Norþworþig* would then probably have been so named to distinguish it from the royal seat of Tamworth. This special meaning of *worþig* must have been forgotten, however, for the generic in Tamworth had been assimilated to *worþ*, the normal form for the area, by the time of the compilation of Domesday Book. One fact is quite clear — the distribution of place-names in *-worþig* does not reflect the distribution of this word in the later Old English period, for that was much wider.

The second derivative of *worþ*, however, namely *worþign*, would seem to be a dialectal variant. Its occurrence in place-names in Herefordshire and Shropshire in particular, as well as in southern Lancashire and western parts of Cheshire, Staffordshire and Worcestershire and northern Gloucestershire (Smith 1956: 277; Smith 1964–65 iv: 139), fits well with its survival in West Midland dialects as *worthine* (*Oxford English Dictionary* s.v.). The boundary for *worþign*-names on Smith's map certainly needs to be pushed further eastwards in both Gloucestershire and Cheshire. I know, because it was in Northenden (*Norwordine* 1086) and Kenworthy (*Kenworthin* 13th century) (Dodgson 1970–81 i: 234–35) in north-east Cheshire that I grew up. In the former name *worþign* gradually became obscured, while in the latter it was eventually replaced by *worþig*. As an element in field-names, *worþign* occurs as far east as Derbyshire, Warwickshire and the West Riding of Yorkshire (Cameron 1959: 755; Gover et al. 1936: 334; Smith 1961–63 vii: 269).

It can certainly be difficult to determine the reliability of distribution maps of words that eventually became current in the standard language or a wider dialect area. Greater reliance can perhaps be placed on distribution maps of words with a permanently more restricted currency. OE *cert*, for example, is only recorded in place-names, although it survives in the Kent and Surrey dialects as *chart*, referring to 'a rough common, overgrown with gorse, broom, bracken etc.'. In place-names its only certain occurrences are in Kent and Surrey and in these two counties it is practically restricted to the light soils of the Lower Greensand outcrop (Darby 1963: 6–18). This locally restricted distribution does not, of course, mean that the word was only current in these areas but merely that it was only thought appropriate for sites with this particular type of light soil. The absence of place-names containing *cert* from other counties with comparable areas of light soils, however, suggests that its distribution was restricted to the South-east.

It is important not to jump to conclusions when interpreting the distribution patterns of place-name elements. There are many factors which need to be taken into consideration. Even experienced scholars make mistakes. It was long thought, for example, that the distribution patterns of place-names in -*holm(e)* and -*hulm(e)* reflected colonisation by Norwegians and Danes respectively. It is this interpretation which lies behind the fact that several maps of Scandinavian settlement in England show an enclave of Danes in the neighbourhood of Manchester (e.g. that in Loyn 1962). It was scholars based in Denmark who first realised that this explanation must be wrong (e.g. Fellows Jensen 1970–73: 201–206; Hald 1978 105–13). This is firstly because the normal spelling of the generic in Denmark is *holm*. The *hulm*-spellings without *a*-mutation only occur in Skåne and Bornholm. The second reason is that spellings in -*hulm* only occur sporadically in the major areas of Danish settlement in England and all these isolated spellings can be explained as conventional latinisations. Kristian Hald thought the *hulm*-forms were archaic West Scandinavian forms. This explanation is not impossible but it is difficult to see why there should be archaic West Scandinavian forms around Manchester rather than in the Lake District, for example. My own explanation is that the *hulm*-spellings represent a dialectal development in south-east Lancashire and north-east Cheshire (Fellows-Jensen 1985: 315) and this explanation has been accepted by John Dodgson (1970–81 v: 237–38). In this case the distribution map of the varying forms reflects not word geography but a phonological development in an English dialect in the 12th century.

There is a hitherto largely unmined wealth of information about Middle English word geography to be derived from records of field-names. These cannot always be pinpointed on the map but it is normally possible to locate them to a parish or township. It will not, however, be possible to compile reliable distribution maps on the basis of field-names before there is a satisfactory coverage in published works of field-names from many more counties than is at present the case. A foretaste of things to come is provided by Kenneth Cameron's edition of the place-names of Yarborough wapentake in Lincolnshire, which has a mouthwateringly rich harvest of field-names (Cameron 1991). As I read through this volume, my attention was drawn to the field-name element *thing*, translated by Cameron as 'possession, property'. In this particular sense the word does not seem to be recorded in the dictionaries of the standard language or the dialects. I noted fourteen different names containing *thing*, eleven of these occurring in coastal parishes on the Humber. In most cases the specific of the name is explained by Cameron as a surname and in six cases he could point to bearers of the surname in the township in question, for example *Robert Fisher* 1606 and *Fishertinge* 1589–91 in Barton on Humber (Cameron 1991: 25). None of the names occurs in more than one record and thirteen of these records are from the 16th and 17th centuries.

I would have been inclined to look upon the use of *thing* in the sense 'property' as an early Modern English development had not Cameron's field-name lists revealed a possible occurrence in the cartulary of Bardney Abbey, compiled in the late 13th century (post 1269). This is *Wadthekersting* in Barton on Humber. Cameron does not attempt to explain this name, considering it to be 'obscure'. It might be suggested very tentatively, however, that the specific could be a place-name in *-kjarr* whose specific shows confusion between Old English *gewæd* and Scandinavian *vað*, both meaning 'ford', although I have to admit that no name resembling this in any way has been found in Barton on Humber or its neighbourhood. Unfortunately it is not only the specific of this field-name that is doubtful. Kristian Hald, who excerpted the field-names in the Bardney cartulary over 60 years ago, noted that *Wadthekersting* was the name of a *semitam*, i.e. 'a footpath', and he considered that *-sting* was probably an error for *-stig* 'path'. It would certainly be inadvisable to date the use of *thing* in the sense 'property' to the 13th century on the basis of this name alone. Forthcoming volumes of *The Place-Names of Lincolnshire* will, I hope, be able to throw more light on this problem but the group of names in Yarborough wapentake can serve as a cautionary example of the danger of relying on lists of field-names reproduced out of context.

Another way of exploiting field-name material is to excerpt all the names from a single source, taking care to include on slips or in the data-base such context as might be relevant for their interpretation. This is a task I set myself 20 years ago with a survey of arable lands, meadow and pasture belonging to the Bishop of Lincoln 1348–49 (Fellows Jensen 1974). The survey, in a 14th–century hand, is contained in MS 366 of Queen's College Oxford. My interest at that time was in the Scandinavian element in English field-names and the survey was particularly suitable for my purpose in that the bishop's lands and the 1,233 field-names lay partly in the Danelaw proper (743 in Lincolnshire, Nottinghamshire, Leicestershire and Rutland) and partly in the counties to the south and west of these (490 in Northamptonshire, Huntingdonshire, Buckinghamshire and Oxford-shire). My study confirmed that distinctively Scandinavian elements occurred much more frequently in the more northerly block of counties. (Cf. the list reprinted here as Appendix 1.) The question arose as to whether the purely Scandinavian field-names could have been coined much earlier than 1348. I could show that at least 28 of the 39 names in Dunholme, Lincolnshire, were already in existence in the 12th century and 11 of the 172 names in Sleaford, Lincolnshire, by 1271. Many of the Scandinavian words in the field-names, however, had entered into Standard English or the local dialects and the names including these can have been coined at any time up to 1348. My conclusion was simply that the vocabulary in the Danelaw in the first half of the 14th century must have contained many more Scandinavian loanwords connected with farming, topography and territorial divisions than did the vocabulary in the other counties involved in the survey.

It is difficult to exploit the evidence in a single written source for the occurrence of individual words in the various dialects. The restricted distribution of a word may reflect other factors than a restricted currency for the word. Middle English (ME) *vyneyard*, for example, is only found in two field-names in Buckden, Huntingdonshire (*Wynyardemade* and *jnfra le vyneyardd'* 57r). Since Domesday Book of 1086 only records vineyards in the south of England, with a concentration in the counties around London, however, it is not surprising that the word *vyneyard* does not occur in the Danelaw counties (Darby 1977: 275–77, 362–63).

The field-name *Warytrefurlong* 47v in Nettleham, Oxfordshire, clearly contains ME *waritre* < OE *wearg-trēow*, presumably in the sense 'gallows'. The more usual term for this instrument of execution is, I would have thought, ME *galwetre*, but OE *gealga* / ON *galgi* occurs most commonly in place-names in the North Country (Smith 1956 ii: 7) and it might be suggested that *waritre* was the southern term. It certainly occurs in an Old English charter dealing with land in Gloucestershire (Smith 1964–65 i: 192) but it must not be forgotten that the same word apparently lies behind the Yorkshire settlement name *Warter* (Smith 1937: 168–69). It would certainly be of interest to plot the occurrences of *galwetre* and *waritre* respectively in Middle English field-names.

The name *Tumberefurlong* 60v in Dorchester, Oxfordshire, obviously contains ME *tumberel*, a loanword from medieval Latin *tumb(e)rellum* 'tip cart, dung cart, trebuchet'. The *Oxford English Dictionary* cites six different meanings for this word and it is impossible to decide which meaning is the correct one in this field-name. It is most likely, however, to be one of the two meanings recorded in *The English Dialect Dictionary*: 'farmcart' (with a general distribution) or less likely 'open rack used for holding fodder for cattle' (noted only in Yorkshire and Lincolnshire). Again this is a word whose distribution in field-names could profitably be plotted with a view to determining both its distribution pattern and its meaning.

The name *Poukepitsclade* 59v, 60r in Banbury, Oxfordshire, contains OE *puca*, ME *pouke*, *poke* 'goblin' or the like. This element has been noted in place-names chiefly in the south and west and the Banbury field-name fits nicely into the distribution pattern (Smith 1956 ii: 74). It should be noted, however, that the element might possibly occur in settlement names in the East Riding of Yorkshire and Norfolk and it would be interesting to record its distribution in field-names.

Finally, I should like to look at a small group of names which might throw some light on the development of the ending *-inge* of the present participle in the various dialect areas. These are names containing the OE element *hangende* 'hanging', used of places on a steep slope or hillside. Starting in the north, we find *Hengandewong* 50v in Sleaford. In this name the participle is actually Scandinavian *hengjandi*. In Newark, Nottinghamshire, *Hangandewong* and *Hangandegorefurlong* 49v have the typically northern ending *-ande*, while *Hangendewong* 54r in Liddington, Rutland, *Hangendefurlong* 58v in Cropredy and *Hangendefurlong* 59r in Hardwick, both in Oxfordshire, all have forms in typically Midland *-ende*. There are four other field-names in Cropredy, however, in which the *-ende* ending has been replaced by *-ing(e)*: *Hangyngfurlong* and *Northangynge-*

furlong 58v and *Holewellehangyngsik* and *Hangynge* 59r. These seem to show that the replacement of *-ende* by *-inge* by association with the verbal substantive was in progress in Oxfordshire in the middle of the 14th century.

In conclusion I would argue on the basis of these appetisers that a data-base containing dated and localised field-names from the whole of the country is a goal for English name-scholars to aim at. The exploitation of a data-base containing material from the Lay Subsidy Rolls by Gillis Kristensson and some of his students from Lund has been criticised as being unreliable for the determination of phonological developments (McClure 1973) but some interesting word-geographical results have nevertheless emerged from their studies. The Leverhulme project in progress at the Centre for English Name-Studies in Nottingham aims to put all English place-names in a data-base but it is beginning with settlement names. The Colloquium might like to express support for the project, recommend that it become permanent, and emphasise to the director the importance of including field-names in the survey.

Appendix

From: Fellows-Jensen G. 1974 English Field-Names and the Danish Settlement. *Festskrift til Kristian Hald*, Navnestudier 13. Copenhagen.

almanna m. gen. pl. 'of the whole community', 1 Nt.
bekkr m. 'stream, beck', 9 L, 2 Nt, 1 Lei, 1 Bk. ME *be(c)k*, modern *beck*.
bōl n. originally 'farm', later used as a unit of area measurement, 2 Nt.
bóndi m. 'farmer', 1 Hu. ME *bond(e)*.
breiðr adj. 'broad', 1 R.
bringa f. 'chest' in topographical sense, 1 L, 1 R.
bý m. 'village', ? 1 L. ME *bī*. Cf. modern *by-law*.
deill m. 'share, portion of land', usually used of a share of the common field (Smith 1956 i: 128). This element is extremely rare in Scandinavia and Hald is probably correct in suggesting that *deill* in English names simply represents a scandinavianised form of OE *dāl* (or *dæl*) ('Vore Marknavnes Alder' *Namn och Bygd* **36** (1948), p. 25), 64 L, 6 Nt, 1 Lei, 2 Bk.
eng f. 'meadow, pasture', often 'outlying pastures', 13 L, 1 Nt, 1 R, 1 Bk. ME *eng*, dialect *ing*.
ferja f. 'ferry', 1 Nt, 1 O. Modern *ferry*, not recorded in common use until 15th century but cf. also OE *ferian* 'to transport'.
flat, OIcel *flǫt* f. 'piece of flat, level ground', 1 L. ME *flat*, Yorkshire dialect *flat* 'division of common field'.

garðr m. 'enclosure', 6 L. Modern *garth*.

gata f. 'way, path, road, street', in some cases with developed sense 'right of pasturage' and in some few others possibly rather a scandinavianisation of OE *geat* 'gate' (Smith 1956 i: 196), 16 L, 7 Nt, 2 R, 7 Lei, 6 Hu, 3 Nth. ME *gate*, Northern dialect *gate* 'way'.

geiri m. 'gore', probably replacing OE *gāra*, 2 L. ME *gaire*, dialect *gair*, *geir*.

gildi n. 'guild', perhaps merely influencing OE *gild*, 1 L. ME *gild(e)*, modern *guild*.

grein f. 'branch, fork', 1 L. ME *grein* 'fork', dialect *grain* 'small, forking valley'.

hafri m. 'oats', rather than OE **hæfera*, 2 L, 2 Nt. ME *haver*.

harðr adj. in comparative *harðari* 'harder', 1 L.

haugr m. 'hill, burial-mound' (or perhaps sometimes the dat. sg. of OE *hōh*, 8 L, 1 Nt, 1 Lei. ME *howe* can represent either *haugr* or *hōhe*.

hengjandi pres. part. 'hanging', 1 L.

hesli n., perhaps merely influencing OE *hæsel* 'hazel', 1 L. ME *hesel*.

holmr m. 'isle, water-meadow, piece of raised ground in marshy area', 19 L, 9 Nt, 2 R, 8 Lei, 4 Bd, 2 Hu. ME *holm(e)*, dialect *holme*.

ODan. **kæki* 'jawbone', in some topographical sense as in Danish Kegnæs (Hald, *Nudansk Ordbog*), 1 L.

ODan. **kæl* 'wedge', as in Kelsit YN, 1 Nt.

kirkja f. 'church', perhaps replacing or influencing the form of OE *cirice*, 2 L, 2 Lei. ME *kirk*.

kjarr n. 'brushwood', later 'bog, marsh', 1 L, 1 Nt, 1 Hu. ME *ker*.

knútr m. 'knot, rocky hill', 1 L.

(h)laða f. 'storehouse, barn', 1 L. ME *lath(e)*, Northern dialect *lathe*.

leirr m. 'clay', 1 Bd. ME *leir*, dialect *lair*.

leirgraf f. 'clay pit', 1 L.

*maligr adj. 'gravelly', as in Swedish Maljen, 2 L.

melr m. 'sandbank', 1 L.

mýrr f. 'mire, bog', 1 Lei. ME and modern *mire*.

rein f. 'boundary strip', 1 L. Dialect *rean*.

skil n.pl., basic meaning 'separation' hence 'boundary', 1 L.

skirr adj. 'clear, bright', perhaps replacing or influencing the form of OE *scīr*, 2 or 3 L.

ODan. *spang* f. 'footbridge over narrow stream' (*Nudansk Ordbog*) or perhaps OE *spang* 'clasp, buckle', English dialect *spong* 'long, narrow strip of ground' (Smith 1956 ii: 135), 1 R (*Spongwong* 54r).

stakkr m. 'rick', 1 L. Modern *(hay)stack*.

stang, Olcel. *stǫng* f. 'pole, stave', used as a standard of measure, 3 L. Cameron notes that the word *stang* as a term of measure remained common in parts of L up to the 17th and 18th centuries.

toft f. 'building site, curtilage', 3 L, 2 Nt, 1 R, 1 Nth. Late OE *toft*.

tunga f. 'tongue', the topographical use seems to be of Scandinavian origin (Smith 1956 ii: 198), 5 Nth.

þorp n. 'secondary settlement', 1 L. Modern *thorpe*.

þvert n. adj. 'athwart', 1 L, 1 R. ME *thwert*, modern *thwart*.

vangr m. 'field', particularly 'in-field', normally used in Denmark for each of the — generally three — large fields in a village, cf. the rare OE *wang* 'piece of meadow-land', open field', 44 L, 57 Nt, 28 R, 5 Lei, 4 Hu, 3 Nth, 1 O.

veiðr f. '(place for) hunting or fishing', 1 L.

vrá f. 'nook, corner of land', 1 L, 3 Nt, 1 Lei. Dialect *wro*.

Scandinavian personal names, not necessarily borne by men of Danish descent: *Auðgrímr* 1 Nt, *Brandr* 1 L, *Grímr* 2 L, 1 Nt, *Haraldr* 2 L, 1 Lei, *Káti* 1 L, *Þórr* ? 1 Hu, *Þorketill* 1 Hu, *Valr* or *Hvalr* 1 L.

County abbreviations in Appendix

Bd	=	Bedfordshire	Nt	=	Nottinghamshire
Bk	=	Berkshire	Nth	=	Northamptonshire
Hu	=	Huntingdonshire	O	=	Oxfordshire
L	=	Lincolnshire	R	=	Rutland
Lei	=	Leicestershire	YN	=	Yorkshire, N Riding

References

Cameron K. 1959 *The Place-Names of Derbyshire*. EPNS vols. XXVII–XXIX. Cambridge University Press: Cambridge

Cameron K. 1985–91 *The Place-Names of Lincolnshire*. EPNS vols. LVII, LXIV/LXV. Nottingham

Darby H.C. 1963 Place-names and the geography of the past. In: Brown A., Foote P. (eds.) *Early English and Norse Studies*. Methuen: London, pp. 6–18

Darby H.C. 1977 *Domesday England*. Cambridge University Press: Cambridge

Dodgson J. McN. 1970–81 *The Place-Names of Cheshire*. EPNS vols. XLIV–XLVIII, LIV. Cambridge University Press: Cambridge

Fellows Jensen G. 1970–73 Review of Dodgson 1970–81 *The Place-Names of Cheshire*. *Saga-Book of the Viking Society* XVIII: 201–206

Fellows Jensen G. 1974 English field-names and the Danish settlement. *Festskrift til Kristian Hald*, Navnestudier 13. Copenhagen, pp. 45–55

Fellows-Jensen G. 1985 *Scandinavian Settlement Names in the North-West*. Navnestudier 25. Copenhagen

Gelling M., Nicolaisen W.F.H., Richards M. 1970 *The Names of Towns and Cities in Britain*. Batsford: London

Gover J.E.B. et al. 1936 *The Place-Names of Warwickshire*. EPNS vol. XIII. Cambridge University Press: Cambridge

Hald K. 1978 A-mutation in Scandinavian words in England. In: Andersson T., Sandred K.I. (eds.) *The Vikings, Proceedings of the Symposium of the Faculty of Arts of Uppsala University, June 6-9, 1977*. Uppsala, pp. 105–13

Loyn H.R. 1962 [1991] *Anglo-Saxon England and the Norman Conquest*, 2nd edn. 1991. Longman: London

McClure P. 1973 Lay Subsidy Rolls and dialect phonology. In: Sandgren F. (ed.) *Otium et Negotium: Studies in onamatology and library science presented to Olof von Feilitzen*. Norstedt and Soner: Stockholm, pp. 188–94

Smith A.H. 1937 *The Place-Names of the East Riding of Yorkshire and York*. EPNS vol. XIV. Cambridge University Press: Cambridge

Smith A.H. 1956 *English Place-Name Elements*, vols. 1–2. EPNS vols. XXV–XXVI. Cambridge University Press: Cambridge

Smith A.H. 1961–63 *The Place-Names of the West Riding of Yorkshire*. EPNS vols. XXX–XXXVII. Cambridge University Press: Cambridge

Smith A.H. 1964–65 *The Place-Names of Gloucestershire*. EPNS vols. XXXVIII–XLI. Cambridge University Press: Cambridge

Svensson Ö. 1987 *Saxon Place-Names in East Cornwall*. Lund Studies in English 77. Lund University Press: Lund

Panel IV   WORD GEOGRAPHY

Discussion

chaired by *Richard Hamer*

Margaret Laing: There is a proposal in relation to Dr Fellows-Jensen's plea about field names that I should write a letter to the directors of the Leverhulme–Nottingham place-name project. This would say that it is the feeling of the Colloquium that the value of the project would be very much enhanced if the field names were included in the survey. Would that meet with approval from the Colloquium?[1]

Gillis Kristensson: I should like to make an additional plea for research of what we call by-names or second names in the Middle Ages. One extremely fine source of our knowledge of Middle English word geography is what is hidden in the second names of persons. In the Middle Ages people were called, for example, 'Peter at the Hille', 'Peter at the Bourne', 'Peter le Longe', so there are adjectives and nouns. Actually there are nouns hidden in these names that had not been known about before in Middle English. We can plot the different forms on the map. I did a test some years ago where I tried to find words with the same meaning as *bourne*. In northernmost England we find *burn* and *beck*, and then in Lincolnshire and Lancashire we find *brook* and *goter*. What is above all valuable is the great amount of material that is hidden here. For instance, from Lindsey in the county of Lincolnshire, there are 22,000 personal names for one single year of the Subsidy Rolls; six years later there is an additional roll, again with about 22,000 names. That is only a part of Lincolnshire.

---

[1] The participants approved and a letter was sent.

The situation concerning field names in August 1993 was reported to the editors by Carole Hough of the Centre for English Name Studies at Nottingham. It is that the fieldnames are unlikely to be entered on the data base over the next 5 years because of the quantity of material. The first phase of the project is dealing with the major place-names. However, provision has been made within the structure of the data base to include the fieldnames at a later stage.

But it takes time and it takes work and it takes money to make use of this material.

Gillian Fellows-Jensen: You have some of it on a data base, do you not?

Kristensson: No. We have it so that we could put it on, but we don't have the money.

Fellows-Jensen: It should be on the same kind of data base as I hope the field names will go on in Nottingham. Perhaps it's on an old-fashioned data base?

Kristensson: We have a lot of it in the old-fashioned form, but we haven't got the money to get it into a modern computer-held corpus. We have had a few people who could do that very well but they are no longer with us. While we are looking for the money, people are disappearing.

Christian Kay: I would like to draw attention to another potential source, which is the Historical Thesaurus Project in Glasgow. I find it quite exciting that we have so many big projects which seem at last to be moving towards a conclusion: like the *Middle English Dictionary* and our Project, and the *Dictionary of the Older Scottish Tongue*. Where I think the thesaurus data would be relevant to what people are talking about is that you can select words which relate to a particular area of meaning. So if you were interested in, for example, something like the concept referred to by *want* and *tharfen* then you might also want to know how many other words could express it. Though I think Terry made a very valid point that you cannot assume that there is isomorphism between concepts from one dialect to another. But, given that, I think there is potential for this kind of study and also for stylistic study afterwards.

Terry Hoad: Bob Lewis mentioned the use of the information on dialect distribution in *MED*, or the selection of examples for it? Do I understand you rightly that from the letter G onwards it's reasonable to draw some conclusions from the material in *MED*, and that before G you'd be well advised not to?

Robert Lewis: Well, I'm the only one to say that. I just think we've become more comprehensive since G. We try much harder than we did before G to represent all dialect texts we know about in our data. I know we have been doing that since Q. But I wouldn't want to make any negative comments about what goes on in A through F. It's just that those volumes are not as full as the later ones.

Matti Rissanen: Dr Lewis kindly mentioned the Helsinki Corpus of English Texts.[2] It is indeed available now. It contains about one and a half million words, from Old English, beginning with *Caedmon's Hymn*, to the beginning of the 18th century. The Middle English part has about 600,000 words.

Jeremy Smith: Two points. First, we've been hearing of great developments of the *MED* and the *DOST*. I think one of the great scandals of the last few years has been the funding problems of the *Dictionary of Old English* in Toronto. That's a major problem for Anglicists and something that ought to be addressed. Secondly, something we could look at further in word geography is extrapolation from Modern English. For example, the use of the words 'gate' and 'yett' in northern England is interesting. In Yorkshire and Cumberland you find [j-] forms rather than [g-]. There seems to have been a clash here because it's a Norse area and so the [j-] type was used to distinguish the sense 'gate' (from OE *geat*, pl. *gatu*) from 'street' (from ON *gata*). I think that kind of investigation can be much extended. Could you say a bit more about the Modern English extrapolation, Terry?

Hoad: Well, we have to decide what our objectives are in word-geographical studies. If we very much focus on descriptions of Middle English — to aid localisation of texts, and so on — then taking into consideration other periods becomes less attractive. If we are interested in more general aspects of English linguistics and historical linguistics then of course doing this poses fascinating problems. We ought then to organise our work in such a way that we don't neglect or exclude other periods of the language before and after the period that we're mostly concentrating on.

---

2 M. Kytö 1993 *Manual to the Diachronic Part of the Helsinki Corpus of English Texts: Coding Conventions and Lists of Source Texts*, 2nd edn. Department of English, University of Helsinki: Helsinki; M. Rissanen, M. Kytö and M. Pallander-Collin (eds.) 1993 *Early English in the Computer Age: Explorations through the Helsinki Corpus*. Mouton de Gruyter: Berlin.

Richard Hamer: One fine thing about the names of places is that places stay put. But I had previously thought that they contained a rather limited range of material, and I have been amazed by the variety in the examples of field names you have given, Gillian.

Fellows-Jensen: There is quite a wide range of material, but mostly nouns and some adjectives. You don't get many verbs apart from a few participles. There must be a couple of hundred different generic words, that is the words denoting the field or the settlement or whatever it is. But all kinds of things can come in as specific elements of names — it is very varied. Every parish will have the usual rather stereotyped names but there is always something that's different or unusual. If you have a lot of fields to describe you would seize on anything that is a bit different. The green field doesn't really describe one field as being distinct from any other and it was used presumably of a field that was lying fallow. But if there was a field marked by, for example, a tree, you may find tree names. Trees and animals occur a lot.

Kristensson: In my opinion one of the best books in the field of lexicography to appear in a very long time was Professor Smith's, *English Place-name Elements*,[3] It covers those elements, mainly nouns and adjectives, that have been shown so far to form part of place-names. It appeared in 1956 in two parts. It reveals an enormous number of words that hadn't been known earlier. About 10 years ago a new *English Place-name Elements* was begun and I think that it would have been about double the size. It would have been extremely valuable in giving us an idea of Middle English and Old English vocabulary. The pity is that the man who started it, Professor Löfvenberg in Stockholm, died and there is no one who is able to carry it on. So, if one could find a good scholar to do that work it would be a great service to the study of English vocabulary. Professor Löfvenberg was extremely well-qualified for this work, and Kenneth Cameron who is now responsible for that part, told me some time ago that he couldn't imagine anyone who could complete the work now.

Fellows-Jensen: This is one of the aims of the Leverhulme Project in Nottingham, where the material is going on to computer. I think that

---

[3] A.H. Smith 1956 *English Place-Name Elements*, 2 vols. EPNS XXV–XXVI. Cambridge.

the days of men like Löfvenberg have gone. Nowadays people get someone to put the material on computer and then a Löfvenberg looks at what the computer spits out. There are several aims of the Leverhulme Project: one is to produce a revised elements volume and that is definitely feasible within a reasonably limited time because it will be based on the already published volumes of names. I'm arguing that it should be extended beyond just the settlement names. Of course, the great problem for the English Place-Name Society is that the records of all the early volumes were lost in the Blitz, so there are no slips. I come from a country [Denmark] that has all its names on slips and you can go and look up any place-name, even for the areas for which there is no publication. There is nothing like that here. You can go to Nottingham but you can't look up a comprehensive collection of slips. You can only look up slip collections for the works published since World War II. All this work though has been done by scholars in their free time or when they've retired. Some of the material is scattered all over the country and, as you know, that for Norfolk is in Uppsala. Do you know what happened to Löfvenberg's slips, Dr Kristensson? Did he leave them to the English Place-Name Society? Or have they been used to stoke a boiler?

Kristensson: They were sent to the EPNS.

Fellows-Jensen: I imagine that the material will be used then. I think that it's no good expecting any eminent scholar to be able to do this work on his own now; it needs a computer to handle all the material, then we need the scholar to look at what comes out and assess it.

Hoad: It presumably also needs more than one person to do that work. There is a supplement that was the work of two people. Weren't the Anglo-Saxon and the Celtic names separately done?

Fellows-Jensen: A supplement was produced largely because there was a lot of criticism of the Celtic element. In this supplement Kenneth Jackson did a full treatment of the Celtic names which had previously been dealt with by Hugh Smith. If you use the old volume you should always refer to the supplement printed in the *Journal of the English Place-Name Society* 1 (1968–69) for the Celtic material. Also many corrections have been published in the *Journal* through the years. You need to look at all the corrections. But one of the things that the Nottingham project will do is to feed into the data-base the old elements volume as well as all the corrections and supplements to it that have appeared since.

Michael Benskin: Is there any intention of putting the field names onto disk so that we can get an index to them? One of the things I find infuriating about EPNS is that, though I can get a list of elements and look up phonological elements by their settlement names, the field names, which are often much more interesting, are just not accessible.

Fellows-Jensen: The idea is that the field names will eventually go in. I don't think they will be the first to be put in because the first aim is to produce a revised elements. That's why we're writing the letter, to say how important it is that the field names should go in too. If the Leverhulme grant isn't renewed at the end of 5 years, and Nottingham doesn't feel able to keep the project on, I'm afraid the field names will never go in. If we can somehow get this project established in Nottingham and Nottingham is convinced that it is a worthwhile project and that people are interested in it, then I think the field names will go in.

Benskin: And yet it would be so much more useful if the field names went in straightaway because at the moment we have no systematic access to them at all. You have simply to read the things section by section, volume by volume.

Fellows-Jensen: They are experimenting with scanning in the published volumes. In that case the field names will go in. But if they start at the beginning, there are very few field names in most of the early volumes. The idea is to use everything that they can. The material will probably be tagged to be dealt with later. The mere fact that it is on the computer will help. It will certainly be analysed into first and second elements.

Benskin: A mere index of field names would still be of enormous value.

Kristensson: This is really important and it is the best thing that could be done for the moment to further the study of Middle English word geography. The material, in one form or another, has to be published. I don't like the idea of additions: there should be an entirely new

English Place-Name Elements, because the additions will be an even larger body of material than what is now available in printed form.

Fellows-Jensen: It will be a new volume, but presumably the original version and the additions will go into the computer and then be run together. They will then be revised by somebody. The additions won't be published separately because such material would be very difficult to use. You don't go through 20 volumes of the *Journal of the English Place-Name Society* looking at all the additions in case you might have missed some of the vital additions. Any new elements volume, even with little human attention paid to it, will be useful.

Hamer: I will briefly summarise. A great deal of work, much of it extremely good, has been done on major aids to study over a very long period, but most of it has been by individuals and individualists. Such great collaborative ventures in the past have largely been devoted to creating dictionaries; Johnson's was to some small extent collaborative, and of course the *OED* much more so. But perhaps too many things have been done by individuals without the support work that can be provided by collaboration.

Dictionaries and other reference works go on being written. We are very fortunate that the *MED* is nearing completion, and *LALME* is now published. Both of these one can regard as the triumphant end of two great opening chapters, and they should be the prelude to a whole range of new scholarly undertakings and better editions of texts. We learn that, if funding is forthcoming, other collaborative ventures may become available to help our researches; and the advantage will be especially great for those who have learned to work with computers.

The other type of collaboration which is very important is that which takes place between people in related disciplines of medieval studies. Too often in the past this has not happened. The present meeting has been an admirable example of this kind of contact among us all, both internationally and between disciplines.